THE POLITICS
OF DEMONOLOGY

The Politics
of Demonology

The European Witchcraze and
the Mass Production of Deviance

Jon Oplinger

Selinsgrove: Susquehanna University Press
London and Toronto: Associated University Presses

Associated University Presses
440 Forsgate Drive
Cranbury, NJ 08512

Associated University Presses
25 Sicilian Avenue
London WC1A 2QH, England

Associated University Presses
P.O. Box 488, Port Credit
Mississauga, Ontario
Canada L5G 4M2

302.5
061 p

The paper used in this publication meets the requirements
of the American National Standard for Permanence of Paper
for Printed Library Materials Z39.48-1984.

Library of Congress Cataloging-in-Publication Data

Oplinger, Jon.
    The politics of demonology : the European witchcraze and the mass production of deviance / Jon Oplinger.
        p.   cm.
    Includes bibliographical references.
    ISBN 0-945636-11-3 (alk. paper)
    1. Deviant behavior—History.   2. Conformity—History.   3. Social control—History.   4. Witchcraft—Europe—History.   5. Political purges—History.   6. Persecution—History.   I. Title.
HM291.0675   1990
302.5'42—dc20   89-43149
                                                                 CIP

TP

To my parents

Contents

Foreword

Legal structure is typically predicated upon the mores and norms of a society at a given time. Over time and space, that which is deemed to be moral or normal changes and is ordinarily reflected in the legal code of that society. As the moral structure and the legal structure of a society become congruent, that which *is* appears to be natural and that which does not fit within the status quo can easily be regarded as deviant. It is upon this shifting boundary between the "normal" and the "deviant" that Professor Oplinger focuses. The construction, maintenance, and policing of such "moral boundaries" constitute the chief work of a social control mechanism. Those who fall outside of the moral boundary are, by definition, deviant and will be dealt with accordingly.

The delineation of such moral boundaries is usually cued by societal elites for the purpose of underwriting their own social hegemony. Professor Oplinger stresses that the ". . . particular perception [that] comes to predominate in the legal structure is a function of who has the most power." Perhaps it would be an overstatement to insist that law is the product of a social monologue of the strong to the weak. However, the point made here is that deviance is an intentional artifact of the legal order and, of course, the legal order is an artifact of social hegemony. Deviance then can be defined so as to meet the needs of the powerful. Indeed, deviance is *produced* or, if need be, *mass* produced to meet those very needs. The critical point is that deviance does not simply "occur" but rather it is intentionally constructed. It is not necessarily a social anomaly that needs to be controlled or eradicated. Rather, it is typically a very normal behavior, or supposed behavior, that is defined into abnormality to meet the social and political needs of the group constructing the definition.

In his consideration of several instances of the mass production of social deviance, Professor Oplinger notes that they are often political purges in disguise. Usually, such purges are the

9

result of a threat to the social system or at least to the status quo. Such threats or perceptions of threats might arise from domestic (internal) sources such as a schism within a hegemonic social coalition (the Cultural Revolution) or they might arise from foreign (external) sources challenging the entire coalition (the Red Scare). Either type of threat to the status quo, whether real or imagined, will likely be met by the quick and efficient production of an abundance of malicious heretics.

Tens of thousands of people in sixteenth- and seventeenth-century Europe died spectacular (and very expensive) deaths for the crime of witchcraft. To ascribe that slaughter to a coincidental rise in Western society's normally high levels of villany and superstition is to abandon the idea that history and politics have any recognizable pattern. Social scientists hold that there is a pattern: the number of witches produced increased dramatically during periods of religious discontinuity such as the Reformation and Counter-Reformation. In such an epoch, the pressures upon the social structure are enormous, and as the prevailing institutions face erosion, the dominant elements of society scramble to adapt to the new social reality or to channel it into forms that are conducive to the maintenance of the elite's social dominance. Indeed, the author notes that ". . . discord, anxiety, and threats to position among the ruling class are directly related to outbreaks of witch-hunting." For the early modern European prince, "God's Lieutenant," the public destruction of God's enemies was both virtuous and practical. Never mind the cost and never mind the numbers if it established a moral boundary. On one side could be found the light of morality and the divine right of kings; on the other, darkness and Satan.

One of the more startling revelations of this study is the great abundance of historical cases of deviance production from which the researcher might draw. It is probably the case that the long-term existence of a social elite requires the periodic mass production of deviance. However, in only some instances does the social elite enjoy the untrammelled control of the machinery for the manufacture of deviance, as was the case with the Inquisition or Joseph Stalin's purges. On other occasions the power of the elite is more circumscribed by various restraint systems. Dr. Oplinger gives us an understanding of, and appreciation for, societal and institutional restraints upon the behavior of those in socially powerful positions. One reason why witch-hunting and killing was far less virulent in Britain than in the

German states might be due to a more moderate political culture in the former. Equally, the explanation might center upon the magnitude of the perceived threat presented to the hegemonic group(s). The greater the threat, the more intense the hunt and the more severe the punishment.

In some societies elite action is virtually unchecked and, therefore, the capacity for repression is without bounds. In other societies such action is checked in varying degrees. Where such restraint is in evidence—where institutional accountability exists to some meaningful degree—the excesses of deviance production will likely be checked. However, while not intending to minimize the importance of restraint mechanisms, it can be argued that the dynamics of deviance production are remarkably similar across time and space. Restraint systems, then, primarily affect he efficacy of the process and the severity of punishment of those on the wrong side of the moral boundaries. If the restraint mechanisms hold and if they are of real substance, one might expect the duration and intensity of a purge to be minimized. In reference to the Red Scare following the First World War, Dr. Oplinger notes that it ". . . was brief because the normal accountabilities and organization restraints could not be held at bay for long in the absence of a persuasive conspiracy." The post–World War II McCarthy Era and the British bout of witchcraft trials were similarly constrained. Such systems can, indeed, facilitate the rise of "Witchfinders General," Joseph McCarthys and Richard Nixons but at the same time constrain their violence.

Finally, Professor Oplinger casts his study in the context of what he terms as a "moral landscape." The moral landscape of a society is far more complex than the simple two-dimensional consideration of normal vs. deviant behavior. Rather, it focuses upon the interplay of competing conceptions of normality, morality, and, hence, deviance. Arguably, the more two-dimensional the moral landscape, the more widely accepted is the elite's definition of normal and deviant. It is when the moral boundary shifts, becomes less clear or, perhaps most important, is challenged by a seemingly significant social group that the landscape becomes multidimensional and the machinery for the mass production of deviance is fired up. Demonologists appear. Repression begins.

All societies strike a balance between sociopolitical legitimacy and repression. As long as the legitimacy of hegemonic social order goes unquestioned, there is scant need for repression.

However, if that legitimacy begins to wear thin, repression becomes a growth industry. If moral landscapes are well defined and widely respected, repression will play a minor role in society. If the landscape is challenged, the challengers themselves will be challenged. The outcome will likely be determined by the persuasive and physical forces of the contenders. What kind of images can they produce? How much legitimacy can they create? How much force can they evoke? Stalin and Hitler could reduce a complex reality to a stark simplicity: us vs. them. In contrast to such dichotomous struggles, one could consider the French Revolution, where the moral landscape was in such disarray that, at times, it appeared as a struggle of all against all.

Professor Oplinger leaves us with several chilling observations. But beyond the obviously important mechanics and technicalities of the various purges, one is left with the realization that the mass production and punishment of deviance is a worldwide phenomenon, is unbound by historic parameters, and is manipulated most effectively by the modern state. Indeed, if the modern Leviathan excels at anything, it is just that.

Mark Bartholomew

Department of Social Sciences
University of Maine at Farmington

Acknowledgments

Why anyone who is not in solitary confinement would bother to read an author's acknowledgments I cannot say, but it is clear to me why they are written. There are always large debts. The librarians and staff of the Mantor Library of the University of Maine at Farmington have been especially helpful to this project; the energetic assistance of Mrs. Shirley A. Martin in her dual capacity as reference librarian and interlibrary loan librarian has been invaluable. Mrs. Patricia Judd, Mrs. Carol Weeks, Mrs. Ruby Tracy, and Mrs. Betty Gosselin have diligently and with unfailing efficiency typed various drafts of the manuscript. Much of this fine work was crowded into an already busy schedule. Drs. Elisabeth Kalau and John Roman, also of the University of Maine at Farmington, have commented critically and most usefully on the manuscript, eliminating in the process a number of flimsy assertions and foolish statements. If any remain it is not their fault. My wife, Jean, has examined my prose with an unblinking eye and remained supportive of a spouse who has for some time lived in that state of highly caffeinated preoccupation achieved only by untenured professors.

THE POLITICS
OF DEMONOLOGY

1

Mass Production of Deviance

"Political history," according to Murray Edelman, "is largely an account of mass violence and the expenditure of vast resources to cope with mythical fears and hopes."[1] This study inspects a subcategory of mass violence: the "mass production of deviance." By this phrase, I am specifically referring to those instances in the history of the state when the identification, processing, and punishment of a particular sort of deviant is extraordinarily intense, when, in other words, the social control system of the state is used to generate mass persecutions. Admittedly, in the long and varied history of destructive campaigns carried out by the state, determining exactly which events fall within this loose definition is ultimately a problem that might be better left to students of Wittgenstein; but clearly included, in my view, are the Great Purge of Stalinist Russia, the terror of revolutionary France, the Cultural Revolution in China, the Holocaust, and, without exhausting the list, the McCarthy Era. Such occurrences and the circumstances surrounding them, although individually unique from the standpoint of history, share common features that can be taken as causally linked to exaggerated outbreaks of deviance production.

Despite the fact that comprehensive and often murderous persecutions of the ideologically unclean are one of the dominant activities of the modern state, such events have been subjected to relatively little comparative analysis by sociologists.[2] This inattention is at the very least curious since the sociology of deviance has much of the conceptual machinery necessary for a thoroughgoing examination of the social forces common to massive political persecutions. Certainly there is no lack of persecutions to compare. It is simply a matter of historical record that repeatedly during this century, tens of thousands, and in several instances millions, of people have been identified by

17

their governments on the basis of tendentious logic and improbable evidence as members of threatening conspiracies. As such they have been punished, and often the punishment has been death. Indeed, it can be suggested that manufacturing and then stamping out imaginary conspiracies is the only undertaking that the modern state carries out with genuine efficiency.

THE MASS PRODUCTION OF DEVIANCE

The *manufacture* of deviance refers to the use of just about any gambit that facilitates the labeling and processing of deviants, and the specific practices covered by this rubric range from the use of a convenient diagnostic stereotype by a mental hospital to the construction and staffing of the Gulag Archipelago. Nevertheless, the manufacture of deviance as a sensitizing concept can be broken down into two component elements: (1) the organization that develops in response to the practical necessities that emerge in the pursuit and processing of deviants and (2) the cognitive landscape that justifies the effort.

The *mass production* of deviance simply refers to situations wherein these selfsame activities have been put on an assembly line basis. Anyone with even a passing familiarity with the Holocaust, the purges in Russia, or for that matter the relatively nonlethal McCarthy Era in the United States must acknowledge that during such periods all of the administrative know-how and technology and a good deal of the energy of a society are mustered in the attack on a celebrated variety of deviant.

I have settled on the phrase "mass production of deviance" because it most accurately depicts the phenomenon to be studied. Deviants are quite literally produced by the modern state as readily as kitchen appliances, rifles, automobiles, medals of military valor, or any other mass-producible thing. And, just as the profitable production of blenders, for instance, depends on bureaucratic organization and an efficient assembly line, so too must the modern state produce deviance if it is to convince its citizens that their well being is menaced by an internal conspiracy. This the modern state does with chilling efficiency. Raul Hilberg, writing about the Holocaust, notes:

The destruction of the Jews was an administrative process, and the annihilation of Jewry required the implementation of systematic administrative measures in successive steps. There are not many ways in which a modern society can, in short order, kill a large number of people living in its midst. This is an efficiency problem of the greatest dimensions, one which poses uncounted difficulties and innumerable obstacles.[3]

It would be misleading, however, to suggest that the administrative resources of deviance production lagged far behind in early modern Europe. In fact, it is abundantly clear that the groundwork for twentieth-century deviance production was put in place in early modern Europe. Hilberg, for example, argues that the Nazi extermination machinery relied heavily on precedent. Continuing directly from the quote above, he states:

> Yet, in reviewing the documentary record of the destruction of the Jews, one is immediately impressed with the fact that the German administration knew what it was doing. With an unfailing sense of direction and with an uncanny path finding ability, the German bureaucracy found the shortest road to the final goal ... for the German bureaucrats could dip into a vast reservoir of administrative experience which church and state had filled in fifteen hundred years of destructive activity.

Certainly the Spanish Inquisition, with its secret prisons, archives of past sins, and theater of iniquity punished (the auto-dafé), also represents a deviance-producing apparatus of remarkable efficiency. The impression is unavoidable that the greater number of deviants tagged and processed in this century is largely a consequence of material technology—meaning simply that the gadgetry associated with the detection, transportation, and punishment of deviants is more "cost effective" now than in the past. The basic outlines of the process nevertheless remain the same.

A small amount of reflection will produce a long list of groups, often imaginary, that have been defined as menacing and persecuted in the interests of the state. However, for purposes of this study the choice is narrowed by the practical necessity of relying on those outbreaks that have been thoroughly discussed in secondary sources. No matter how single-minded or energetic, an individual scholar could never in a lifetime sift through the primary source material stemming from the mass production of deviance. With this restriction in mind, I have concentrated on a comparison of the European Witchcraze, the Great Purge of Stalinist Russia, the two major episodes of Red baiting in the United States (the Palmer Raids and the McCarthy Era), and the Holocaust.

The European Witchcraze has been selected because it encompassed a great amount of time and territory, allowing varied and repeated comparison of culture, political situation, and legal structure. In specifics, the procedures of the Spanish Inquisition, the religious and secular courts in Northern Europe, and common law in England differed substantially, providing a variety of comparisons that can be employed in the development of empirical generalizations. These are extended in subsequent chapters to the rich information base available on the twentieth-century episodes of the mass production of deviance. This explanatory tactic is not intended merely as a demonstration of the journalistic chestnut that political purges are witch-hunts. Rather, it is being used as a device to refine theoretical propositions into middle range theory; to demonstrate that genocide and political purges are manifestations of a common class of social phenomena—the mass production of deviance—and can be explained on the basis of a single *explanans*.

All evidence indicates that the witchcraze was a classic instance of the mass production of deviance. Norman Cohn writes:

> The great witch-hunt can in fact be taken as a supreme example of the massive killing of innocent people by a bureaucracy acting in accordance with beliefs which, unknown or rejected in earlier times, had come to be taken for granted, as self-evident truths. It illustrates vividly both the power of the human imagination and its reluctance to question the validity of a stereotype once it is generally accepted.[4]

In recent years archival sources have been carefully studied to produce detailed accounts of witch-hunts in several regions of early modern Europe. Indeed, some of the most detailed and, by all appearances, reliable data on the mass production of deviance derive from the archives of the Spanish Inquisition.[5] The same could be said of the Salem Witch-Hunt, which is especially well documented since it was the inspiration for much contemporary social commentary. These commentaries are perceptive and very revealing of social process.

To be sure, the use of the European Witchcraze as a source of comparative data involves some distressing trade-offs. Leaving aside the loss of records through time, there is the fact that people in the sixteenth and seventeenth centuries were not as interested in and therefore did not always record the sort of information thought to be important today. Lamentably, from the point of view of a sociologist, often status and occupation were not recorded.

At the same time there are unique advantages to using the witchcraze as a source of comparative data. To begin with, any possible influence exerted by the actual rate of deviant behavior is largely eliminated. "Common sense" often leads to the supposition that the social control apparatus of a society is simply a utilitarian response to the provocation of deviant acts and that the scope of its activities are in keeping with the frequency of misdeeds. That this is almost never true is one of the more interesting findings of the sociology of deviance. By all indications, the relationship between rule breaking and rule enforcing is very elastic and, since people cannot do what witches in Europe were accused of doing, the European Witchcraze provides a classic example of this elasticity. Admittedly, as Keith Thomas points out, it was entirely possible for a person to attempt to do what witches were reported to do, but, by every indication, this dangerous practice was uncommon.[6] It is simply a cold historical fact that the vast majority of those dragooned into the role of witch were innocent in both thought and deed; their confessions were an artifact of inquisitorial procedure.

THE TWENTIETH CENTURY

Social process in this century is no different; during the McCarthy Era in the United States and the Great Purge in Russia, there is little, in retrospect, to support the notion that there was a dramatic upswing in communist (or fascist) activity, despite the firm conviction on the part of powerful interests that this was so. Of course, genuine fascists and communists exist, but we have a pretty good idea how many there actually were within Russia and the United States during the periods in question—very few.

It is true, of course, that large numbers of people once practiced Judaism within the territories encompassed by the Third Reich. But to define, as Hitler did, the members of this religious community (or any other) as a discrete biological entity is an exercise in fantasy. Obdurate reality, however, is seldom, if ever, an obstacle to the mass production of deviance. It was never so within the Third Reich, which identified Jews (roughly one percent of the population of Germany in 1933) on the basis of social criteria—there was no other way to do it—and then proceeded to murder them on the basis of their alleged biology. In short, during all of these examples of the mass production of deviance, the state was being protected from the inroads of a conspiracy that was dramatically overblown or, as during the witchcraze and the Holocaust, entirely fictitious.

The record of the nation state in this century is clear; motivated by cupidity, fear, hatred, and zeal, citizens of the modern state have enthusiastically and efficiently destroyed vast numbers of their fellow citizens. No less preoccupied with myth and fantasy, the modern state differs from its early modern predecessor fundamentally in that it is potentially more destructive to its citizenry. The comprehensively destructive nature of modern warfare, in other words, has its internal counterpart: the mass production of deviance.

The Great Purge (1936 to 1938) under Stalin is an instance of the mass production of deviance in the context of a modern nation state during which the apparatus of social control had almost absolute freedom of action. Source materials available to Sovietologists include the transcripts of the show trials, reports by dissidents, Soviet newspaper accounts, published party documents, and captured archives.

The designs of a remarkably deadly personality can be taken as the principal factor behind the purge, but it is also obvious that there were forces at play during the purge that Stalin neither wanted nor controlled. Comprehensive statistical data, as would be expected, are not available and probably not extant. However, the overall scope of this event can be inferred from demographic data, and the social forces behind the purge, as well as many of its component elements, have been subjected to systematic investigation by Sovietologists.

By comparison, Red baiting in the United States provides recurring episodes of the mass production of deviance within the context of a pluralistic society in which the social control system is bridled by countervailing institutions. The dynamics of the Palmer Raids are especially clear. The post–World War II period is more complicated, but it is still fundamentally a repetition of an established pattern. As such, it is especially illustrative.

The use of the Holocaust in this analysis arises from two considerations—both practical. First, the Holocaust is exceedingly well documented and is the subject of a vast body of historical analysis. Second, and more compelling, to treat the Holocaust as an entirely separate category of event, as a historical aberration, implies that there is no need to fear the recurrence of a comparable horror. This attitude places undue faith in human courage and rationality and underestimates the power of the state to structure the social reality of its citizens. In this century, an egomaniacal orator convinced an educated nation that Jews were a biological evil. This collective delusion then became the basis for action; at great effort and by means of a carefully developed industrial technology, millions of people were murdered by men who chose to consider their crime to be an act of self-sacrifice performed in the service of the state.

No other single deed quite approaches the Holocaust in the dimension of its inhumanity. Even so, from the standpoint of the sociology of deviance, it was not utterly unique. The Holocaust shares certain features with other episodes of the mass production of deviance and is subject to comparative analysis.

METHOD

It is by now clear that the debate over the relative merits of "scientific" survey sociology and historical sociology is fast becoming immortal. In fact, both approaches are fundamental to the discipline and each employs a similar strategy of explanation. Austin Turk argues that the "logic of historical explanation is indistinguishable from the scientific explanation."[7] And, further:

> We sociologists need historical data for the same reasons we need comparative socio-structural and cross-cultural data: to determine the range of applicability of our reality models and the explanatory power of our theories.[8]

Whether historical, cross-cultural, or socio-structural, the key phrase is "comparative data." Ernest Nagel pursues this issue directly. "Controlled investigation," as he calls it,

> does not require, as does experimentation, either the reproduction at will of the phenomena under study or the overt manipulation

of variables; but it closely resembles experimentation in other respects. Controlled investigation consists in a deliberate search for
contrasting occasions in which the phenomenon is either uniformly
manifested (whether in identical or differing modes) or manifested
in some cases but not in others. . . . It is clearly immaterial whether
the observed variations in the assumed determining factors for observed changes in the phenomenon are introduced by the scientist
himself, or whether such variations have been produced "naturally"
and are simply found by him.[9]

On this basis, I take the method of comparative historcal
investigation to be simply an application of Mill's Method of
Difference.[10] Moreover, historical comparisons have the advantage of establishing temporal connections between events. The
causal inferences are not "cut and paste" as is sometimes the
case in other forms of comparative endeavor; historically, "e-
ffect" has trailed "cause" through time.

THEORETICAL FRAMEWORK

It is idle to suppose that a purely inductive assault can be
made on the questions surrounding the mass production of deviance. Any approach to a problem is theory-laden, and some
consideration of theoretical issues is necessary. It is partly the
objective of this essay to demonstrate that the most elegant explanation for the mass production of deviance lies in an adapta-
tion of a "tempered" conflict theory exemplified in the thinking
of Austin Turk.[11] This view of social deviance stems logically
from three critical, and for conflict theorists, standard, assumptions about the nature of society. It assumes: (1) that society
is animated and shaped by the struggle for scarce goods; (2)
that this struggle is dominated by those with power; and (3)
that this domination is reflected in the legal system. The law,
in other words, protects the interests and world view of the
powerful.

On this basis it is expressly understood that criminality is
an artifact of the legal system in force. Deviance is not thought
in this scheme to derive from some internal miscue within the
person, some individual defect of biology, psychology, or social
experience that lies within "defective people." Rather, deviance
is conceptualized as a social *status* that is determined by those
in power. This status may be ascribed to individuals on the

basis of being discovered engaging in an act that is threatening to the powerful, or, in the words of Turk, merely because "of real or fanciful attributes, because of what they are rather than what they do, and justified by reference to real or imagined or fabricated behavior. . . ."[12] Those persecuted during outbreaks of deviance mass production most often hail from this latter category; guilt is assigned, and a conspiracy manufactured, on the basis of imaginary or fabricated wickedness or simply on the basis of an alleged connection with such fictions.

Conflict theory argues that it is not the nature of the act but the social and legal context in which the act occurs, *or is said to occur,* that defines deviance and criminality. Across different normative systems equivalent behavior takes on very different qualities. The laws now protecting the rights of children have the broadest possible support within this society; however, any attempt by a time-traveling American reformer to impose a similar set of laws upon the society of Imperial Rome would have met with widespread and highly placed resistance, if not the attribution of madness. But even had our reformer stayed at home and strayed only a little distance in time—back to nineteenth-century America—our reformer would have received much the same reception and, if a woman, undergone far greater risk of incarceration in a mental hospital. Considering the history of child labor laws in this country, it is safe to assume that the laws now protecting children against exploitation would have seemed unreasonably fastidious and maybe a little insane to most nineteenth-century Americans.

Simply because certain values are widely held within society and the laws sustaining them have broad support, it does not follow that these standards are immutable and in some way "natural." From the perspective of conflict theory, the "fact" of social order, which is perhaps the primary explanatory concern for functionalism, is taken to be largely an artifact of the stable configuration of power, and widely agreed-upon norms are thought to reflect the successful imposition of the views of a dominant group or, in a pluralistic society, a coalition of groups—not some systemic tendency towards consensus. The furious legislative battles over child labor, a moral issue now long settled and thought to be perfectly obvious, are a case in point.

Functionalism is a light-year removed from this stance. The fundamental assumption here is that society is, when everything is as it should be, an orderly and balanced system. Normative consensus is taken to be the natural and healthy state of society, and conflict is regarded as symptomatic of a temporary misalignment of parts (subsystems). Power is seen as a fundamentally systemic property, and the exercise of power by individuals is basically derivative; that is, power is conferred upon certain individuals for the betterment of the social system. Deviance, necessarily, is viewed in systems terms. Norm violations are seen either as destructive activities that derive ultimately from systemic strains or, in specific forms and at managed frequencies, as socially beneficial (functional).

MORAL BOUNDARIES

It has become an act of faith in Durkheimian sociology to believe that a certain amount of deviance is necessary for the efficient functioning of any social body. Working from this frame of reference, Kai Erikson argues that when society calls to task someone who has strayed from the norm, it is making a public declaration about the latitude of acceptable behavior; it is establishing, in Erikson's terms, *moral boundaries*.[13] These are said to shift as the structure of society changes or as the external environment becomes threatening. Deviance, in short, is thought by Erikson to function to highlight frontiers of social approval and thereby to safeguard group solidarity. He writes:

> Deviant behavior is not a simple kind of leakage which occurs when the machinery of society is in poor working order, but may be, in controlled quantities, an important condition for preserving the stability of social life. Deviant forms of behavior, by marking the outer edges of group life, give the inner structure its special character and thus supply the framework within which the people of the group develop an orderly sense of their own culture identity.[14]

Erikson's concept of moral boundaries was developed in the context of small group research and was later applied to the study of deviance in seventeenth-century Massachusetts. It is undeniably an effective conceptual device when applied to small groups,[15] but in applying it without qualification to Puritan society, it seems that Erikson has skirted an important issue. Puritan society was complex and highly stratified, and when Erikson's Durkheimian perspective is forced upon it, major questions arise. If the crisis of confidence in Massachusetts during

1692 was so universal, as Erikson maintains, why was the witch-hunt opposed by certain factions, and why were the powerful and highly placed citizens relatively immune from prosecution during this episode? Erikson, in his analysis, divided colonial society into "the people" and the "ruling cadre"; and it is quite evident from a careful reading of his monograph that the Salem Witch-Hunt was not a creation of the community as a whole but of powerful elements within it.[16] It would seem, then, that moral boundaries are better conceptualized as manipulative devices put to the service of powerful interests rather than as a systematic property of society.

MORAL LANDSCAPES

Regarding the imagery of deviance itself, I suggest that it is far more useful to think in terms of moral landscapes rather than a normal curve of conformity and deviance.[17] The image of a three-dimensional moral landscape is conceptually truer to what is being described because it drives home the central fact that within complex society the view of a particular group derives from its economic and social vantage point. From the perspective of those who are secure and powerful—who, if you will, are on high social ground—the moral landscape can look very different from that seen from the vantage of those who have been frustrated in the struggle for resources. Indeed, the landscapes are different. What is more, many factors in combination affect the appearance of the moral landscape. From the position of those in power, the menace of youth unrest, for example, is far less serious in the light of tranquil times than in wartime.

It is simply a matter of ordinary experience to realize that complex society is an arena for invidious comparison. The model of a moral landscape admits that events and practices that are seen as virtuous and benign from the vantage point of one group will often be seen as wicked and menacing in the view of another. As George Vold explains, many acts of deviance are merely the actions of a good soldier as seen by unfriendly eyes.[18] Which particular perception (which landscape) comes to predominate in the legal structure is a function of who has the most power. It is this wrangling over which construction of reality is the morally correct reality (the "real" reality) that is the central struggle in complex society during which changes in the political definition of deviance come about as the ability of dominant groups to coerce, propagandize, and inveigh is brought into play, as the powerful, in other words, seek to impose their moral landscape and their interests on the whole of society.

I am specifically proposing that the concept of a moral landscape can be used as a root metaphor in the construction of a theory of sufficient scope to encompass variations on the theme of the mass production of deviance.[19] I suggest also that Erikson's notion of a moral boundary is conceptually useful in conjunction with the metaphor of landscape in that we may regard it as a reification of the actions taken by powerful groups to dramatize the reality of their scheme of values—their moral landscape—and to impose it on the rest of society. The repeated and very dramatic labeling and punishment of a particular category of people has the effect of driving home their wickedness and, by extension, the righteousness of the social construction of reality of those in power. Few institutions have been more expressly designed or better able to do this than the Inquisition.

Developed over the course of three centuries to combat the enemies of the church, inquisitorial procedures were readily adopted by secular courts because they offered an efficient method of suppressing groups whose interests were at odds with those of the state. Furthermore, and far more important, they could be used to legitimize the moral landscape of those in power. Any apparatus of social control structured along inquisitorial lines has the capability of generating thousands—and with modern refinements, millions—of ritually charged interactions between the agents of the powerful and selected examples of wickedness for the purpose of dramatizing the contours of righteous behavior. During the sixteenth and seventeenth centuries, the Christian states of Europe drew upon the ancient embodiment of evil, the witch, to enable this dramatization. Configured anew as the devil's servant and as a member of a "new" cult of satanic agents, the public trial and execution of witches provided visible evidence of the vast diabolical conspiracy that menaced the early modern states of Europe.

Relying heavily on the work of the rationalist historians, Elliot Currie sets out the essential differences between witch-hunting under English Common Law and the inquisitorial systems found on the Continent:

In continental Europe, people accused of witchcraft were brought before the elaborate machinery of a specialized bureaucratic agency with unusual powers and what amounted to a nearly complete absence of institutional restraints on its activity. . . .[20] [In contrast] there was no Inquisition in Renaissance England, and the common law tradition provided a variety of institutional restraints on the conduct of the witch trials. As a consequence, there were fewer witches in England, vastly fewer executions, and the rise of a fundamentally different set of activities around the control of witchcraft.[21]

Currie refers to these two extremes as *restrained* and *repressive*. The central features of a restrained system, using England as the exemplar, are accountability to outside social institutions, the presence of effective restraints within the control organization, and a reduced demand for the production of deviants. In a repressive legal system all of these restrictions on the apprehension and processing of deviants are lacking. The regional history of witch-hunting bears strong witness to the impact of these contrasting systems of social control on the production of deviants, and it is incontestably true that the number of people tried and executed for the crime of witchcraft was enormously greater—probably two or three hundred times greater—on the Continent than in England. At the same time, however, it must be emphasized that despite its restrained legal system, English witch-hunting did at times take on continental dimensions, notably during the Civil War when a fifth of all English witches were executed. Such occurrences cannot be dismissed as the work of unusually successful confidence men, as Currie suggests, nor is it useful to simply pass them off as quirks of history. It may, however, be argued that such brief but intense whirlwinds of persecution in England represent periods when powerful elements within English society were attempting to establish a moral boundary.

The productivity of a social control system, and therefore its ability to impose a moral boundary, can be predicted on the basis of the value that is assigned to "catching" and punishing deviants and the degree to which those who carry out these activities are subject to restraint. Embedded within this relatively self-evident statement are four categorical variables.[22] They are:

1. *Accountability*: the existence of institutional structures outside the social control apparatus that have the capability of exerting pressure on functionaries within the social control system; the degree, in

other words, to which the social control system is subject to the inroads of other social institutions.

2. *Organizational Restraint:* the degree to which checks on the use of power are structured into the social control system itself. Within a legal system characterized by organizational restraint, there are laws or internal regulations that *in the normal course of events* limit the number of deviants that can be processed. For example, are there restrictions on the use of coercive strategies and are the actions of social control agents subject to internal review?

3. *Internal Demand:* Currie has carefully argued that when the functionaries within the legal system are highly motivated to apprehend and punish a particular sort of deviant, the number of formally tagged deviants will increase. Implicitly, Currie used the rate of confiscation as an index of motivation, insisting, quite reasonably, that witch-hunters often hunted witches because it was profitable to do so; but other factors are equally important. The fundamental point is that internal demand refers to a motivational system that is internal to the institution of social control.

4. *External Demand:* the value that is placed on the suppression of a particular sort of deviant by powerful interest groups that are not directly connected with the social control system. The level of external demand is high when powerful outside institutions (i.e., the crown, church, politburo, senate, fuehrer chancellory, etc.) place great emphasis on the pursuit of a particular variety of deviant.

It is important to emphasize the distinction that has been made between the demand for tagged and processed deviants that arises from within the social control system, which I have called internal demand, and the demand for officially labeled deviants that arises from powerful outside groups. The history and circumstances surrounding the Great Witch-Hunt argue that deviance is mass produced when powerful groups believe their values and interests to be embattled and find it to their advantage to establish a moral boundary. *External demand is the overriding consideration in the explanation of the mass production of deviance.* The events surrounding the many localized panics and purges that, taken together, comprise what is known as the Great Witch-Hunt demonstrate that when a powerful elite feels that it is menaced, accountability is forestalled, organizational restraints abandoned, and internal demand brought to a boil. To be very sure, the mass production of deviance is more readily accomplished (and far more difficult to shut down) under a repressive social control system, to use Currie's terminology, than under a restrained social control system, but it is nevertheless a fact that the mass production of deviance also arises within the context of restrained systems. Stated more directly, restrained social control systems, here defined as control systems that are usually characterized by accountability, organizational restraint, and low internal demand, are unrestrained in the context of a high level of external demand.

The purpose of this essay is to construct a theory and thereby to avoid what may be described as the Horatio Nelson approach to problem solving, a broadside of concepts. Finer explanatory tactics are possible. The mass production of deviance as a general phenomenon can be presented as a series of relational statements. Realistically, it is seldom possible to fashion an elegant deductive structure out of comparative data, and most comparative investigations attempt, usually only implicitly, the *causal process* form of theory, the heart of which is a set of causal statements—propositions—stipulating deterministic or probabilistic relations.[23] Causal process theories are characterized chiefly by the fact that each proposition is given equal weight. This theory form, apart form being intuitively more satisfying, has the substantial advantage of being easier to construct. Nevertheless, it still carries the structures that enforce clarity and permit falsification: definitions of concepts, operational definitions, and the overt invocation of general laws.

A THEORY OF THE MASS PRODUCTION OF DEVIANCE

1.0 The higher the level of external demand, the higher the rate of deviance production.

1.1 The greater the perceived threat to the status and resources of dominant groups, the higher the level of external demand.

2.0 The less a social control system is subject to accountability and organizational restraint, the greater the potential for deviance production.

2.1 The potential for the exercise of accountability is inversely related to the concentration of power within society.

2.2 The greater the immunity of the resource base of an apparatus of social control to the inroads of other organizations, the greater the resistance to the exercise of accountability.

3.0 The potential for the mass production of deviance is greatest in societies characterized by great concentration of power, a high level of external and internal demand, and an unrestrained social control system.

4.0 Within a society that is normally characterized by a restrained social control system, the advent of a high level of external

demand will foster a relaxation of both accountability and organizational restraint.

4.1 Over time, the maintenance of a high level of external demand
will bring about changes in procedural law that will enhance
the ability of dominant groups to manufacture deviance.

Embedded within propositions 1.0 and 1.1 is the implication
that a reduction in the level of external demand will be followed
by a reduction in the rate of deviance production. By extension,
it would be expected—and is here asserted—that a reduction
in the level of external demand stems from the perception on
the part of key people within dominant groups that their status
and interests are no longer in jeopardy. Furthermore, it may
also be suggested that a reduction in the rate of deviance production will follow from the perception on the part of dominant
groups that the mass production of deviance is itself a menace
to their interests. This perception is assumed to develop because
members of dominant groups are directly imperiled or because
occurrences connected with mass production of deviance are
damaging to the self-concept of leading actors within powerful
groups.

Additionally, certain consistencies in the behavior of the
European ruling class during the witchcraze have implications
that can be usefully presented as hypotheses. Invariably, it
would seem, powerful interest groups seek to label their enemies
as wicked and a menace to the general welfare. These tactics
not only enhance their own moral capital, but they enlarge the
field of common interests in jeopardy; and, to the degree that
a powerful faction is successful in such endeavors, the potential
for the establishment of countervailing interest groups is reduced.[24] Obviously, from the standpoint of the mass production
of deviance, the success of this strategy is directly tied to the
ability of an interest group to substantiate the existence of a
broadly perilous reality. In turn, the disappearance of a menacing reality from the cognitive map of powerful groups will bring
about a falling out among members of a coalition established
on the basis of common peril. Accordingly, I offer the following
hypotheses:

5.0 The broader the perceived threat to status and self-intereest,
the more likely it is that powerful groups will act in concert.

5.1 The more concerted the actions of powerful interest groups,
the higher the level of external demand.

5.2 The more concerted the actions of powerful interest groups, the less potential there is for the exercise of accountability (as per 4.0).

6.0 Coalitions of interest groups will tend to break down in the absence of the perception that they are facing a common menace.

According to Carl Hempel, the purpose of general laws is "to connect events in patterns which are usually referred to as explanation and prediction."[25] It is fundamentally true that a chasm separates Red baiting in the United States from the slaughters comprising the Great Purge and that yet another separates the Great Purge from the Holocaust. Even within Stalin's very lethal camps, there was at least the fiction of rehabilitation and survival. Hitler's death camps made no such pretense; they were designed to kill all. I do not suggest that the McCarthy era, the Great Purge, and the Holocaust are identical events—just the simple enumeration of differences would require volumes and could never in the realm of particulars be regarded as exhaustive. The differences are not at issue. It is suggested only that these and other events, including the Great Witch-Hunt, share certain underlying features, that they are linked by common social processes, and that it is useful to try and understand what these processes are.

2

The Production of European Witches

European witchcraft is witchcraft. That is, it falls into a broad set of notions about the origins of evil and the nature of wickedness that can be found worldwide. At the core of these sentiments, in every culture, lies a category of rituals and mysteries that is aligned with the belief that some people can cause harm to others through preternatural means (*maleficium*).

Witches can be conceived of as the contradiction of the standards of normality and virtue imposed upon people by society; that is, witches are an embodiment of what is thought to be abnormal and evil. Accordingly, European witches, just as witches in other regions of the world, were thought to fly through the air on a variety of conveyances, change themselves into animals, become invisible, hold orgies, eat human flesh, cause sickness and death to both people and livestock, use magical ointments, ruin crops by provoking bad weather, "run in families," and by and large, be *women*.

It is axiomatic among social anthropologists that witchcraft can be understood only in the context of social structure and the nearly universal tendency to direct suspicion toward the distaff is a prime example of this.[1] Men dominate society (there are no matriarchal societies *sensu stricto*) and women who have, for whatever reason, transcended traditional roles are often accused of witchcraft.

This is a fundamental theme in early modern European society, and it is useful at this juncture to bring in some specific cross-cultural examples. For instance, Scarlet Epstein notes that the introduction of irrigation and consequently cash cropping into a Mysore village in southern India brought considerable wealth to some farmers.[2] A number of these men provided their wives with substantial amounts of cash, enabling them to enter the local money market by offering short-term loans at high interest. Traditionally, borrowing between men involved much larger sums, at low interest, which were often not repaid for many years; these transactions were part of the normal patron-client relationship in this region. Money lent by women, however, generated new and unhappy relationships. Village men do not like women who are independent and they particularly do not like being indebted to them. Such women are often accused of witchcraft. Mysore villagers are well aware that accusations of witchcraft occur between people who have strained relationships, a situation they usually ascribe to the "meanness of women."[3] The primary focus of witchcraft accusations in this setting seems to be women who are beyond the confines of their proper (i.e., inferior) status. This is very typically the case.

Among the Nupe of Nigeria, accusations of witchcraft are also commonly directed at *out of status women*—in this case, women traders. S. F. Nadel argues the following:

> The witch is accused of doing mystically precisely what women, in virtue of their economic power, are accused of doing in real life. So that witchcraft beliefs and fears paraphrase a true state of affairs and the anxieties and frustrations arising from it.[4]

These frustrations and anxieties have been exacerbated by the vast (Nadel's word) increase in trade among the Nupe. Women traders, in the Nupe view, are bad women and bad wives; they are independent and loose and often refuse to have children. "Women alone are evil witches."[5]

These two examples (many others could be adduced) suggest that social change fosters an increase in accusations of witchcraft. At least that is the standard view of social anthropologists who have studied Africa; but it also seems that women in stable communities are often inordinately the focus of suspicion.[6] Edward Harper has gathered some remarkable information on the status of women—particularly widows—among the Havik Brahmins of India.[7] His thesis is that people

> who lack power and prestige, who generally do the bidding of others, and who have minimal control over their own social environment are likely to be portrayed as dangerous or malevolent beings in that society's belief system.[8]

The social position of Havik women provides a lesson in the creation of powerlessness. Havik brides are essentially transferred from one patrilineage to another and male authority over females is virtually absolute. Unlike women in other castes, Havik women cannot enter into financial transactions, worship high gods, or have knowledge of sacred rituals. A woman depends totally on her husband and his lineage. Brothers may *not* marry women from the same family and should avoid marrying women from the same village. That is, brothers should avoid bringing women into the patrilineage who are likely to form alliances. Within the patrilineage, women who bear children into it or are born into it (mothers, sisters, and daughters), are revered; but women who marry into the patrilineage are despised—until they bear children. Fights between women along this division are common. Women are viewed as lustful and prone to lure men away from purity and worship; they provoke jealousy and cause brothers to fight.[9]

Within the Havik Brahmin community, being a widow is the nadir of existence. Havik widows must shave their heads and wear special clothing. They cannot remarry. Widows are universally thought to be dangerous. It is believed that they poison people by means of an obnoxious (but nontoxic) fluid obtained from a local lizard. *All* of the Havik widows in the village studied by Harper were accused of poisoning people by at least one informant.[10] Havik widows are feared in other ways as well: for instance, dreaming of a widow and even the sight of a widow are bad auguries. These women epitomize the degradation of status; yet they have transcended traditional female roles only in the sense that the death of their husbands has removed them from direct male domination. They are, in Nupe terms, "women alone."

Such sentiments are so similar to the European attitude toward women during the fifteenth, sixteenth, and seventeenth centuries that they could have been lifted directly out of any of the many early modern treatises on witchcraft during this period. This, especially, is true of the *Malleus Maleficarum*, a pioneering and influential witch-hunters handbook, notable, among other things, for raising misogyny to an art form. In this book, women are relentlessly depicted as spiteful, lustful, weak in mind, and susceptible to the blandishments of the devil.

EUROPEAN DEMONOLOGY

Bad events demand explanation and all societies have "theories of misfortune." Society is made up of sets of reciprocal expectations; when these expectations are violated and misfortune results, witchcraft is often taken to be the operational explanation. In the classic phrase of E. E. Evans-Pritchard, "Sufferers from misfortune seek for witches among their enemies."[11] Stated more directly, fear, envy, rage, hatred—in sum, the emotions that stem from social tension—lead to accusations of witchcraft.[12] Witchcraft beliefs are a general phenomenon for the simple reason that the normal arrangements of community—and much more so the displacements of social change—generate frustration and hatred.

It is important to understand that European cosmology was for a period of centuries phrased in terms of an elaborate demonology and that witchcraft was then an official theory of misfortune.[13] In the twentieth century, witchcraft is, of course, no longer an official explanation, but it remains a compelling unofficial theory in rural areas of Europe.[14] European countrymen are reluctant to overlook good explanatory bets in the face of a very unlikely series of misfortunes. This attitude is exemplified by the cliché heard in rural Galicia: "Yo no creo en brujas—pero hay" (I don't believe in witches—but they exist).[15]

Perhaps the most surprising feature of the witchcraze is the time of its occurrence. The infamous mass-trials, which frequently led to the deaths of large numbers of people thought to be witches, did not occur during the Middle Ages; rather, they are a fundamental characteristic of the supposedly more humanistic and rational Renaissance and Reformation. This timing, which is by now well documented, provides the key to an understanding of the witchcraze.[16]

The concept of witchcraft held by Europeans in the sixteenth and seventeenth centuries was the result of a confluence of several streams of thought regarding the nature of evil and the origins of misfortune. There was, first of all, the basic notion found in Roman law, of maleficium: wicked people can bring harm to others by preternatural means. This idea was closely linked to the common worldwide figuration of the "night witch," who flies though the air, devours babies, and so on. Regional terms–Bruja, Hexen, Stregoni—which are typically translated into English as "witch," embody this basic concept. But, in addition, witchcraft was, in the mind of the European elite, a notion that was subsumed under the concept of demonology. The witch was conceived of as being someone who had bound herself or himself to the devil by a contract (often in writing—if we are to believe the trial records) and was therefore the devil's servant. It is the legend of Faust come to life. Further, the witch

was regarded as a member of an organized sect that met periodically at a sabbat and orgiastically worshipped Satan in a
rough inversion of ritual Christianity. In this sense, witchcraft
was feared as a particularly terrible form of heresy, and those
who practiced it were considered far more dangerous and insidious than the standard sort of heretic that the Inquisition had
been battling since its inception.[17] By the latter part of the fifteenth century, much of the European elite thought itself directly
threatened by a new and terrible organization of witches, led
by the devil, whose ultimate objective was the destruction of
Christianity.[18]

European society, as it approached the Reformation, was hag-
ridden by the specter of witchcraft. There are a number of indications that trace the development of this obsession. Between
1320 and 1420, thirteen treatises on witchcraft are known to
have been written; but during the period beginning with Johann
Nider's *Formicarius* (1435–1437) and lasting until the publication of Sprenger and Institoris's *Malleus Maleficarum* (1487)
fifty years later, we know of twenty-nine such treatises.[19] In
the age of the printing press, many of these were published
and widely circulated. Without question, the most influential
of these early books on witchcraft was the *Malleus Maleficarum*,
which took its title from the term often applied to Inquisitors—
"Hammer of Heretics."[20] Between 1487 and 1520 it was reprinted
fourteen times.[21]

There is a dramatic connection between many of the men
who provided the intellectual foundations of the witchcraze
and the Council of Basel (1431–43), which was an outgrowth
of the Church's concern over schism and heresy.[22] *Formicarius*,
the first work to establish the misogynystic tone of witch theory,
was written by Nider in Basel while the Council was in session.
Martin Le Franc, author of *Le champion des dames* (circa 1440),
a poem that discusses the sabbat and the insidious role of
women, was secretary to the "pope" elected by the Council.
Nicolas Jacquier, author of *Flagellum haereticorum fascinari-
orum* (1458), which argued the reality of "flying witches," was
a strong advocate of church reform at the Council and was
also a principal inquisitor at the large witch trial at Arras (1459)
in France. This trial, as with many early trials, was characterized
by the lack of any clear distinction in the minds of the inquisitors
between ordinary heresy and witchcraft.[23]

It was in the region surrounding Basel, the Jura of France
and Switzerland, that the separate concepts of heresy and witch-

craft inseparably fused, forming the fatal image of the witch as an apostate servant of the devil. It is entirely possible that this new image of witchcraft was not so much a cause as a consequence of the desire of the Dominicans (the order responsible for carrying out the Inquisition) to obtain jurisdiction over witchcraft as well as heresy.[24] The Dominicans certainly advanced this argument with great vigor.[25] Jean Veneti argues in his *Tractus contra Daemonum Invacatores* (1450), for example, that witchcraft was a new form of heresy unrelated to old-fashioned activities of solitary, peasant witches, who were often looked upon by authorities as ignorant, superstitious rustics.[26] The new cult of witches represented an organized conspiracy.

Norman Cohn makes it clear that the Renaissance witch theorists drew upon an established pattern when they developed the stereotypical image of the devil-worshipping witch.[27] This is a fantasy that has considerable antiquity in European history and was, perhaps, first used to chastise Christian communities of the second century A.D. Even at this early date, accusations focus on orgies, babies eaten in strange rites, and the worship of a god in animal form. Such tales, of course provide a recurrent theme in Western civilization and, once Christianity became the established religion, were invariably used to vilify other "heretical" sects and Jews (and still are, for example, in *The Protocols of the Elders of Zion*). More recently, a number of African independence movements have been accused of similar activities.[28]

The gradual transformation by which the local peasant accused of using witchcraft to kill a neighbor's cow becomes the devil's servant has been studied by Richard Kieckhefer. Prior to 1300, witch trials were so rare, or so few trial records have survived, that they provide no pattern worth mentioning. Between 1300 and 1330, witch trials were infrequent and largely a consequence of political mudslinging between members of the ruling class. The trial of Joan of Arc (1331) provides a convenient benchmark for the end of this period. The one hundred years that follow were marked by a gradual (very gradual at first) increase in the number of records that specifically mention Satanic interference in the affairs of men. This increase, in Kieckhefer's opinion, does not merely reflect an increase in the survival of records but is genuine. However, from the 1430s on, there is clearly an abiding concern on the part of religious and political authorities to defend against *diabolical* witchcraft, and by the second half of the fifteenth century, the proportion of witch trials that specifically mention this new menace is high.[29]

The trial records for the period between 1435 and 1500 provide clear evidence that the fear of a Satanic element in the activities of witches was primarily, if not exclusively, elitist in origin. Those records that bear the mark of peasant culture—the use of vernacular, etc.—rarely mention the devil and deal strictly with maleficium whereas accusations that stem from the judiciary (i.e., the elite) invariably invoke the devil as a cause of mischief.[30]

It is possible to trace this same evolution of thought in the Papal Bulls that make specific reference to witchcraft, sorcery, and magic. As would be expected, every Pope of the fourteenth and fifteenth centuries inveighed against the use of sorcery and magic in some form. But in the fifteenth century these edicts become much more strident. In four bulls, issued between 1434 and 1445, Pope Eugenius IV instructed the Inquisition to move against magicians because they sacrificed to demons, desecrated the cross, and, above all, made pacts with the devil. The implication is that now magicians were under the control of the devil whereas before it was generally supposed that magicians had operated with greater independence. The following Pope, Nicholas V, in 1451 allowed the Inquisition to proceed against simple sorcery.[31] The landmark decision, so to speak, came in 1484 when Pope Innocent VIII issued the bull *Summis desiderantes affectibus* at the urging of the prominent Dominican Inquisitors Institoris and Sprenger. These individuals needed the support of the Holy See to overawe local authorities who had resisted the witch-hunt they had introduced into South Germany. The bull directly admonishes those who

> blasphemously renounce that Faith which they received by the Sacrament of Baptism, and at the instigation of the Enemy of the Human race they do not shrink from committing and perpetrating the foulest abominations and excesses to the peril of their souls, whereby they offend the Divine Majesty and are a cause of scandal and dangerous example to very many.[32]

Furthermore, the pope castigated those evidently numerous clerics and laymen who interfered with his inquisitors, and he empowered the Bishop of Strasbourg to use the threat of excommunication in the event that this interference should continue. Most important, the bull was included as a preface

to the *Malleus Maleficarum* (1487) written by Institoris and
Sprenger and was taken by the Inquisition and by many secular
authorities as a mandate to pursue the war against the "new"
witchcraft.

The *Malleus Maleficarum* deserves attention. It had the seal
of papal approval, and its scholastic organization and wealth
of anecdotal material, gathered by the authors during trials that
resulted in the burning of at least forty-eight witches, made
it intellectually fashionable. Just the same, the direct influence
of the *Malleus Maleficarum* on the popular mind was limited.
The book was written in scholarly Latin and was probably
largely inaccessible, even to the typical village priest. But in
reaching the audience it was directed toward, the Inquisition
and its secular support, the *Malleus Maleficarum* was effective
on two levels. As a theoretical treatise it persuasively linked
the maleficia of popular sorcery with the activities of the devil.[33]
It is obvious that the authors of the *Malleus Maleficarum* specifically sought to deny leverage to those who would oppose the
idea that witchcraft was heresy; their purpose is set out clearly
on the title page, which declares, "To disbelieve in witchcraft
is the greatest heresy of all." And, on a purely practical level,
it was in every sense a handbook offering a wealth of advice
to the novice witch-hunter, as well as samples of a variety of
useful bureaucratic forms—that is, depositions, questionnaires,
and so on.

Institoris and Sprenger argued that the menace of witchcraft
was so widespread that the aid of secular courts was needed.
(It was obviously needed, from their point of view, in territories
that did not permit the Inquisition to operate.) In the sixteenth
and seventeenth centuries the secular state was to follow this
advice with alacrity. In fact, as H. C. Eric Midelfort notes, "The
state proved more efficient in this ecclesiastical role than perhaps it ever was in any other role it has assumed."[34]

By the end of the fifteenth century, the only major facet of
the witchcraze that had not been fully developed was the sabbat,
which would be elaborated upon in the sixteenth century. In
sum, the epistemic process that was initiated in the minds of
the European elite in the fifteenth century began to bear fruit
by the mid-sixteenth century; and from then on, until the witchcraze had run its course, the devil was a permanent fixture
in the witch trials of Europe.

The hallmark of this preoccupation with the devil and his servants was the *Devil-book*. Unlike the formal treatises of the fif-

teenth century, these books were metaphysical potboilers aimed
at a general audience. Enormously popular, devil-books depicted
to an agitated public the powers of witches, magicians, and
the devil and generally disseminated the notion that the devil
was everywhere. Dozens of these books were written, and over
one hundred thousand copies were printed and reprinted between 1552 and 1600 for the German market.[35] Throughout
Europe the witchcraze was characterized by a steady stream
of broadsheets and pamphlets on the subject of witch trials,
and for the period after 1580, and particularly between 1590
and 1610, a bombardment of demonologies fell upon the literate
and quasi-literate public.[36] These works by many of the notables
and leading intellectuals of Europe—Remy, Del Rio, Boquet,
Bodin, James VI of Scotland, and others—were either written
or reprinted in the vernacular, and were accessible to a very
substantial public. Geoffrey Parker notes that from 1550 to 1650,
in France alone, 235 books and pamphlets were published on
witchcraft, "creating the impression that a comprehensive alternative religion existed, posing a major threat to Christianity."[37]
This literature fueled the reality upon which the witchcraze
was based.

THE DARK FIGURE

The witchcraze is generally thought to span the period from
1550 to 1680[38] and to have brought about the execution of something in the neighborhood of one hundred thousand people
for the practice of witchcraft. This, at least, is the generally
accepted "dark figure"; however, many authorities suggest that
the number of people put to death was much larger.[39]

On the Continent and in Scotland the penalty for witchcraft
was typically death by fire. In England where, on the whole,
very few people were executed for the crime of witchcraft, the
maximum penalty was hanging. The Caroline Code (Constitutio
Criminalis Carolina) initiated under Charles V in 1532 was probably the most influential criminal code, affecting much of what
is now Germany and Switzerland. It states (article 109):

Item, when someone harms people or brings them trouble by witchcraft, one should punish them with death, and one should use
the punishment of death by fire. When, however, someone uses
witchcraft and yet does no one any harm with it, he should be

punished otherwise, according to the custom of the case; and the judges should take counsel as is described later regarding legal consultations.[40]

"According to the custom of the case" meant, in actuality, that if a confessed witch had been cooperative (had accused others), she or he might be given a lesser sentence, or, if sentenced to death, the witch might be given the luxury of being beheaded or strangled before her or his corpse was consigned to the fire. But in Europe, witches often died horribly, burned alive.

By all indications the pattern of witchcraft prosecution ran counter to that of normal crime. Despite the views emphasized in the popular press ("crime waves" are often enforcement waves), the frequency of most crimes is (and evidently was) rather constant; that is, changes in frequency are gradual. But, in sharp contrast, witchcraft trials are statistically more like epidemics. The witchcraze was characterized by localized plagues of witches.[41] There is no evidence for an evenly distributed Continent-wide increase in the frequency of witch killing. Witch killing was *always* geographically limited, with some regions of Europe putting witches to death in batches while others, during the same period, killed few or none.

The key word here is *epidemic*. In community terms, the witch killing epidemics were characterized by the *panic-trial*, which has been defined by Midelfort as a trail that resulted in more than twenty executions in the space of a year.[42] By this criterion there were dozens (and very likely hundreds) of panic-trials in Continental Europe during the witchcraze. Many of these trials took hundreds of lives. From the German southwest alone, which was notorious for killing witches, there is documentary evidence for forty trials that resulted in the execution of ten or more individuals in a year's time.[43] Overall, there are extant records indicating that some 200 of the 299 towns in the region of southwest Germany studied by Midelfort experienced "some sort of epidemic between 1500 and 1680."[44] Moreover, it is likely that many witch-hunts have gone undetected since documentation may have been destroyed or lies buried in disorganized archives.[45] It was the panic-trial that accounted for most of the deaths brought about by the witchcraze.

The more typical sort of trial, which resulted in the execution of only one or two stereotypical witches, continued between peak years of witch killing and also made a contribution to the slaughter. This type of trial existed long before the witch-craze and lasted long after it, in fact, well into the eighteenth century in some areas.

The critical role of the panic-trial was entirely understood by contemporary critics. The Jesuit Friedrich von Spee wrote in his *Cautio Criminalis* (1631) that during his years as a confessor to witches (an experience that reportedly turned his hair snow white) he had yet to encounter a single person who had actually done the things to which she or he had confessed under torture. His views on the place that torture occupied in the process of the panic-trial are clear:

> . . . A single innocent person, compelled by torture to confess guilt, is forced to denounce others of whom she knows nothing; so it fares with these, and thus there is scarcely an end to accusers and accused, and as none dares retract, all are marked for death.[46]

Such criticism was not new; in 1563 Johann Weyer in *De Praestigiis Daemonum* writes that people suspected of witchcraft were

> ". . . constantly dragged out to suffer awful torture until they would gladly exchange this most bitter existence for death," and that it was obvious that they would confess to "whatever crimes were suggested to them rather than be thrust back into their hideous dungeons amid ever recurring torture."[47]

Both Weyer and von Spee had a clear understanding of the larger perspective and significance of he panic-trial. Von Spee writes:

> We see again that a witch trial, once begun drags on through several years, and that the number of condemned grows so that whole villages are wiped out, and nothing is concluded before the trial reports contains the names of further suspects. If this should continue, there will be no end of witch burnings before the whole country is depopulated. Thus, finally, every prince has had to stop the trials. Down to today, every trial of this sort has had to be stopped by an edict. They never find their own conclusion.[48]

It is exactly the perception of modern scholars although, in fact, it is something of an exaggeration. Most panic-trials stopped before the imposition of authoritarian edicts, but exactly why they came to a halt remains a puzzle. Much more is known about the genesis of panic-trials than is known about what brought them to a halt. Nonetheless, it should be emphasize that in some cases reality approached the image of the runaway panic-trial provided by von Spee.

Decimation has a precise meaning and it must be understood that a panic-trial could literally decimate communities that sustained them. Examples of this type of trail are found throughout Europe, but they seem to have been most characteristic of the German-speaking regions.[49] E. William Monter suggests that "probably more witches were killed within the confines of present-day Germany than the rest of Europe together."[50] The litany of panic-trials from this region is astonishing, and it is clear that while the slaughter of witches was localized, it was otherwise essentially unrestrained. Only a few of the more extreme cases will be mentioned.

Probably the most notorious example occurred in Bamberg. Here, Prince-Bishop Johann Georg II burned approximately 600 people in the space of ten years, 1623–33. His victims were tried in a special "witch-house" equipped with two dozen or so cells and an elaborate torture chamber.[51] Bishop Philipp Adolf von Ehrenberg of Würzberg, at about the same time, is reported to have executed 900 suspected witches. Although it is only reasonable to suspect some exaggeration, for the period from 1627 to 1629, the best documented, there are precise records of 156 people being put to death in twenty-nine separate bonfires.[52] To continue, records state that in the bishopric of Eichstatt (Franconia), 274 witches were executed in one year alone (1629); and in Trier, in the Rhineland, the archbishop-elector presided over a witch hunt that burned 368 witches in only five years. In two of the small villages thus affected, only one woman was left alive. Finally, since the picture should be clear by now, in 1589 in the tiny area under the control of the convent of Quedlinburg, 133 witches were executed in a single day.[53]

Outside of what is now Germany, panic-trials were most common in Lorraine, Switzerland, the Franche-Comté, the Pyrenees, the Low Countries, Scotland, and Sweden.[54] As a matter of record, the careful and reliable Spanish Inquisitor Salazar writes that the French Judge Pierre de Lancre burned at least 80 witches in the French Pyrenees during the course of his commission, which is known to have lasted for only four months. De Lancre is the author of the *Tableau de l'inconstance des mauvais anges et demons* (1613). This work elaborates the notion of the witches' sabbat to the point where Satan, along with legions of demons and witches, was supposed to fly to abandoned fields for revels at the rate of two, three, sometimes four, times a week. These phantasmagoria were often accepted as the truth and had considerable influence beyond the local region.[55]

In Lorraine, the French Judge Nicholas Remy claimed to have knowledge of 900 people executed for witchcraft in the space of fifteen years. He is casual about the number that he personally sentenced to death but does provide a figure of 200 "more or less" sentenced to the stake for "making hail."[56]

James VI introduced the witchcraze into Scotland in a response to the attempt on the part of an assembly of 200 witches at North Berwick to raise a storm at sea and drown the king and his bride. The resulting trials advertised the king's faith and are likely to have been, in part, an attempt to smear a political opponent, the Earl of Bothwell; but the cycle of accusations eventually involved about 100 ordinary people, of whom many were executed.[57] Including this episode and until 1735, Scotland executed "something over a thousand people," the majority during five intense nationwide hunts.[58]

In Calvinist Geneva and the surrounding territory, local beliefs linked plague and witchcraft; accordingly, during epidemics the toll of people suspected of witchcraft—and therefore of spreading diseases—was high. Twenty-nine such unfortunates were executed during a plague in Geneva in 1545; and during the epidemic of 1571, 36 people were put to death. In the French-speaking cantons of what is now Switzerland, "It seems that almost every village had some trials for witchcraft."[59]

The witchcraze came late to Sweden although reports of witchcraft were common at the ethnic border separating Scandinavians from Lapps. Under the rule of Queen Christina, witch-hunting was scattered and feeble, and not until her exile during the 1660s did panic-trials occur. The worst outbreak took place in the town of Mora in 1669, when accusations by children brought about a trial that resulted in the burning of 85 people for witchcraft.[60]

Panic-trials were extraordinarily numerous in the German southwest, and it is useful to look in detail at a number of such episodes. The witchcraze in southwest Germany had an abrupt beginning. In the town of Wiesensteig several women were arrested following a severe storm on 2 August 1562. They were promptly killed. Over the weeks that followed, 41 women were executed for witchcraft and sorcery, and on 2 December

1562, 20 more women were killed. The archival sources no longer contain the trial records (they were probably lost when much of the town burned in 1648), but there is substantial indirect evidence supporting the figure provided by a pamphlet dated 1563 revealing "The True and Terrible Acts and Deeds of the Sixty-Three Witches and Sorceresses Who Were Burned at Wiesensteig." While the exact nature of the trials is unclear, there is solid evidence of the antecedent conditions. Wiesensteig was already the scene of bitter religious factionalism when, in 1562, the combined misfortune of summer hailstorms and an epidemic evidently provided a catalyst.[61]

Over the course of thirty years, at least 150 people were executed in Rottenburg, a town of roughly 2,750 people. The considerable majority were women. Midway through this period of destruction, the town fathers imposed a halt to the killing of witches, insisting that if the burnings were to continue at the established pace, there would be no women left. Unhappily, this cautionary edict had only temporary impact, and the town soon enthusiastically returned to witch killing.[62]

Ellwangen, a small town in southwestern Germany, provides an archetypical instance of a panic-trial. The documentation is extensive. The questioning of a single individual—a seventy-year-old woman—led to a cycle of torture and accusation that brought about the death of close to 400 people between 1611 and 1618. More than 250 people were executed in repeated mass burnings during the first two years alone![63]

The monasterial lands of Obermarchtal, which comprised a population of about 700, provides another example of just how devastating a panic-trial could be. Witch killing began in 1580 and continued by small fits and starts well into the eighteenth century. The valley suffered one major panic-trial. The documentation provides little indication of preliminary events aside from suggesting pervasive and bitter impoverishment. As might be expected, all of the witches in this territory were poor peasants. In 1580 a man was executed for his connections with the devil. There were no further executions for witchcraft until 1586. Then, abruptly, from June of that year until some time in 1588, 53 people were burned, including 42 women, and 11 men. In short, in less than 2½ years, roughly 7½ percent of the resident population of Obermarchtal died as witches. It is clear from the extant records that the local judiciary placed extraordinary emphasis on determining the identity of the accomplices of the accused witches. This emphasis, in combination with the use of torture, resulted in the chain reaction so feared by von Spee.[64]

The broad outline of European witch production has been established, but, in summary, a number of points should be brought into sharp relief. First, European witchcraft was unique only because of its conceptualization by a Christian elite as a particular heresy. The French demonologist Jean Bodin, writing in 1580, presents the contemporary view very cogently: a witch is "one who knowing God's law tries to bring about some act through an agreement with the Devil."[65]

Second, this unique conceptualization of witchcraft was entirely self-serving to the growing apparatus of social control in post-Renaissance Europe. The record of the Inquisition and the writing of the scholarly inquisitors lends support to the position taken long ago by the rationalist historians. George Lincoln Burr observes:

> When, in the lands where the Inquisition had found entrance, heresy was at last utterly rooted out—when the souls of the faithful were safe and the hands of the inquisitors idle—then, as was natural, the hungry organization cast its eyes about for other victims.[66]

Third, the European witchcraze is not a feature of the dark, "superstitious" medieval period; it is, instead, part and parcel of the Reformation and Counter-Reformation. The witchcraze and the modern nation state emerged together and are a product of the same strategy of social control.

3

The Origins of the European Witchcraze

Party-line explanations for the almost universal occurrence of witchcraft in tribal societies and among peasants invoke a variety of appeals to functionalism.[1] There is overwhelming empirical support for the contention that witchcraft provides an explanation for misfortune. Stated more simply, if you ask people why they have suffered this or that calamity, they will say that it was brought about by a witch.[2] Furthermore, since all societies that believe in witchcraft have established methods for dealing with its onslaughts, it can be argued that witch beliefs allow the sufferer to focus his or her anxiety on what they believe to be a logical cause for their misfortune and to take specific remedial action. This is thought to be psychologically desirable and is therefore said to be functional. In addition, accusations of witchcraft are a mainstay of the social sanctioning system. In any kinship-based society, unorthodox and erratic personalities are the usual target of accusations of witchcraft. Nadel, in his analysis of witchcraft among the Nupe, declares categorically that accusations of witchcraft are "an attack upon behavior and character traits held undesirable."[3]

Witchcraft beliefs also serve the established order in that, as Lucy Mair puts it, "The mystical agencies of deserved punishment call witches to their aid."[4] Alan Macfarlane discovered in his study of English village life during the sixteenth and seventeenth centuries that during this period traditional networks of exchange and responsibility came under pressure. Those institutions that had traditionally aided the poor, such as neighborly support, church relief, and manorial organization, were especially taxed. In England, the sixteenth and seventeenth centuries saw the creation of a category of poor within the village who had ties with the property-holding members of the village. The vagrant poor were not a problem because they could be simply driven away; but the village poor were properly owed support. It was this category of people, the village poor with a righteous claim on local charity, who were most often the target of accusations of witchcraft.[5] Those villagers who had refused to give aid and comfort—"God's good"—to their needy neighbors often felt themselves to be afflicted by witches. George Gifford, a local commentator, says that "It is not godly zeal but furious rage" that led to accusations.[6] The advent of the Poor Laws altered this situation, and accusations of witchcraft fell off following their implementation. The Poor Laws allowed the English villagers to deal with their poor neighbors as abstractions, bureaucratically, at the distance of formality.

Although it must be acknowledged that witchcraft beliefs clearly have a number of recognizable effects within society and can in that sense be regarded as a solution to social problems, it is a mistake to consider witchcraft beliefs to be a perfect or final solution. Nadel, for example, argues that the impact of such beliefs within society should be thought of as something rather like a drug with side effects that poison the system.[7]

WOMEN AND WITCHES: A LINKED STATUS

The structural vulnerability of women worldwide to accusations of witchcraft has already been discussed. In Europe it has been suggested that this vulnerability intensified as a result of demographic changes in the early modern period and because of the special liability of particular female roles in light of the teachings of continental demonology. For instance, in England midwives were not especially likely to be accused of witchcraft and Macfarlane in his careful study found nothing to support the idea that villagers in Essex were more prone to suspect midwives than other women. But on the Continent, in the context of full blown demonology, midwives were felt to make up a sizable part of the devil's constituency. Even by peasant standards, the economic position of midwives was miserable and the their status so low in some areas that they were looked down upon by barbers and executioners. The son of a midwife was often excluded from membership in a guild.[8] Most damning was the belief that the devil and his servants used newborn babies in the preparation of a special ointment that enabled witches to fly. Being the logical source for this commodity, it was believed that midwives stole newborns and delivered them to the devil. Naturally, the unexplained death of a newborn infant was often accompanied by a charge of witchcraft.

Christina Larner emphasizes that in many respects witch-hunting must be considered to be essentially *woman hunting*.[9] The European stereotype of a witch as an old, ugly, solitary, poor woman is the personification of social vulnerability. Admittedly, there were local exceptions, but as a rule of thumb, something on the order of 80 to 90 percent of all people executed as witches were women.[10]

It can hardly be overlooked that witch-hunting in Europe was associated with an unparalleled eruption of misogyny. It has been argued that this broad attack on the image and status of women has its origins in the profound demographic changes that have been documented on the Continent and in England for this period.[11] During the sixteenth century the pattern of European marriage underwent a fundamental change. Towards the end of the fifteenth century and increasingly throughout the sixteenth century, the mean age of first marriage for women rose dramatically throughout much of Europe. Michael Flinn notes that although

> figures of under twenty at one extreme or over thirty at the other may be found in some parishes, the range of mean ages of women at first marriage for all parts of the *ancien regime* of Europe for which we now have calculations is generally much narrower, and national means based on all available figures within countries all fall within little more than a two-year range between 24 and a half and 26 and a half.[12]

In addition, the percentage of women who did not marry before the age of fifty—who were spinsters—ranged between 10 and 20 percent; and the percentage of unmarried women of all categories (i.e., young, widowed, or a spinster) was in the neighborhood of 50 percent or more.[13]

There is evidence that in at least some parts of Europe, if not generally, the transition from a pattern of early marriage for the vast majority of women to the late marriage pattern of early modern Europe was rapid. In Geneva it was especially rapid. Only 15 percent of Genevan women at first marriage were over twenty-three years of age in the 1580s; but in the decade that followed, almost 40 percent were over the age of twenty-three, with a *median* age of twenty-two at first marriage.[14] To Monter:

> The statistical demonstration seems clear; between 1590 and 1620 native born Genevan women moved from a "transitional" marriage pattern with a bare majority of teen-age brides, to an almost "completed" marriage pattern.[15]

This transition seems to have been linked to economic factors. The cause of the transition to the European marriage pattern (meaning late marriage) in this region, according to Monter, is

> something familiar to historical demographers—famine—reinforced by something familiar to traditional historians—war. The region around Geneva suffered a memorable famine in 1586–1587, its worst in a century; then it experienced its worst war in centuries between 1589 and 1593. Taken together, they wreaked havoc on the countryside.[16]

Flinn also advocates the position that economic factors as much as anything are behind the transition to late marriage. He argues that the European experience as a whole was generally similar to that of postfamine Ireland roughly three centuries later.[17]

In a society that had little place for women outside of the family or the convent, the presence of a substantial percentage of women who were *not* directly under masculine control must have been hard to digest. Women were taken to be a seditious element, especially liable to be influenced by the devil.[18] The vulnerability of women to diabolical influence is one of the central themes of the *Malleus Maleficarum* and, indeed, all demonologies. The poverty of these women looms large. Among the three motivations that bring people to witchcraft, according to James VI in his *Daemonologie* (1597), is "greedy appetite of gear, caused through great poverty."[19] Poverty is also a standard fixture in the confessions of the relatively small percentage of women who seem to have genuinely believed that they were witches. Such women typically reported that the devil offered them money and security. Invariably the amount of money offered was pitifully small (a few coins that often turned to stones or leaves by the next day), and, as a rule, the devil promised simply that these women and their children would not suffer for want of food and clothes.[20] These cases are especially poignant. Elizabeth Southern, for example, was promised two and sixpence by the devil; but according to Elizabeth, he later reneged "and complained of the hardness of the times."[21]

SOCIAL STRAIN

It is a standard anthropological homily that social strain will bring about an increase in the number of accusations of witchcraft. Indeed, some anthropologists have used the frequency of witchcraft accusations as an index of social strain.[22]

The concept of social strain follows logically from the treatment of society as a system in that it can be argued that when the component elements of this system become discrepant, the result is something identified as *social strain*. Robert Merton, in his well-known work on social structure and anomie, employs this theme to argue that social structure pressures individuals into nonconforming behavior. In Merton's view, the clash between preferred goals and practical means fosters deviant behavior.[23] The *strain* lies in the disjunction of system elements and *not* in the individual.

But, while the distinction between psychological strain and social strain is theoretically useful, it is also analytically troublesome. The tendency is to automatically view psychological strain as a symptom of "deeper" (i.e., more abstract) system strain. This conceptual thicket can be avoided simply by abandoning much of the intellectual baggage of functionalism and defining strain as something that resides in the psychological realm. And, in fact, psychological reductionism is often bootlegged into the analyses of functionalists. Albert Cohen, in his analysis of deviance, comments, "It is apparent that the actual sense of frustration, despair, injustice—in general, of strain—does not depend on any one of these (goals, means, norms) but on the relationship among them."[24] In other words, system disjunction is one cause of psychological strain. More to the point, reductionism beckons because in the final analysis it is people and not systems that act. It is an interesting intellectual exercise to argue that the social disruptions occasioned by discrepant system components somehow motivated the people of early modern Europe to burn witches; but it is not true to say that discrepant system components burned witches. Social change can be said to foster strain because the alterations of social conditions identified as "change" often adversely affect the life chances of particular categories of people, or so devastatingly impinge on the security of their world view that it results in feelings of anxiety, frustration, anomie, and rage.

THE SOCIAL SETTING OF SIXTEENTH- AND SEVENTEENTH CENTURY EUROPE

Not only were the sixteenth and seventeenth centuries periods of wrenching social change, they were also the occasion for frequent and bitter hard times. Voltaire, in his *Essai sur les moeur et l'esprit des nations* (1756), argued that the seventeenth century was in turmoil over the "three things that exercise a constant influence over the minds of men: climate, government, and religion."[25] Many contemporary historians are willing to declare roundly that the early modern era (1500 to 1700) was a period of unusual privation and widespread anxiety. The mechanisms marshalled to support this assertion range from the grand processes of social change—such as the "crisis of feudalism"—to those already noted by Voltaire.

The documentation of frequent and intense hard times for the sixteenth and seventeenth centuries has gone far beyond the simple enumeration of wars and famines (in itself compelling). On the matter of climate, Parker notes:

> All evidence, whether gathered by historians, meteorologists or solar physicists, points to a climate of greater extremes of weather and in particular to cooler and wetter summers in the temperate zone, during the seventeenth century, with a particularly severe period between 1640 and 1660.[26]

The effect of this on food supplies was devastating. Ester Boserup states flatly, "The worst period of famines in western Europe seems to have occurred in the seventeenth century." Henry Kamen, in *The Iron Century, 1550 to 1660,* discusses the unusual intensity and frequency of famine, warfare, and disease.[27] All of these conditions are intimately related; and what H. R. Trevor-Roper has chosen to label the "General Crisis of the Seventeenth Century" was rooted in demographic and economic factors found in the sixteenth century.[28] Population increased, prices rose, and wages fell.

The best single index of mounting privation is probably the price of wheat. The cost of this commodity rose steadily throughout Europe for the period from 1500 to 1650. Generally the price of necessities rose and the standard of living declined in measure.[29] In this connection, Parker notes that the habit of separating the poor into the "deserving poor" and the "undeserving poor" became common in the sixteenth century for the simple reason that the poor were so universally present during this period.[30] This overall historical perspective on the early modern period certainly corresponds to the view of contemporaries. It is the Hobbesian world depicted in the *Leviathan* (1651) and portrayed in the paintings and engravings of Pieter Breughel and Jacque Callot.

From this standpoint, it is not surprising that historians have been quick to ascribe the witchcraze to the privations of this period. Paralleling Max Marwick, V. G. Kiernan argues that "The dementia of the witchcraze . . . was a more faithful index of the depth of the social and spiritual crisis than the falling-out of Protestant and Catholic."[31] Parker, less grandly, simply states, "It is true that accusations were lodged in years of dearth."[32] Similarly, Kamen says:

> In every European country the most intensive outbreaks of witch persecution were in time of disaster. Taking the long view, the equation of crisis and witchcraft becomes even more striking. It was the very period of greatest price rise—the late sixteenth and early seventeenth centuries—that saw the most numerous cases of accusation and persecution of witches.[33]

An inspection of other periods in European history offers support for this explanatory focus. The fourteenth century, also a period of unusual privation, was characterized by massive outbreaks of the most bizarre sorts of collective behavior as well as an apparent upswing (albeit mild) in formal accusations of witchcraft.[34] Kieckhefer, noting a spurt of witch trials around 1375, suggests that these may have resulted from the social tensions brought about by the large scale migration of peasants to urban areas following the plague.[35]

All of this notwithstanding, the concept of strain does not alone provide anything like a forceful explanation for the mass production of witches in early modern Europe. Two compelling objections have been raised by Christina Larner. First of all, it is undeniable that the persecution of witches has been a major preoccupation within societies that do *not* seem to have under-gone either massive social change or unusual privation. Larner notes of Scotland, where the destruction of people supposed to have been witches approached continental dimensions, that the social and economic structure was relatively unchanged for a period a great deal longer at both ends than that covered by the witch prosecutions.[36]

Conversely, it is possible to point to societies that experienced massive social change but did *not* experience anything like the mass production of witches. For instance, England underwent a dramatic social transformation during the early modern period but, at the same time, executed very few witches.

Second, the peasantry, which naturally bore the brunt of hard times everywhere, could not on its own legally kill a suspected witch. The production of witches in England was minimal even in the face of the absolute conviction on the part of the English peasantry that witches were exceedingly active. The requisite legal machinery to control witches was in the hands of another group. It cannot be emphasized enough that witch-hunting was an activity that could only be undertaken by those who had control of the legal system. Witch-hunting, to put it directly, was a ruling class activity.

> Peasants left to themselves will identify inividuals as witches and will resort to a variety of anti-witchcraft measures in self-defense, [but] they cannot pursue these measures to the punishment, banishment or official execution of even one witch, let alone a multiplicity of witches without the administrative machinery and encouragement of their rulers. When encouragement is forthcoming, however, they can supply an almost unlimited number of suspects.[37]

The point is that the concept of social strain cannot be regarded as a necessary cause of the European witchcraze; nor can it be invoked willy-nilly as an efficient cause unless it can be demonstrated that powerful groups in Europe were so pressured. Larner makes this very clear:

> The principal factor which makes the social strain explanation unsatisfactory when applied to the continental witch-hunt ... is the conspicuous and unequivocal way in which the ruling elite controlled and manipulated the demand for and the supply of witchcraft suspects. The behavior and motivation of the elite therefore, seems more important in explaining witch-hunting ... than the experiences of the peasantry.[38]

In Scotland there was a very strict link between expressions of official anxiety and the outbreak of national witch-hunts. This was generally the case throughout most of Europe during the sixteenth and seventeenth centuries. The impression obtained from the English evidence is that periods of dearth and rapid social change had the general effect of increasing the capacity of the peasantry to act as a reservoir of potential deviants that could be drawn upon as the ruling class saw fit. During periods of relative tranquility among the ruling class, the impact of a strained, witch-ridden peasantry on the production of official deviance was small. Such periods are characterized by a high rate of acquittals. The evidence for Essex County supports this assertion. Overall, the number of people hanged for witchcraft in England was very small, and the largest trial executed only 19 people. C. L'Estrange Ewen estimated the number of people executed for the crime of witchcraft in England to be a little less than a thousand. But Ewen's estimate was largely an extrapolation from the Assize records of Essex County, which are the best preserved for the period; a more recent estimate by Larner—of about 500 executions—takes into account new information that strongly indicates the situation in Essex County was atypical.[39] From all present indications, accusations and prosecutions for witchcraft were far more common in Essex County than in either Sussex or neighboring Hertfordshire County (both of which have reasonably good documentation for some of the early modern period). In Sussex County only 2 of 546 indictments were for witchcraft, and in Hertfordshire, 17 of 1018. But in Essex County, from 1559 to 1603, 5 percent of the indictments were for witchcraft, second only to theft. Moreover, during the decade of 1580 to 1589, it was fully 13 percent.[40]

Essex County was densely populated, and relatively advanced agriculturally, and it was a center of cloth manufacture. In short, it is reasonable to argue that Essex County was undergoing a considerable degree of social change relative to rural—by sixteenth-century standards—Sussex and Hertfordshire. It was probably also experiencing far more social strain. It can be argued that this greater level of strain accounts for the far greater number of executions for witchcraft in Essex County. Nevertheless, it is important not to exaggerate the impact of social change in Essex County. The vast bulk of the witch killing in Essex was concentrated into two episodes. The first of these, as noted, brackets the 1580s and is roughly correlative with the height

of the Catholic missionary movement, which was considered
(with some justification) by the Crown to be a political conspiracy.[41] The second, in the seventeenth century, involved the-
appearance of an especially persuasive witch-hunter in Essex
County against the backdrop of the English Civil War, a period
when *all* strata of English society were experiencing social
strain. Without these two "epidemics," the overall number of
indictments and executions in Essex County would have been
dramatically lower.

It is quite clear that during tranquil periods, the English gentry, who controlled the court system (and especially the Grand
Jury), was inclined to be distrustful of the evidence marshalled
against a particular individual. Generally, the rate of conviction
was low and it was only during periods of ruling class anxiety,
which are marked by direct statements of alarm, that the rate
of conviction increased dramatically. But at the same time, it
is very clear that the typical Essex villager was always obsessed
(the word is not too strong) with the perils of witchcraft. The
local observer George Gifford comments repeatedly on the very
high level of anxiety. He recreates an exchange between two
villagers in *A Dialogue Concerning Witches and Witchcraftes*
(1593). When asked why he should think that he has been bewitched, one speaker answers:

> Trust me I cannot tell, but I feare me I have, for there be two
> or three in our towne which I like not, but especially an old woman,
> I have been as careful to please her as ever I was to please mine
> own mother, and to give her ever and anon one thing or other,
> and yet me thinkes she frowns at me now and then.[42]

Even more informative are the frequent references to suspected witchcraft in the casebooks of two Essex doctors. In the
casebook of Richard Napier, spanning a period of thirty-four
years (1600 to 1634), there are 120 references to patients complaining of afflictions that they thought to be the result of witchcraft; and, in the casebook of William Lilly, covering the years
from 1644 to 1666, there are at least 50 cases of suspected
witchcraft. Yet none of these complaints were ever broached
in court; there is not the slightest hint that any of this suspicion
and enmity ever came to any official recognition.[43] It is very
hard to avoid the conclusion that the ruling class was, by and
large, indifferent to such matters except during periods when

it was pressured and anxious and particularly when this anxiety derived from perceptions of an internal conspiracy.

In England the judiciary seems to have accepted the concept of maleficium in principle; that is, most magistrates believed that it was possible to harm others by occult means. But in practice, during most periods of English history, there was a tendency to be skeptical that this or that suspect was in fact guilty.[44] Judicial skepticism, plus the nature of English common law, very clearly reduced the severity and the frequency of panic-trials in England.

On the Continent, however, the demonological conception of witchcraft was embraced wholeheartedly by nearly everyone in the powerful classes. As a practical matter there were no thoroughgoing Continental skeptics, and even the most cele-brated criticisms of the witchcraze were really directed against judicial procedure. The result of this Neoplatonic reality was that when a genuinely frightened judiciary dipped into the reser-voir of the local peasant population for witches, it would be inundated with accusations. Even to territories under the control of the Spanish Inquisition, which tended to use torture only sparingly, the prodding and intimidation of inquisitors, coupled with peasant preoccupation with witchcraft, could generate a multitude of official deviants in a very short time.

MONITORING DEVIANCE: THE SPANISH INQUISITION

The Spanish Inquisition was virtually a state within a state and was protected by law even from the inroads of the crown. Nor was it under direct Papal authority; the Spanish crown and not Rome appointed the Inquisitor General. Every organiza-tional feature of the Spanish Inquisition was bent to the purpose of maintaining its immunity from outside influence. It main-tained its own sources of income, and all of its members were sworn to secrecy. Even the king could not obtain information that the Inquisition did not wish to divulge. Functionaries of the Inquisition could not be tried by secular authority. In all cases except rape, treason, and highway robbery, the jurisdiction of the Holy Office prevailed. The Inquisition had its own minis-try, its own court system (the Tribunals), its own prison system, and its own intelligence service. It even had its own fraternity (The Brotherhood of Saint Peter the Martyr). All functionaries within this internal state system were carefully screened. A certificate of family purity (limpieza de Sangre), which attested to a multigenerational absence of family heretics, was required.[45]

Organizational immunity and an all-pervasive secrecy are the keys to the power of the Spanish Inquisition. Its activities, ancient archives, and even the names of the people in its prisons were inaccessible to outsiders. Suspects who came under the control of the Inquisition often simply disappeared without a trace into special secret prisons. Kamen notes of these institutions:

> Prisoners were cut off strictly from all contact with the world outside and even within the prison were secluded from each other whenever possible. On finally leaving the gaol they were obliged to take an oath not to reveal anything they had seen or experienced in the cells. Small wonder if this absolute secrecy gave rise to the most blood-curdling legends about what went on inside.[46]

Despite this image, the use of torture by the Spanish Inquisition, in comparison to much of Europe, was relatively mild and subject to close supervision. La Suprema (The Supreme Council of the Inquisition) was quick to rebuke overzealous inquisitors, and it is estimated that only about one-third of those individuals accused of crimes that warranted the application of torture were, indeed, tortured.[47]

The fact that the Spanish Inquisition did not produce vast numbers of deviants (during most periods of its existence) was almost entirely due to its highly developed system of organizational restraint. Gustave Henningsen writes:

> There was one redeeming feature of this state within a state: its tremendous self-control. La Suprema was vigilant in ascertaining that its laws and regulations were strictly adhered to, and this was primarily ensured by the inspections which each provincial court was subjected to from time to time and which could last for years. The inquisitor general was always ready to listen to complaints of abuse, and it was possible for these complaints to be anonymous. Thus in order to control the tribunals la Suprema applied the very same methods towards its own officials as ordinarily applied to heretics.[48]

The Spanish Inquisition, then, unlike the secular courts of northern Europe, had a finely tuned ability to control the activities of its functionaries. The operations of this internal dynamic during the Great Basque Witch-Hunt illustrates the control that a bureaucratic structure can exert over the production of deviants.

THE GREAT BASQUE WITCH-HUNT

Much of the massive correspondence of the principal inquisitors involved in the Great Basque Witch-Hunt has survived, providing a clear picture of the production of witches in this small sector of early modern Europe. In the fall of 1608 the spy network of the Spanish Inquisition reported that witchcraft was being practiced around the Basque town of Zugarramundie. The Tribunal at Logroño responsible for the Province of Navarre in northern Spain promptly dispatched a commissioner and notary to investigate. Their report confirming the presence of witches in large numbers reached the inquisitors Alonso Becerra Holquin and Juan de Valle Alvorado at Logroño on 12 January 1609. In the careful, plodding fashion of most inquisitors, they searched the Tribunal archives for guidance and finally unearthed instructions (complete with questionnaires) given to their predecessors some eighty years before. Precedent in hand, they interrogated four suspect witches who had been delivered to Logroño. Held in isolation at the Tribunal's secret prison on the strength of accusations that were unknown to them, the four suspects spun a tale that confirmed the worst fears of the inquisitors. Other suspects were similarly treated with similar results.[49]

Altogether, thirty-one witches were sentenced at the auto-da-fé held at Logroño on 6 and 7 November 1610. Six *negativos* (suspect witches who had refused to confess their crimes to the Inquisition) were burned at the stake along with the remains of five other witches who had died in prison. Confessed witches, and an assortment of ordinary heretics, were given lesser sentences.[50]

An auto-da-fé (act of faith) was the public face of the Spanish Inquisition. A ceremony of extraordinary pagentry and solemnity representing the Day of Judgement, it was at the very least spectacular theater, and it drew people from many miles around. Preparations for the auto-da-fé at Logroño, which ultimately cost 2,451 reales (a very considerable sum), included the construction of a stage, reviewing stands, and a high terraced platform for the presentation of those to be sentenced. The principal inquisitors, as was standard, were provided a special box installed at the highest level of the reviewing stands. Roof tops and windows in the buildings surrounding the square were preferred vantage points and claimed a high price on the day of the ceremony. A letter to the Inquisitorial Commissioner provides some sense of the compelling nature of these festivities.

> . . . I can assure Your Grace that never before have so many people gathered together in this town. It is estimated that over thirty thousand souls have assembled here from France, Aragon, Navarra, Vizcaya and various parts of Castilla. The reason for such enthusiasm was the publication of the announcement that the vile sect of witches was to be revealed at this auto de fe.[51]

The procession of the Green Cross (the symbol of the Inquisition) opened the auto-da-fé. All of the tribunal apparatus and local religious orders, as well as parish priests—altogether about a thousand people—participated in the pageant, which wound its way through Logroño to the town square. At dusk the stage was illuminated by dozens of lanterns and a vigil was maintained over the Green Cross through the night.

The following morning (a Sunday) the prisoners, barefoot and wearing sambenitos that advertised their fate, were led in solemn procession to the stage.[52] Even death did not afford escape from the Inquisition. The effigies of the five dead witches (also garbed in sambenitos) and their coffins accompanied the living.

Official and unofficial reports of the auto-da-fé at Logroño and of the deeds of the witches sentenced were numerous and spread alarm.[53] It is also clear that a number of French officials attended and that they took elaborate notes. The Supreme Council was aware of their interest and instructed the Tribunal at Logroño to send a short report of what they had uncovered to one M. de Gourgues "since he is a judge of witches in that country . . . [and] we may perhaps in this way serve God's cause."[54] Popular accounts also influenced de Lancre in France, who devoted a chapter in his book to the auto-da-fé at Logroño.

Reports of witchcraft persisted throughout the summer and fall of 1610, convincing the Supreme Council that the cult of witches was established over a much wider area. The course of action decided upon was a "preaching crusade," which was duly sent to Navarre. This was a standard tactic of the Inquisition and had been employed during an earlier outbreak of witchcraft in this area, in 1527. It is clear that the effect of the auto-da-fé at Logroño, remembered as the one that "burned the witches," in combination with the preaching crusade, dramatically exaggerated the level of peasant fear.

Henningsen notes that a few months following the auto-da-fé, the entire region was "ablaze" with talk of countless bewitched children who had been spirited away by witches to attend the local sabbat. The report of the Jesuit de Solarte to his Bishop shows that many towns within the afflicted area had "bewitched" children and that the parents of these children, as might be expected, frequently took matters into their own hands by attacking and now and again killing the village witch.[55]

Many of the battalion of ecclesiastics sent to proselytize among the witches used the confessional to urge people to turn themselves into the Inquisition. At the same time, however, the confessional provided evidence of false confessions and false accusations. As the witches began to confess in droves, the skeptics found a champion in the remarkable Inquisitor Alonso de Salazar Frias, who had recently jointed the Tribunal. Increasingly at odds with his two colleagues, it was Salazar who was dispatched into Navarre to read the *Edict of Grace* issued by the Inquisition and to hear the confessions of "witches" choosing to come forth under its protection. This too was a standard measure. The stated purpose of the Inquisition, after all, was to readmit heretics to the faith. Much of Salazar's correspondence and some small portions of his visitation books (in which he recorded the confessions) have survived. His report to the Inquisition makes astonishing reading:

In a letter which I addressed to Your Highness from Fruenterrabia, on 4 September, I reported how, as a sequel to the Edict of Grace . . . 1,546 persons of all ranks and ages came forward to avail themselves of it. . . . I now report that—during the period from 22 May, when I set forth on the visitation, to 10 January of this year, when I concluded it—a total of 1,802 cases has been dispatched. . . . The figure can be broken down into the following groups: 1,384 children, of twelve or fourteen years of age and under, were absolved *ad cautelam*. Of those older than twelve or fourteen, 290 were reconciled; 41 absolved *ad cautelam* with abjuration *de levi*; 81 retracted the confessions which they had made to the Holy Office . . . ; and finally, 6 confessed to have relapsed by returning to *aquelarres*. Among the 290 whom I reconciled there were a hundred persons over twenty . . . many of them being sixty, seventy, eighty or even ninety years old.[56]

Salazar is referring to 1,802 cases, not people, and by Henning-sen's reckoning there were 1,777 confessed witches involved. Salazar concludes:

> I have not found a single proof nor even the slightest indication from which to infer that one act of witchcraft has actually taken place. . . . Rather I have found what I had already begun to suspect in these cases before my experience during the visitation; that the testimony of accomplices alone—even if they had not been submitted to violence and compulsion—without support from external facts substantiated by persons who are not witches is insufficient to warrant even an arrest.[57]

At the bidding of a more credulous inquisitor it is clear that the Inquisition would have moved against many of these people. In this same general area, in Cataluna, the secular authorities hanged more than three hundred witches in the space of less than three years and would have hanged more had not the Holy Office intervened.[58]

However, it is not correct to conclude that in another legal system, such as held sway in what is now Germany, the authorities would have encountered as many "voluntary confessions." The Inquisition (both Spanish and Roman) was notoriously lenient relative to secular systems of control.[59] This was particularly true of the Inquisition's treatment of children (note the 1,384 children absolved in Salazar's report). And, under the Edict of Grace, those of any age who came forward voluntarily could expect to get rather light treatment (to be reconciled). In contrast, those who refused to confess ("negativos") were invariably "re-laxed" to the secular authorities and burned. It is reasonable to assume that the auto da-fé at Logroño had brought this essential fact home to the peasants of Navarre.

Under the ministrations of Salazar the plague of witches quickly subsided. What is clearly demonstrated by this remark-able episode is the manner in which the forces of order can turn on or off the flow of deviants. Salazar's understanding of this process was profound: "No hubo brujas ni embrujadas hasta que comenzó a tratar y escriver dellos" (There were nei-ther witches nor bewitched until they were talked and written about).[60] The figures from the first and second half of Salazar's visitation journey demonstrate how the source of confessions and accusations slowed to a trickle when not actively bolstered by the agents of control (1,546 vs. 256).

Salazar's increasingly bitter dispute with his coinquisitors was ultimately settled in his favor by the Supreme Council. Salazar had come to the Tribunal following a career in ecclesiastical law, whereas his opponents on the Tribunal were trained purely as ecclesiastics. Salazar, moreover, was the protegé of the Inquisitor General.[61] Given the careful approach of the Supreme Council and its preoccupation with heretics (Luteranos), it is not hard to see why Salazar's careful reasoning was upheld. In one of his many rejoinders he states:

> . . . It is not very helpful to keep asserting that the Devil is capable of doing this or that, simply repeating over and over again the theory of angelic nature, nor is it useful to keep saying that the learned doctors state that the existence of witchcraft is certain. This is only a needless annoyance since nobody doubts this. The real question is: are we to believe that witchcraft occurred in a given situation simply because of what the witches claim? It is clear that the witches are not to be believed, and that the judges should not pass sentence on anyone unless the case can be proven by external and objective evidence sufficient to convince everyone who hears it. However, who can accept the following: that a person can frequently fly through the air and travel a hundred leagues in an hour; that a woman can get out though a space not big enough for a fly; that a person can make himself invisible; that he can be in a river or in the sea and not get wet; or that he can be in bed and at the aquelarre at the same time. . . . Indeed, these claims go beyond all human reason and many pass even the limits permitted the Devil.[62]

The response of the Supreme Council was decisive. It issued a set of precise instructions that limited the use of coercion in cases of suspected witchcraft. And, probably more important, the Supreme Council established an *Edict of Silence,* which prohibited all public discussion of the activities of witches. Henceforward, according to the edict, all those with knowledge of witchcraft were to "feel free to come to us [the inquisitors], and *only to us.*"[63] The impact of these instructions, particularly with the Edict of Silence, was to dry up almost immediately the source of the Basque witches. Seven years after the outbreak of witchcraft, a local priest wrote to the Tribunal at Logroño:

> I cannot describe to Your Eminence the momentous impact the instructions have had. They have quietened the consciences and souls of so many persons who, on account of violence, pressure,

or coercion had confessed to being witches and had incriminated many others. The instructions have also served to resolve the state of irresolution to which the priests and confessors had been reduced over this problem. For many of these witches went to them with tears and grief in order to revoke their confessions but on account of the fear they have always lived in of being punished, it was quite impossible for the confessors to persuade these people to report themselves to the agents of the Holy Office and repeat their statements there.[64]

In 1617 Salazar wrote to the Supreme Council about the situation in the general region of Navarre. Noting that the panic had swept up something like eighteen hundred witches and four thousand suspects, he commented:

> No one could have imagined that with the imposition of silence on the witch question it would have been possible to combat the craze to such an extent that today it is as if the problem had never existed.[65]

* * *

The Spanish Inquisition was a remarkably efficient institution for the detection, processing, and public presentation of deviance. Over the course of five generations it had developed into a mechanism that maintained the production of public deviance in Spain at fairly constant levels. In the instance of the Basque Witch-Hunt, and in others, the discovery by the Inquisition of a few deviants regarded as the vanguard of a conspiracy brought about an intensification of effort that quickly made the feared conspiracy a documented reality. However, the last thing the leaders of the Inquisition wanted at the beginning of the seventeenth century was an unrestrained flow of thousands of deviants (and particularly deviants of the wrong sort) into the system. Even as it was, the Tribunal at Logroño was taxed beyond its limits.

The fact that the Basque Witch-Hunt was so suddenly brought to a halt was, at one level, the result of the personality and insight of Salazar; but the more fundamental reason was organizational. The extraordinary ability of the Spanish Inquisition to produce candidates for the status of deviant was balanced by a variety of bureaucratic strategies—edicts of silence and so on—which allowed the leadership of the Spanish Inquisition to frustrate the tendency of zealots in the lower echelons to follow the dictates of their imagination. When things got out of hand, the Supreme Council simply short-circuited the production line.

Such was not the case in much of northern Europe. The apparatus of social control in those regions of Europe where the witchcraze was most intense differed from the Spanish Inquisition in two essential respects: (1) the use of torture was largely unrestricted and (2) there was simply no institutionalized means of shutting down a witch-hunt in these areas once it had begun.

4

The Political Geography of Witchcraft

As suggested in the introductory chapter, the various questions surrounding the "mass production" of deviance ultimately focus on issues that are either cognitive and emotional or administrative and legal. The specific problem of the origin of the European witchcraze is thus rooted in two fundamental questions: (1) why did the demand for the production of witches increase so dramatically and (2) what institutional changes allowed this demand to be fulfilled?[1]

It would seem beyond dispute that facilities for the prosecution of suspected witches became more efficient through time. The later Middle Ages and the Renaissance brought a shift from restorative interpersonal justice to rational-legal, bureaucratic justice.[2] In less abstract terms, the shift, on the Continent, is from *accusatorial* to *inquisitorial*.

There were variations on the theme, but evidently, as a guiding principle under accusatorial law, both the accused and the person bringing the accusation came to court "on equal footing."[3] A trail was a contest between accuser and accused, relying on symbolic acts and phrases that had to be carried out and uttered just so. Procedures were oral, public, inflexible, and, as a practical matter, often weighted in favor of the accused. Bringing an accusation against someone often meant undergoing a trial by ordeal so that the issue of guilt or innocence could be judged by God.[4] It also meant leaving oneself open to retaliation in the event that the court, or God, did not rule in one's favor. If the plaintiff lost his case he could be saddled with a penalty (the *talion*) as severe as the one that had faced the accused. Proof, moreover, had to be "clearer than the noonday light."[5]

In short, bringing an accusation against someone was risky business. The whole thrust of this legal system was to discourage malicious accusation, which it would seem to have done quite effectively. No one with common sense would have made an accusation in court unless heavily pressed by circumstances or in effective control over the judicial mechanism. These hazards and limitations applied to normal crime and much more so to cases of alleged witchcraft. It was obviously very difficult to obtain a judgment in one's favor in cases of maleficium. After the ordeal was abandoned as a formal procedure, witchcraft became, for all intents and purposes, unprovable in the absence of a confession.[6]

Aspects of accusatorial law prevailed throughout Europe until the fourteenth century and in some areas until much later. Unsurprisingly, the continued reliance upon accusatorial procedures in some German-speaking areas was a sore point to the authors of the *Malleus Maleficarum* since it greatly interfered with their production of witches.[7]

Inquisitorial procedure, which was used by both ecclesiastical and secular courts, developed in response to three tightly interwoven factors. First, the Fourth Lateran Council of 1215 abolished the ordeals and, with them, an entire system of legal proof. Technically from then on, mortal men, and not God, determined guilt or innocence. The resulting judicial system—Roman law—was dependent on the supporting testimony of two eyewitnesses and could not, *without torture*, deal with covert crime.[8] It is presumably for this reason that a person undergoing torture in the inquisitorial system was sometimes officially referred to as a "witness."

Second, there is a good deal of support for H. C. Lea's contention that the inquisitorial process and the Inquisition itself were both a direct response to the spread of heresy—especially the teachings of the Catheri and the Waldensians. The suppression of heretical sects could not be accomplished by means of a judicial system that relied on the principle of the ordeal; heresy (and, subsequently, witchcraft) came to be regarded officially as *crimen exceptum*, demanding special methods.[9] These special methods were refined by degrees into standard inquisitorial procedure.

Third, the secular establishment adopted the procedures of the Inquisition with enthusiasm since its methods could be bent to the needs of the weak postfeudal governments emerging during this period.[10] The nation state and inquisitional procedures develop hand in glove.

INQUISITORIAL PROCEDURE

By the latter part of the thirteenth century, the basic principles of inquisitorial procedure had been established. First of all, the state or the church took over the role of the accuser. Defendants could be held without counsel and in secrecy for extended periods. Central to inquisitorial procedure was the use of torture, which was seen as necessary to overcome the power of the devil, who, naturally, protected heretics and, in time, would be thought to protect witches.[11]

The methods used to extract a confession were every bit as persuasive as those in use today, and when employed without restraint, as they often were, they would infallibly produce either a confession or the death of the person interrogated. In those cases in which a person had been tortured to death, it was argued that the devil had killed the "witness" in order to prevent him or her from revealing the truth. Should the accused confess and then, upon reflection, withdraw his or her confession, she or he could be tortured anew and/or considered relapsed heretics. Such people were usually burned. By degrees, inquisitorial procedure became more efficient, and in some of the German-speaking regions of Europe, the responsibilities of judge, prosecutor, and defense counsel were taken over, at lest in theory, by a panel. At times all these functions were vested in a single individual.[12]

Scholastically influenced, the Inquisition often used formularies of questions and answers in Latin that were "translated" for the accused.[13] The stereotypical answers to these questions provided by suspected witches, so impressive to the demonologists of early modern Europe, are readily explained as a function of standard questions put to the accused during interrogation. The judges in Alsace relied on a typical set of queries:

> How long have you been a witch? Why did you become a witch? How did you become a witch, and what happened on the occasion? . . . What is the name of your master among the evil demons? What oath were you forced to render him? . . . How was the sabbat banquet arranged? . . . Who are your accomplices in evil? . . . How are you able to fly through the air?[14]

It is clear and unsurprising that there is a direct relationship between the severity with which torture was applied and the level of productivity in burning witches. Those areas that killed the greatest number of people were also the most notorious for the use of torture. The panic-trials did, in fact, take place largely according to the scenario presented by von Spee; an individual would be accused, incarcerated, and tortured into a confession—often in a matter of days. His or her confession would implicate other people in Satan's plot, usually because under torture the accused suddenly recalled seeing those people at a sabbat. The newly accused would themselves be put to torture and the process repeated. When entirely unbridled, inquisitorial procedure resulted in an almost exponential increase in the number of deviants.

In actual practice, however, it was only at the height of panic-trials that full potential was achieved. In the more usual case, local restrictions on the use of torture were adhered to in some degree with a corresponding diminution in the production of deviants. For example, throughout much of France there was typically a series of investigatory procedures short of torture. Only as a last resort was torture permitted—*after* the judge had put the matter to a legal advisory council. Generally the use of torture properly required that there be at least "half proof" (i.e., one eyewitness) or circumstantial evidence of the sort that "no innocent person can know."[15] Similarly, judicial officials of the Jura Alps (Switzerland and France) were characterized by a certain lack of gullibility regarding accusations of maleficia. According to Monter, judges were wary of "implausible suspects who invariably turned up in the second and third layer of a chain-reaction panic as confessed witches named new 'accomplices.'"[16] Of equal importance was the fact that judges tended to adhere to the strict limits put on the use of torture by the Caroline Code. Under such limitations, "most women and about half the men could withstand torture and maintain their innocence."[17] The clear result of these restrictive practices was a lack of full-fledged mass-trials of the type found repeatedly in southwestern Germany. In sharp contrast to the situation found in the German southwest, the typical trial of the Jura region was the *small panic-trial* (Monter's term), which executed six or seven people and then terminated. Bluntly stated, rates of conviction tended to be low since fewer people were tortured into confession.

COMMON LAW

The sharpest contrasts in regard to the impact of different legal systems on the production of deviants derives from a comparison of English and Continental witch production. As noted, there are two main strategies underlying Western law—the inquisitorial and the accusatorial. On the Continent, the early abolition of the principle of the ordeal channeled the development of law towards inquisitorial procedures and the institutionalization of torture. But in England, trial by jury came to replace trial by ordeal with the result that English criminal procedure continued to evolve along the accusatorial track.[18]

Additionally, in England maleficia were by and large treated as "normal" crime. That is to say, the crime of witchcraft, in the English legal system, resulted from the *harm* done to another person; the means of bringing about this harm were largely irrelevant. The crime was *not* in the pact with the devil, an idea that was poorly developed (despite the fact that it is mentioned in the 1604 statute). Indeed, in England, Continental demonology was very much an alien notion.

It would be difficult to exaggerate the impact of these contrasting attitudes and legal systems on the production of God's enemies. The dark figure of one hundred thousand derives almost totally from Continental witch-hunting. A glance at the area that is now Germany reveals that conservatively tens of thousands of people were executed for the crime of witchcraft. In England, on the other hand, the figure was somewhere in the neighborhood of five hundred; panic-trials occurred but rarely.

Although it is impossible to estimate European population levels with any degree of accuracy, it is here assumed that the early modern population of Germany was substantially larger than that of England, which evidently had a population of roughly four million by 1600.[19] However, even if the population of what is now Germany had been many times that of England, comparison between the killing rates would still be impressive. By way of underscoring this contrast, it should be noted that there is solid documentation for the execution of over three thousand people in the region of southwestern Germany studied by Midelfort; yet these figures surely do not tally the total number of witches actually killed.[20] Mention may also be made of the duchy of Bavaria where, by every indication, close to two thousand people were executed for witchcraft.[21] Turning to the British Isles, England, which had a far greater population than Scotland, executed less than half as many witches as were put to death in the north.

It is this stark contrast in the pace of witch killing that so impressed the rationalist historians, notably Lea, who saw the witchcraze as a result of the Counter-Reformation and the laws of confiscation.[22] Elliot Currie's important discussion of Continental and English legal practices continues this tradition. In Currie's view, witch hunting was something of a racket in England (and, at times, it was) and a major extractive industry on the Continent—which, in reality, it was not. Currie argues that "the witchcraft industry in continental Europe was a large and complex business which created and sustained the livelihoods of a sizable number of people."[23] This was certainly the view of some contemporaries, especially in German-speaking regions. A popular maxim was "Burn the poor and soak the rich," and many authors wrote explicitly of the cupidity and venality of jurists.[24] Perhaps the most biting comment came from Cornelius Loos, a Catholic priest, who complained in *De vera et falsa magia* (1592):

> Wretched creatures are compelled by the severity of torture to confess things they have never done and so by the cruel butchery innocent lives are taken and *by a new alchemy gold and silver coined from human blood.*[25]

All this aside, confiscation does not offer a satisfactory explanation for the witchcraze. Although it must be acknowledged that killing witches offered a financial windfall to a few, for the most part a large witch trial was a burden on the community that sustained it. The laws dealing with confiscation— which applied to other types of crime as well—seem to have been mandated in an effort to recoup at least some portion of the expenses incurred in controlling wickedness. Again and again witches are listed in trial records as indigent, and the general impression is that such efforts at recouping expenses were usually only partially successful. Certainly some categories of people did benefit from a witch trial. In Scotland and generally everywhere:

> The people who gained from a witch-hunt were minor officials: the witch watchers and jailers, the organizers of an execution, the clerks of courts and above all witch-prickers.[26]

Burning a witch was a very costly business.

> The total process of pursuing a witch to execution could be expensive to a parish. The witch had to be fed and guarded prior to

the execution. Messengers . . . required a fee and expenses, the commission itself had to be paid for. The hangman and his assistants
required payment, and those who supplied rope and fuel and re-
freshments for the hangman. A witch's estate was automatically
forfeited to the crown, but this was hardly a major source of revenue.
The locality would extract their expenses first. In 1649 the expenses
for imprisoning and executing Margaret Dunham were 92 pounds
14 shillings (Scots), and from this they deducted 27 pounds ". . .
Margrit Dinham had if her ain," leaving the parish of Lauder a
deficit of some 65 pounds 14 shillings.[27]

In the Caroline Code, the law of confiscation was "a classic
of incoherence," with the result that each of the multitude of
independent German-speaking territories followed their own
policies. In some areas confiscation was total, but in other areas
nothing at all was confiscated.[28] Confiscation, where it did take
place, was usually around 10 to 15 percent of the witch's total
assets, which, as Midelfort points out, is "less confiscatory than
many modern inheritance taxes."[29] More central to the issue,
there does not seem to be any strong connection in southwestern
Germany between the pace of witch killing and the practice
of confiscation. Those areas in southwestern Germany that did
not practice confiscation also burned witches with enthusiasm.

By and large, internal comparisons in other regions of Europe
likewise do not reveal any linkage between the practice of confiscation and witch-hunting. Nor, on close examination, does there
seem to be any compelling reason to expect such a link. Larner
estimates that in about 90 percent of the cases the execution
of a witch was a financial burden to the community.[30] In England
the most intense episodes of witch killing took place during
the period when confscation was not permitted. The short-lived
Act of 1542, which ordered confiscation, was not marked by
an increase in the number of witches executed, and at all times
witches were typically described in the records as having "no
goods."[31] To be sure, it was possible for certain individuals to
profit from witch scares through a variety of schemes, but such
narrow opportunities cannot be regarded as major enterprises.
In Scotland, the central government benefited from confiscation
in those evidently rare instances when the estate of the witch
exceeded the local costs of execution. But a much more important source of revenue came from the selling of commissions

to hunt witches. Nevertheless, there is absolutely no connection between shortfalls in the public treasury and outbreaks of witch-hunting. The motive for witch hunting at this level seems to have been entirely ideological and not financial.

Overall, there does not seem to be any particular connection between the distribution of the laws of confiscation and the geography of witch-hunting. Taking the regions of present-day Spain, Germany, and Scotland as examples, it can be noted that although all three areas practiced confiscation, they exhibited the widest possible variation in the rate of witch killing. Furthermore, in Spain, the one area where confiscation was a major source of revenue, the execution of witches was a comparatively rare event.[32]

In sum, the financial interest that some control agents had in the pursuit of witches cannot be accepted as a major explanatory factor for either the origin or the intensity of the witchcraze. On a more general level, it can be argued that the motivation of lower- and middle-level control agents, internal demand, is not the central factor in the mass production of deviance.

As other comparisons are made, the pattern of European witch-hunting emerges in finer detail. The Spanish Inquisition provides a clear example of an institution of social control that is characterized by a high degree of organization restraint. It was, of course, the several established mechanisms of internal restraint within the Inquisition—edicts of silence and so on— that were put into operation by the Supreme Council to end the Great Basque Witch-Hunt.

Southwestern Germany, in sharp contrast, provides an example of the deviant-producing capacities of inquisitorial system that were essentially devoid of effective organizational restraints. These were the control systems that generated the panic-trials that time and time again executed people supposed to be witches by the hundreds. Often the functionaries of such systems seem caught up in an internal dynamic of their own manufacture, and once underway these people found it very difficult to shut down a witch-hunt until after it had reached catastrophic dimensions.

In the broader context of Europe, as organizational restraints were introduced by increments into the picture, the production of deviance drops in rough proportion. For instance, the internal restraints within the judicial system(s) of France, and particularly the arrogation by Parlement of the use of torture, reduced the number of witches executed. Torture, when it was applied by the Parlement of Paris, was relatively mild, and confessions, as would be expected, were infrequent. Soman writes:

> The jurisprudence of the Parlement of Paris stands in striking contrast to the conditions in the Holy Roman Empire, where confession rates of 40–90% were common in the seventeenth century, depending on the scrupulousness with which the regulations of the 1532 *Carolina* were observed.[33]

Similarly in Denmark, in 1547 two specific internal restraints were introduced into Danish procedural law for the express purpose of curtailing the production of witches: (1) torture could not be applied until *after* an individual had been sentenced to death and (2) the legal system could not proceed against someone simply because they had been accused by a witch.[34] As a direct result of the introduction of these restrictions, the production of Danish witches plummeted to almost nothing.

The absence of institutional accountability is a fundamental element in the social conditions that foster the mass production of deviance. The apparatus of social control must have a free hand if it is to successfully mass produce deviance. The scramble by Institoris and Sprenger to obtain the support of the Church after they had been confronted by local opposition is an obvious case in point. It is entirely realistic to view the whole developmental thrust of the Inquisition as an attempt to establish its invulnerability to outside restraint. It is wrong, however, to suppose that a system of social control is ever totally immune to outside accountability. Such a system would be a state. Always there is accountability at some level if only at the very top.

To be sure, the Inquisition (and inquisitorial procedure) developed because of an internal dynamic, but it is equally true that it was allowed to develop. From its earliest beginnings, the Inquisition was put to use as a political tool—God's work had very pragmatic results.[35] A particularly compelling example of inquisitorial politics is provided by the fate of the Knight Templars. By the beginning of the fourteenth century, this enormously wealthy monastic order—in some respects the first multinational corporation—had dangerously antagonized the Dominicans who staffed the Inquisition. At the behest of the King of France (Philip IV), the Templar hierarchy was seized in closely planned raids and promptly tortured into confessions of sodomy, devil worship, and infanticide, etcetera. Thus, by a single stroke, which could not have been achieved without the myth of demon-worshipping heretical sects and the official use of torture, a major nonterritorial military power was crushed and the treasury of the Île-de-France replenished.[36]

The level of upper-class demand for the manufacture of deviants of a particular sort is by every indication the transcending element in the mass production of deviance. Despite the fact that the peasantry in all parts of early modern Europe was tormented by the prospect of maleficium, witches were only produced in sizeable numbers *only after the ruling class became alarmed*. Only when the "new cult of witches" became a fixture within the construction of reality of the European elite did the production of witches assume major proportions. In early modern Europe, there was always a clear relationship between expressions of concern on the part of the ruling class and the production of witches; and the peasantry was a factor in this equation only insofar as its fears influenced and reinforced the concerns of the elite. It is indisputable that the politically powerful on the Continent placed far more emphasis on hunting witches than did their counterparts in England. The demand, in other words, was higher; and this too accounts for vastly greater slaughter on the Continent. While it is certainly true that the English gentry and aristocracy believed in witches, they feared them less. England had only a "weak tradition of heresy," and two critical notions that made a conspiracy of witches plausible, the demonic pact and the sabbat, were poorly developed.[37] Even a determined effort by their King, James I (James VI in Scotland), to advance these fashionable Continental views among the English met with little success. The statute introduced in 1604 soon after James assumed the English throne contained specific Continental ideas on demonology and made the penalties for witchcraft more severe; but on balance there is little to indicate that these changes had any effect on the pace of English witch killing. Indeed, James shortly came to adopt English attitudes and became something of a skeptic on matters of witchcraft.[38]

All the same, it is clear that English witch-hunting did, at times, assume Continental dimensions. The special conditions surrounding the severe outbreaks of witch-hunting within the usually restrained legal system of England and the single such episode in colonial New England emphasize the critical importance of the level of external demand in mass production of deviance. These episodes make it clear that discord, anxiety, and threats to position among the ruling class are directly related to outbreaks of witch-hunting. More than fifty years ago this strong connection between witchcraft and a troubled ruling class was noted by Kittredge:

> If we look at Great Britain for a moment, we shall see that such outbreaks are likely to coincide with times of political excitement or anxiety. Thus early in Elizabeth's reign, when everything was more or less unsettled, Bishop Jewell ... made a deliberate and avowed digression, in a sermon before the queen, in order to warn her that witchcraft was rampant in the realm, to inform her (on the evidence of his own eyes) that her subjects were being injured in their goods and their health, and to exhort her to enforce the law. The initial zeal of James I in the prosecution of witches stood in close connection with the trouble he was having with his turbulent cousin Francis Bothwell. The operations of Mathew Hopkins (in 1645–1647) were a mere accompaniment to the tumult of the Civil War; the year in which they began was the year of Laud's execution and of the Battle of Naseby. The restoration was followed by a fresh outbreak of witch prosecution—mild in England, ... but very sharp in Scotland. With facts like these in view, we can hardly regard it as an accident that the Salem witchcraft marks a time when the Colony was just emerging from a political struggle that had threatened its very existence. For several years men's minds had been on the rack.[39]

Two of these instances can be examined in depth—the Salem Witch-Hunt in New England and the witch-hunt that took place in the eastern counties of England during the Civil War (1642– 49). The latter episode was the direct result of the exploits of one of the great moral entrepreneurs of all time, Mathew Hopkins, self-styled "Witchfinder General of England," whose short career (from 1645 to 1647) brought about the death of a significant percentage of all those executed for witchcraft in England.

England's Continental Interlude

It is of primary importance to understand that the Hopkins episode took on many of the aspects of a full-fledged Continental panic-trial. In fact, except for the minor particular that Hopkins's victims were hanged rather than burned, it would be very difficult to differentiate this mass killing of suspected witches from a Continental outbreak.

Mathew Hopkins, who is described by Ewen as a "Puritan run to seed," seems to have been a lawyer of very modest achievements.[40] His career as a witch-hunter was probably a compensatory device. Although both he and his colleague John Stearne, of whom even less is known, denied making money, records suggest a tidy profit.[41]

The witch-panic introduced by Hopkins and Stearne was sustained by two conditions. First, Hopkins and Stearne, who were essentially professional accusers, managed to advance Continental ideas on the nature of witchcraft. Hopkins was evidently familiar with King James's *Daemonologie*, and many of the indictments handed down during this period are for participating in the sabbat, signing a pact with the devil, ritual intercourse with the devil, and so on.[42] Such activities were rarely mentioned in the typical English indictment prior to Hopkins. More important, when Hopkins was in charge, confessions were gathered in a quasi-Continental manner. Out-and-out torture was, of course, not permitted, but Hopkins utilized every possible method short of that, including starvation, prolonged interrogation, deprivation of sleep, intensive pricking with a pin to locate the mark left on the suspect's body by the devil, and walking the suspect around until his or her feet blistereed.[43] The witch-hunters principally succeeded in encouraging further accusations and in vastly increasing the number of convictions. According to Keith Thomas:

> There is every reason to think that what he did was to turn a higher proportion of informal popular allegations and suspicions into actual prosecutions, twisting them from charges of *maleficium* into allegations of devil-worshipping.[44]

Second, the Civil War and its aftermath produced "unusual anxieties and insecurities." The campaign of Hopkins and Stearne took place against this background, which had the immediate effect of throwing England into a "state of judicial anarchy" wherein the "local authorities were in control."[45] While the use of the phrase "judicial anarchy" is perhaps extreme, there is hard evidence that local gentry, at least for the years when Hopkins was on the loose, were in effective control at the expense of the central authorities. According to Ewen:

That Hopkins' enterprise against the supposed public evil achieved great success was largely due to the unsettling effect of the civil war, causing the regular assizes to be suspended and superseded by quasi-justice dealt out by special commissioners.[46]

The effect of the Civil War on English society was profound. "It was not only," writes Ollard,

that the uncertainties and apprehensions enter[ed] into relations, transactions, and decisions of almost everybody. There [were] also immediate effects on trade and communication, on law and order, on education, and, most instantly and universally felt of all, on money and prices.[47]

Mathew Hopkins, in short, profited from a deterioration of the moral landscape of all strata of English society, and particularly that of the aristocracy. He also profited from the general "breakdown of government."[48] The effect of all this is impressive. Thomas estimates that between 1645 and 1647, approximately two hundred people were convicted of witchcraft in the eastern counties. Stearne himself refers to two hundred executions for the entire stretch of the campaign.[49]

The first trial at which many of the Hopkins's suspects appeared was held in 1645 at Chelmsford (Essex County) under the authority of the Essex Summer Session Assizes. These proceedings brought about the death by hanging of nineteen women out of thirty-two people indicted. In addition, four more died in prison, and, as noted in Ewen's account, five more died subsequent to the trial by the "visitation of God."[50] This trial was not conducted by justices of the Assize, but by justices of the peace presided over by the earl of Warwick, whose judicial status was uncertain.[51] Parliament also became directly involved through the granting of a special commission of Oyer and Terminer to a number of prominent clergymen and justices of the peace. Under this aegis, a trial condemned two men and sixteen women to death but was forced to adjourn before its work had been concluded because of "the neere approaching of the Cavaliers."[52] One hundred and twenty people, evidently there on a variety of charges, remained in prison; little is known of what became of them.

Less is known of Hopkins's and Stearne's activities in Suffolk, except that here the destruction of life seems to have been, if anything, even greater. Pamphlets and depositions provide information on one hundred and twenty-four suspected witches, of which sixty-eight were condemned and executed. Imprisonment claimed more.[53] In addition to Essex and Suffolk Counties, Hopkins subsequently took his campaign into other areas with, one gathers, diminishing results.

It is clear that Hopkins moved rapidly from one area to another. He was, for instance, in Norfolk in early June (1645), and by July 20 he had moved on: in the interim twenty witches had been executed.[54] It is also clear that he *had* to keep moving. He was vigorously opposed in several towns, very often from the pulpit. It is interesting that the writers of the *Moderate Intelligencer* (4–11 September 1645) asked why Satan approaches "none but poor women."[55] Hopkins's own pamphlet, *Discovery of Witches* (1647), is largely a rejoinder to the many attacks to which he had been subjected. In Essex it appears that the witchfinders were a part of a faction favoring indictments that were vigorously opposed by another faction. The witchfinders were interfered with and threatened, evidently by the same group that ultimately succeeded in indicting Stearne and forty others for conspiracy. This opposition effectively drove the witchfinders from the county. In other areas, citizens appealed to Parliament to rid themselves of Hopkins, and in Norfolk he was charged with cruelty and fleecing the county treasury.[56] The witchfinders, for their part, seem to have sincerely felt that they were performing a public service. But as the country became more secure and administratively stable, Hopkins's crusade met with even more effective resistance. His activities came to a close with his death by consumption in 1647. With the return to more settled times, Stearne did not, and probably could not, continue.

In the final analysis, the great success of Mathew Hopkins as a witch-hunter can only be partially explained. With due caution, it can be supposed that Hopkins and Stearne brought about the execution of more than one hundred people in the space of two years. When contrasted with the usual pace of English witch killing, this is a *very* large figure. It must be emphasized also that witchfinders were very unusual in English history. One operated at Newcastle and along the Scottish border near Berwick, and another is suggested by court records during the period of the influx of Roman Catholic missionaries (1570–95), which was also a time of political tension.[57]

Considering the date of its occurrence, the Newcastle episode is of some interest. Here, the town fathers, influenced by the lingering effects of the Civil War and the raging national hunt for witches just across the border, sent to Scotland for a celebrated witchfinder. The most satisfactory account of this event is found, oddly enough, in *England's Grievance Discovered in Relation to the Coal Trade* by Ralph Gardiner (1655):

> John Wheeler . . . about the year 1649 . . . being at Newcastle heard that the magistrates had sent two of their Sergents . . . to agree with a Scotch-man, who pretended knowledge to finde witches by procking them with pins, to come to Newcastle, wher he should try such who should be brought to him and to have twenty-shillings a piece, for all he could condemn as witches.
>
> The magistrates sent their bell-man through the town, ringing his bell, and crying, all people that would bring any complaint against any woman for a witch, they should be sent for, and tryed by the person appointed. Thirty women were brought into the townhall, and stript, and then openly had pins thrust into their bodies, and most of them were found guilty, near twenty-seven of them by him, and set aside.[58]

The fact that Hopkins and Stearne, and at least one other individual, had such success precisely during the unsettled times of the Civil War or immediately thereafter is unlikely to have been a coincidence. In the last analysis, however, it is impossible, given the extant information, to untangle which of the conditions arising out of the times was the more important: Was it the partial disarray of the court system—evident at Chelmsford—or the high degree of anxiety among the aristocracy and the gentry (then at war with each other) that encouraged this slaughter?

It would seem that Hopkins was essentially a catalyst.[59] His method of extracting confessions was widely known but usually tolerated by powerful factions. And even when an objection was voiced to higher authority, little came of it aside from the rapid departure of Hopkins and Stearne. Neither man was ever brought to justice. Evidently the special commission of Oyer and Terminer constituted by parliament was a response to the news that Hopkins was extracting confessions by very harsh methods.[60] But, here again, there is no hint that this body called Hopkins to task, except on the matter of swimming witches; and, indeed, according to a pamphlet published in 1645, it stayed to condemn eighteen witches to death before the timely arrival of the Cavaliers forced its adjournment. Had it not been for this interruption it seems likely that many more would have been executed; yet it seems that the participation of Hopkins in this trial was relatively peripheral.[61]

Notestein weights evenly the influence of the organization of the court system, the energy and personality of Hopkins, and social strain in his explanation of the witch-hunt.[62] On the matter of social strain, he notes:

> Every energy was directed towards the prosecution of the war. The strain might very well have shown itself in other forms than in hunting down the supposed agents of the Devil. As a matter of fact, the apparitions and devils, the knockings and strange noises, that filled up the pages of the popular literature were indications of an over-wrought public mind. Religious belief grew terribly literal under the tension of the war. The Anglicans were fighting for their kind, the Puritans for their religion. That religious fervor which easily deepens into dementia was highly accentuated.[63]

Macfarlane, who has closely studied Hopkins's escapades in Essex County, also argues that a combination of factors was at play.

> If we minimize the personal influence of Hopkins and Stearne in the Essex prosecutions, we are left with the central problem: Why were there savage prosecutions in 1645? The answer seems to lie in a combination of particular factors, especially the disruption of local government and justice by the Civil War and, possibly, the economic, spiritual, and other tensions which war created, with beliefs in witchcraft which, though usually kept just below the surface, were no less widespread and powerful than they had been in the sixteenth century. Wallace Notestein, having dismissed the suggestion that Puritanism was to blame for the prosecutions, suggested the lack of government as a major factor. If he had been aware of the existence of Assize court records for the year 1645 he would not have stated that "England was in a state of judicial anarchy" in that year. If this had ever been true, it was in 1643 when the Assizes do not appear to have been held. Thus lack of government, by itself, cannot explain the 1645 trail.[64]

In sum, there are reasons to believe that it would be a mistake to attribute the plague of witches that appeared so suddenly during the English Civil War either to the partial decay of the legal system or to the force of Mathew Hopkins's personality. Rather it seems that menacing and unsettled conditions of the Civil War fostered a high level of upper-class demand for an abundant supply of the "Enemies of God." The zeal for hunting witches in counties under parliamentary control was criticized in royalist circles, and considering the highly misogynistic nature of Cromwell's forces, it can hardly be assumed a coincidence that it was only during this period in English history that women were burned for witchcraft (specifically for bewitching their husbands, an activity defined in law as "petty treason").[65] The conflict between Parliament and the king aligned Puritan against Angelican and produced a fevered environment in which accounts of the devil's mischief blossomed in the popular press. In this atmosphere, it is unsurprising that Hopkins's Continental notions often received a welcome audience.

5

The Salem Panic-Trial

When attention is paid to the circumstances surrounding the Salem Witch-Hunt, the overwhelming impact of *external demand* emerges with greater clarity. During all other periods of colonial history, formal accusations of witchcraft were relatively rare and trials for witchcraft rarer still. When they did not feel themselves to be immediately threatened, the skepticism of Puritan magistrates was robust. Acquittals and successful appeals are recorded. Now and again, cases were simply tossed out of court by the Puritan judiciary and, on one occasion, a self-confessed witch was punished for perjury. His admission of "having familiarity with the devil" was taken to be an obvious lie.[1] But during the witch-panic, there were literally hundreds of accusations of witchcraft, and for those cases of alleged witchcraft that went to trial, the conviction rate was 100 percent— there were reprieves but *no* acquittals in 1692. Fully half of all those executed for the crime of witchcraft in new England, *at any time*, were hanged in Salem Village during the summer of 1692.[2]

The sequence of events is well known. The farming community of Salem Village, less than a day's ride from Boston, was small, unprosperous (only about one hundred men appear on contemporary tax rolls), and contentious even by Puritan standards.[3] Beginning in the fall of 1691, a small group of prominent young girls was, in the words of Cotton Mather, "led away by little sorceries." Dabbling in "little sorceries," in fact, seems to have been rather common at this time, and, as with many people in New England, the girls evidently used such homespun devices as the white of an egg in a glass, or a key inserted between the pages of the Bible, to tell the future. Such practices were vigorously denounced (and advertised) from the pulpit. Considering the circumstances, it is not in any way surprising that fortune-telling should have come into some vogue at this

85

juncture. "It was," in the words of Charles Upham,[4] "the darkest and most despondent period in the civil history of New England." Upham has described the larger social and political context from which the witch panic developed.

> The people . . . had, a few years before, been thrown into dismay by the loss of their charter, and, from that time, kept in a feverish state of anxiety respecting their future political destinies. In addition to this the whole sea-coast was exposed to danger: ruthless pirates were continually prowling along the shores. Commerce was nearly extinguished, and great losses had been experienced by men in business. A recent expedition against Canada had exposed the colonies to the vengeance of France.[5]

In 1684 the charter upon which the special nature of Puritan society ultimately rested had been abrogated in one stroke by the English Crown. For a time, an unwelcome royal governor (Sir Edmond Andros) dominated the administration and proved so unpopular with the Puritans that they had taken the dangerous step of overthrowing him and restoring the old charter rule. But everyone in Massachusetts knew that the charter, once "as precious to the Massachusetts theocracy as the tablets of the law to the children of Israel," was irrevocably dissolved.[6] For the two years preceding the witch-hunt, Increase Mather had pressed Court and Parliament for a return to the old charter. By the early part of 1692, it was learned in New England that Mather's efforts had largely been a failure and that a new governor, William Phips, would shortly arrive with a new charter. Prompted by the doleful nature of Puritan literature, many in New England now felt that doomsday was upon them.[7]

Against this anxious background, private concerns over "little sorceries" were soon translated into behavior. The small and timid cabal of village girls began to act strangely, and by the early part of February their antics were beyond anything that could have been overlooked. A contemporary, Robert Calef, describes their behavior as "getting into Holes, and creeping under Chairs and Stools and sundry odd Postures and Antick Gestures, uttering foolish, rediculous Speeches. . . ."[8] It has been argued that today such behavior would be regarded as symptomatic of hysteria.[9] In any case, local remedies had no effect.

According to Samuel Parris, minister of the church at Salem Village and father of one of the afflicted, these disquieting symptoms spread "plague-like." Ten to twelve local girls soon began to manifest behaviors that became increasingly more extreme and bizarre.[10] By late February community leaders, thoroughly alarmed, had agreed that witchcraft was the source of their afflictions. On 29 February (1692 was a leap year), three local women—the best available targets—were accused of witchcraft and arrested: Tituba, a slave in the house of Samuel Parris and likely mentor of the girls; Sarah Good, a stereotypical witch figure; and Sarah Osburne, an older woman of independent habits.

On the following day, two members of the General Court of Massachusetts conducted a public examination of the three women in the meeting house of Salem Village. Both Sarah Good and Sarah Osburne were completely bewildered by the proceedings and denied that they were witches. Sarah Osburne commented that she was "more like to be bewitched than that she would be a witch."[11] More astute, Tituba, who alone would survive, confessed in imaginative detail, describing the devil (apparently) as "a thing all over hair, all the face hairy, and a long nose."[12]

Had the Salem episode held to the typical New England pattern of witch-hunting, it would have ended with the trial of these three women. But it did not end there; it took wings. By the middle of March the occurrences at Salem Village were attracting widespread attention; furthermore, adults, as well as children, were beginning to publicly manifest peculiar behavior. Calef describes one such episode.

> Mr. Parris invited several Neighboring Ministers to join with him in keeping a Solemn day of Prayer at his own house; the time of the exercise those Persons were for the most part silent, but after one Prayer was ended, they would Act and Speak strangely and Rediculously, yet were such as had been well Educated and of good Behavior . . .[13]

On Sunday, 20 March, Deodat Lawson, who had once occupied the same position as Mr. Parris, delivered the mandatory antiwitchcraft sermon at the Salem meetinghouse. This event too deteriorated into the same sort of spectacle as Mr. Parris's Solemn Day of Prayer.

> On Lords Day, the Twentieth of March, there were sundry of the afflicted Persons at Meeting. . . . They had several Sore Fits, in time of Publick Worship, which did something interrupt me in my First Prayer, being so unusual. After Psalm was Sung, Abigail Williams said to me, "Now stand up and Name your Text": And after it

was read, she said, "It is a long Text." In the beginning of Sermon, Mrs. Pope, a Woman afflicted, said to me, "Now there is enough of that."

In Sermon time when Goodw. C was present in the Meetinghouse Ab. W. called out, "Look where Goodw. C sits on the Beam suckling her Yellow bird betwixt her fingers"! Anne Putnam another Girle afflicted said there was a Yellow-bird sat on my hat as it hung on the pin in the Pulpit: but those that were by, restrained her from speaking loudly about it.[14]

On the following Monday, Martha Cory was examined at the meetinghouse and promptly dispatched to the Boston jail. She was joined two days later by four-year-old Dorcas Good, the daughter of Sarah Good. Martha Cory was then the wife of a prosperous landowner and a covenanting member of the church, but earlier, as a young woman, she had given birth (or so it was rumored) to an illegitimate child.[15] Dorcas Good was naturally tainted by her mother and had apparently been badgered into making a detailed confession.

On 24 March, Rebecca Nurse, a seventy-one-year-old matri-arch, who is described by Starkey as "the very essence of what a Puritan mother should be," was arrested, examined, and re-manded to prison.[16] The successful labeling of a perfectly re-spectable and convenanting member of the church was a turning point; it totally undermined any remaining sense of security and stability in the mind of Samuel Parris. In his sermon book for 27 March, he penned ruefully, "There are devils as well as saints . . . here in Christ's little Church."[17] In the "invisible world" of a great many of the Puritan select, the moral fortress of Puritan New England had been breached. On 11 April, the "number of Accused and Accusers being much increased," an examination was held for the first time outside of Salem Village, in Salem Town, before "a very great assembly" of six magistrates, several ministers, and Deputy Governor William Stoughton, who was both a magistrate and a minister.[18] In the upshot, many more were incarcerated, including the first man, John Proctor, who had tried to assist his wife too assiduously during her interrogation. In Upham's analysis this meeting was a major turning point that:

changed in one sense the whole character of the transaction. Before it had been a Salem affair. After this, it was a Massachusetts af-fair. The colonial government at Boston had obtruded itself . . . and without call or justification, had taken the whole thing out of the hands of the local authorities into its own management. Neither the town nor the village of Salem is responsible, as a principal actor, for what subsequently took place. To that meeting of the deputy-governor and his associates in the colonial administration, at an early period of the transaction, the calamites, outratges, and shame that followed must in justice be ascribed. *Had it not taken place, the delusion, as in former instances and other places here and in the mother-country, would have remained within its original local limits, and soon disappeared.* That meeting, and the proceedings then had, gave to the fanaticism the momentum that drove it on, and extended its destructive influence far and wide.[19]

By mid April the crisis was snowballing and events from this point forward became so hectic that the documentation glosses over important points. There is, for example, only general agreement on the number of people officially accused— about 150 (unofficial accusations abounded and involved something like 400 to 500 people). In March, 6 people were incarcerated, and by the end of April, 22 had been officially accused.[20] During May and June the number of official accusations increased dramatically. Part of the reason for this acceleration in the pace of witch-hunting clearly stems from the acceptance of "spectral evidence." People were accused on the basis of having appeared in someone's dream or hallucination— that is, in spectral form. Also, by 1 April it was generally acknowledged that the Salem witches had been attending a sabbat and by May it was known that their chosen spot was a pasture owned by Samuel Parris, notwithstanding the fact that he was never accused. Once the existence of the sabbat was established, the witches were seen as highly organized, and accusations were leveled in very large numbers.

In late April, George Burroughs who had been minister of Salem Village several years before, and who had made enemies in the process, was accused of being the wizard responsible for the cult of witches. Burroughs had long since left Salem Village for a position in Maine; nevertheless, officials were sent to arrest him. In the last days of April, the General Court of Massachusetts ordered "a solemn day of fasting," but this brought no abatement to the plague of witches. In May, thirty-nine more people were officially accused and jailed. Even more alarming to Puritan New England, people of substance were now being accused. Two important selectmen of Salem Town proved to be the first of this stripe, and in time the spiral of accusations would close in on the centers of power in Boston.

The new governor, a native of Maine, arrived from England

in mid-May and promptly set about constituting a court of Oyer and Terminer to be presided over by William Stoughton. On 2 June the first trial was held and brought about the conviction of Bridget Bishop. She was hanged a week later. The second trial, on 29 June, tried five more women. One defendant, Rebecca Nurse, was at first acquitted; but Chief Justice Stoughton insisted on further deliberation. She was finally convicted with the others. All five women were hanged on 19 July.

The events of June established the pattern for the remainder of the summer. At fitful intervals of two to three weeks, trials were held that were then closely followed by executions. Throughout the summer the rapid pace of accusations and arrests continued. The fact that many of the accused managed to escape—the soundest course of action once accused—is witness to the chaotic state of the control system. All the same, the jails were kept crammed to capacity.

At its most extreme, the Salem Witch-Hunt may have rivaled the efforts of Hopkins in England half a century earlier. In late June, a resident of Andover determined that his wife had been bewitched, and two of Salem's Village's "enchanted" girls were promptly brought to the scene. By then perceived as official witchfinders, the girls arrived in Andover as celebrities. They quite naturally responded with enthusiasm, and in just one day's time identified forty witches. More would have been revealed had not the local justice, a man named Bradstreet, flatly refused to sign additional warrants. Bradstreet was then accused and quickly went into hiding.[21]

The last of the executions came on 22 September when eight people who had accumulated from two trials were hanged. At this point, nineteen people had been hanged, and one man, who had unwisely chosen to stand mute before a Puritan Court, had been pressed to death. This resulted from an established legal gambit (Peine fort et dure) designed to force defendants to enter a plea. In addition, two more people died in prison so that altogether twenty-two people, at a minimum, had been killed in one fashion or another.[22]

At the very least, an examination of the Salem Witch-Hunt points to the essential understanding that societies with restrained legal systems are entirely capable of mass producing deviance under conditions of acute tension. On a broader level, it can be argued that when societies characterized by restrained social control systems are threatened, when, in other words, there has been a dramatic deterioration in the moral landscape of the powerful arising from either internal discord or external aggression, there is an increase in the control measures employed to deal with the category of deviant that is thought to embody the menace to social order. The level of demand, in short, becomes so high that it temporarily overrides the restraints normally in place within a restrained legal system. The documentation available on the Salem Witch-Hunt allows an analysis of this process.

THE MORAL LANDSCAPE OF PURITAN NEW ENGLAND

"Human society in Puritan thought," according to Foster, "was an organic union among men created unequal. Differences existed everywhere, in riches, in birth, in intellect, and most importantly, in power."[23] During the early history of the Massachusetts Bay Colony, those differences were masked by the sense of destiny that dominated Puritan reality. Virtually everyone perceived their interests to be in concert with those of an ecclesiastical elite, "God's chosen saints," who were regarded as the predestined custodians of God's earthly commonwealth.[24] However, by the latter part of the seventeenth century, this sense of common purpose had eroded and the ecclesiastical and commercial segments of Puritan society began to pull in different directions. Moseley notes:

> With continuing economic success, a merchant elite began to supplant the clergy's social power and symbolic prestige. Instead of a holy commonwealth, Boston was fast becoming a trading center, linking the New World with the Old. Ministers had to pay heed to the wishes of a growing commercial aristocracy.[25]

The cleavages within Puritan society are the point of departure from which an analysis of the Salem Witch-Hunt must proceed. It is undeniable that the social forces that encouraged the witch-hunt to escape beyond the limits of Salem Village also brought it to a halt. The Salem Witch-Hunt did not just gradually run out of steam; it was shut down, abruptly, by a coalition of powerful men who brought pressure to bear on the judicial machinery.

There had always been some opposition to the witch-hunt. From the very beginning in Salem Village, a few people were of the opinion that what the afflicted girls needed was either a husband or a good thrashing.[26] In more tranquil times the latter view probably would have prevailed; but for the community leaders of Salem Village, the spring of 1692 was not a time of security. There were directly threatened. Paul Boyer and Stephan Nissenbaum have penetrated as close to the heart of this matter as the extant record will allow. There were solid structural reasons for the contentious nature of Salem Village. It had no clear political status and had always been a stepchild of prosperous Salem Town. Bickering between the residents of Salem Town and Salem Village over the operation of the local militia and the right to maintain a church and pastor, both symbols of independence in New England, is apparent in the records from an early date. As would be expected, the maps of Salem Village dating from this general period show no systematic layout since Salem Village was not a planned community. Additionally, the tax rolls demonstrate: (1) a high rate of population turnover, (2) an increase in the number of landless men, and (3) a diminution in the mean size of holdings among men who did own land.[27]

Over time, a sharp division developed between those who identified their interests with the commerce and external connections of prosperous Salem Town and those who stood to benefit most from the independence of Salem Village. This division hardened irrevocably in 1689 when a formal move for the political separation of Salem Village was made.[28] Much of the resulting dispute swirled, in typical New England style, around the village church and its pastor. In Salem Village this pattern of disputation appears to have been remarkably developed since all three of Mr. Parris's predecessors had been driven from their posts—as Parris himself would be in 1695.[29] Naturally, those supporting political separation from Salem Town also supported the symbols of separation—Mr. Parris and the church—while those against separation opposed Parris.

The feud arose, in part, from a critical lack of institutional apparatus in Salem Village. Boyer and Nissenbaum argue the following:

> The Village's institutional arrangements were unusual—indeed nearly unprecedented—in seventeenth century Massachusetts. Salem Village was virtually the first Massachusetts community to enter for a protracted period this grey area in which its separate existence was given legal recognition, but in such a way as to deny it any real autonomy.[30]

In short, Salem Village's relative poverty, economic divisions, and vague political status left it ripe to be torn apart by social stress—as it was.

To contemporaries, however, the problems of Salem Village were not political and economic; they were moral. In the contemporary view, Salem Village (and New England) was incurring the wrath of God because it had departed from the path of righteousness. God, in the language of the Puritan Jeremiads, "had lengthened the devil's chain."[31]

In Salem Village, the pattern of witchcraft accusations followed the lines of the pro- and anti-Parris factions. The constituency of these factions differed strikingly in church membership, place of residence, and landholding. Typically, those who lived close to Salem Town and were not members of the Salem Village church formed the anti-Parris faction; and those who lived farthest away from Salem Town and were covenanting members of the Salem Village church formed the pro-Parris faction and favored independence from Salem Town. A map of residence patterns in Salem Village illustrates just how striking this pattern was. Boyer and Nissenbaum have plotted the residences of accused witches, defenders of those accused of witchcraft, and the accusers of witches in and around Salem Village and Salem Town.[32] The geography of these roles is striking. Those located close to Salem Town and along the Ipswich Road, which led to Salem Town (i.e., those who had economic ties with the commercial life of Salem Town), were members of the anti-Parris faction and were often counted among the witches or their defenders. Those most removed from Salem Town acted upon a different set of interests and formed the constituency of the pro-Parris faction. In a nutshell, the wealthiest and most prominent members of the pro-Parris faction, through the agency of their afflicted children, directed accusations of witchcraft at the more vulnerable members of the anti-Parris faction. The typical accusation, as it comes down to us through pamphlets and an occasional legal document, was made by Mr. or Mrs. so-and-so (or one of their daughters) against Goodwife or Goodman so-and-so. The title of Mr. or Mrs. was a sign of prominence and respect, whereas that of Goodman or Goodwife (or often just "Goody") was a mark of ordinary respectability—or less. The prominent Putnam family exemplifies this pattern. They comprised much of the strength of the pro-Parris faction and were, in the words of Robert Calef, the "chief prosecutors of this business."[33] In specifics, eight of the Putnams—most notably twelve-year-old Ann Putnam—were directly involved in the formal accusation of forty-six witches.[34] This general pattern was also apparent to Upham in the nineteenth century.

> The persons who were apprehended had, to a considerable extent, been obnoxious and subject to prejudice, in connection with quarrels and controversies. . . . They were "Topsfield Men" or the opponents of Bayley or of Parris, or more or less connected with other feuds.[35]

Once the accusations had moved beyond the first three likely targets, the labeling of witches rapidly became political. This, of course, fits the universal pattern since, as Evans-Pritchard has already told us, "Sufferers from misfortune seek for witches among their enemies."[36] Examples from Salem Village are numerous: Daniel Andrew and Phillip English were accused shortly after their election to office in Salem Town; the husband of Rebecca Nurse was a leader of the anti-Parris faction; and many of the accused witches were associated with the Porter family—the most prominent family within the anti-Parris faction. Boyer and Nissenbaum write:

> As the accused are examined from the perspective of factionalism, they begin to arrange themselves into a series of interconnected networks. These networks were not formally organized or rigidly structured, but there were nonetheless real enough. The kinds of associations which underlay them were varied: kinship and marriage ties were crucial, but marriage, in all likelyhood was simply the final step, the institutionalization of less tangible bonds built up gradually over a period of time.[37]

It is clear, then, that the outbreak of witchcraft in Salem Village was rooted in the conflicting interests of the factions present in Salem Village. Furthermore, it would seem that the reasons for the continued "plague-like" spread of witchcraft beyond the Salem community are to be found in the larger configurations of power and self-interest within the Boston ruling class. In a very real sense the feuds of Salem Village were a microcosm of the conflicts that were dividing Puritan society within the larger arena of Massachusetts as the merchant class began its ascendancy. For the heirs of a select group that thought of themselves as "the shock troops of a Calvinist internationale," the present situation was perilous.[38]

In the minds of the Puritan saints, the various issues surrounding the conduct of the witch-hunt began to hinge on the question of spectral evidence. It was obvious to everyone that if this category of evidence was disallowed, the witch-hunt would end. But in the climate of alarm that gripped the Community of saints during the early spring of 1692, the arguments against spectral evidence carried little weight despite the fact that during an early examination, one of the defendants had neatly destroyed the veracity of spectral evidence upon the bedrock of Biblical authority. When Susanna Martin—by all reports an especially salty personality—was questioned about the career of her specter, she retorted, "He that appeared in the shape of Samuel, a glorified Saint, may appear in anyone's shape."[39]

In the view of most Puritan divines, stern measures were required; and it is very clear that stern measures were employed. Two Boston merchants, Robert Calef and Thomas Brattle, provide vivid accounts of the practices—reminiscent of the methods used by Hopkins—that were permitted throughout the hunt. In a lengthy letter dated 8 October 1692 and circulated in manuscript form, Thomas Brattle registers his opposition:

> First, as to the method which the Salem Justices do take in their examinations, it is truely this: A warrant being issued out to apprehend the persons that are charged and complained of by the afflicted children (as they are called); said persons are brought before the Justices, (the afflicted being present.) The Justices ask the apprehended why they afflict those poor children; to which the apprehended answer, they do not afflict them. The Justices order the apprehended to look upon said children, which accordingly they do; and at the time of that look, (I dare not say by that look, as the Salem Gentlemen do) the afflicted are cast into a fitt. The apprehended are then blinded, and ordered to touch the afflicted; and at that touch, tho' not by the touch (as above) the afflicted ordinarily do come out of their fitts. The afflicted persons then declare and affirm, that the apprehended have afflicted them; upon which the apprehended person, tho' of never so good repute, are forthwith committed to prison, on suspicion for witchcraft.[40]

Calef also comments on the techniques used to extract confessions:

> There are numerous Instances . . . of the tedious Examinations before private persons, many hours together, they all that time urging them to Confess (and taking turns to persuade them) till the accused

were wearied out by being forced to stand so long, or for want of sleep, etc. and so brought to give an Assent to what they said; they then asking them, Were you at such a Witchmeeting, or have you signed the Devil's book, etc. upon their replying, yes, the whole was drawn into form as their confession.[41]

He also quotes a petition written by some of the accused witches from Andover detailing how it was that they came to confess. According to Burr this is the same document referred to by Thomas Brattle in the letter quoted above, as "a petition lately offered to the chief Judge."[42]

And, the Authority in Andover . . . sent for the (afflicted girls) to come together to the Meetinghouse in Andover. . . . We were blindfolded, and our hands were laid upon the afflicted persons, they being in their fits at our coming into their presence (as they said) . . . and then they said they were well, and that we were guilty of afflicting them; whereupon we were all seized as Prisoners by a Warrant from the Justice of the Peace, and forthwith carried to Salem. . . . We were all exceedingly astonished . . . and affrightened even out of our Reason; and our nearest and dearest Relations seeing us in that dreadful condition, and knowing our great danger, apprehending that there was no other way to save our lives . . . but by confessing ourselves to be such and such persons, as the afflicted represented us to be, they out of tender love and pity perswaded us to confess what we did confess. And, indeed that Confession . . . was no other than what was suggested to us by some Gentlemen. . . . Also the hard measures they used with us rendered us uncapable of making our defense; but said anything and everything which they desired, and most of what we said was but in effect a consenting to what they said. Sometime after when we were better composed, they telling us what we had confessed, we did profess that we were Innocent and Ignorant of such things. And we hearing that Samuel Wardwell had renounced his Confession, and quickly after Condemned and Executed, some of us were told that we were going after Wardwell.
Mary Osgood, Mary Tiler, Deliv. Dane, Abigale Barker, Sarah Wilson, Hannah Tiler.[43]

Brattle's letter was written during or shortly after the executions; and, although Calef's essay More Wonders of the Invisible World, was written some time after the fact (1697), he also lived through the witch-hunt. Calef, who clearly had access to information provided by Brattle (the petition above, for example), and evidently from other sources as well, can be regarded as the chief spokesman of the commercial faction. There were other critical essays circulated during the witch-hunt. These cover basically the same territory as the Brattle letter and reveal the same bent of mind.[44] At all events, as the number of executions mounted, private doubts turned to open discontent. Even so, the witch-hunt did not end until, finally, a coalition of powerful ecclesiastics signaled that the time had come to halt the production of witches.

There seems to have been a number of reasons for this. *First, prominent people were being accused.* According to Boyer and Nissenbaum, these included by the end of the summer: a number of merchants and landowners of "great estate" in Boston; the wife of the prominent minister John Hale, a man who had, until that point, supported the trials; one of the most celebrated men of New England, John Alden; two members of the distinguished Bradstreet family; Nathaniel Saltonstall, who had resigned in protest from the Court of Oyer and Terminer; and Lady Phips, the wife of the governor.[45] Rumored appearances in spectral form included none other than Cotton Mather and his mother.[46] As a general rule, such accusations were simply ignored, and when the girls accused Samuel Willard, the president of Harvard College and a pastor of Boston's First Church, they were sternly told by the court that they were in error.[47]

As more and more prominent people were accused, key people became deeply troubled. In the end, they began to voice the opinion that the evils associated with the cure for witchcraft were outstripping the dangers that witchcraft posed. "This consulting of these afflicted children," declares Brattle, "seems to me a very grosse evill. . . . I know there are several worth Gentlemen in Salem, who account this practice as an abomination."[48]

Some years after the witch-hunt, John Higginson, senior pastor at Salem Town, wrote a brief "epistle to the reader," which introduced an essay on witchcraft by a very prominent actor in the Salem drama, the Reverend John Hale. In his letter, Higginson laconically reviewed the sequence of events, as he saw it, that fostered this disillusionment:

It pleased God some few years ago, to suffer Satan to raise much trouble amongst us . . . the beginning of which was very small and looked on at first as an ordinary case which had fallen out before at several times in other places, and would be quickly over. But in the progress of the matter, a multitude of other persons . . . were Accused, Examined, Imprisoned, and came to their Trials, at Salem, the County Town, where about Twenty of Them suffered as Witches; and many others in danger of the same Tragical End: and still the number of the Accused increased unto many Scores; amongst whom were many Persons of Unquestionable Credit, never under any grounds of suspicion of that or any other scandalous Evil. This brought a general Consternation upon all sorts of People, doubting what would be the issue of such a dreadful Judgement of God upon the Country.[49]

Second, as powerful people, or those close to them, were accused, they were thrown into the camp of the opposition. John Hale, for example, promptly shifted his alliance when his wife was accused.[50] Governor Phips falls into this category, and Cotton Mather may be yet another example. Mather's considerable concern over the validity of spectral evidence was voiced soon after his and his mother's alleged appearance in spectral form.

Third, at the same time that the witch hunt was becoming daily more voracious, the external situation was becoming less and less threatening. That is, the moral landscape was no longer as menacing to the ruling class as it had been in the spring of the year, and, in this improved setting, the extreme measures being taken no longer seemed justified. The executions of the summer, and particularly the mass hanging of 22 September, undoubtedly forced this reconsideration. It can be noted that Governor Phips, while infamous in the Puritan view, was still a vast improvement over his predecessor, and the feared French attack showed no signs of materializing. The social and political crisis was, in other words, clearly winding down.

In combination, these factors had the effect of bringing together a coalition of powerful ecclesiastics who formally questioned the manner in which the witch-hunt was being conducted. It is important to understand that this attack on the witch-hunt did not take the form of an attack on the principal figures behind the hunt or on the reality of witchcraft itself. The only issue that was directly broached was the validity of spectral evidence, upon which most people had been convicted and many executed. All concerned, nevertheless, were entirely aware of the consequences of disallowing spectral evidence: it was largely a symbolic issue.

The witch-hunt ended suddenly. Over the course of the summer there had been a number of occurences to signal that support for the hunt was not overwhelming. Five days after the first execution, a group of twelve prominent Boston ministers,

including Cotton Mather, addressed a letter of encouragement
and advice to Governor Phips. In it a "very critical and exquisite
caution" was recommended since the "daemon may assume the
shape of the innocent."[51] It was, overall, an ambiguous document, no doubt reflecting their collective state of mind. After
the trials resumed at the end of June, one member of the court,
Saltonstall, resigned in protest. He too was accused. Over the
summer, as the number of executions steadily mounted, more
and more "country preachers," as Starkey refers to them, went
on record as opposing the hunt; a few actively aided the escape
of accused witches. In August, a woman was reprieved because
of pregnancy; in September, six more reprieves were given out.
Throughout, the circulation of critical manuscripts increased.

It was the execution of the last large group of people on 22
September that galvanized key figures into action. On 3 October,
Increase Mather (the father of Cotton Mather) presented a sermon
to a formal gathering of minsters at Cambridge. This message,
later published as *Cases of Conscience Concerning Evill Spirits
Personating Men* (1693), was signed by fourteen prominent ministers and circulated in manuscript form almost immediately.[52]
The title of the sermon conveys the message: it was an unquali-
fied condemnation of the use of spectral evidence. In it Mather
argues, "It is better that ten suspected witches should escape
than one innocent should be condemned."

Increase Mather's sermon, endorsed by the Boston ministers,
became the pivot upon which subsequent events turned. Governor Phips acted officially on 12 October and forbade, temporarily, further incarceration and prosecution, noting as he did so
that the devil had taken the shape of people who were "to
my certain knowledge" innocent (i.e., Lady Phips). From mid-
October on, the residents of the towns of Topsfield, Glouster,
Haverhill, Chelmsford, and Andover petitioned for the release
of friends and kin.[53] On 18 October, two ministers and twenty-
four residents of Andover, a town that stood to be decimated
if the prosecutions were to be allowed to recommence under
existing standards of evidence, presented a letter to the governor
and General Court that portrayed the afflicted girls as "distem-
pered persons."[54] A week later a bill was introduced into the
General Court calling for a fast and a convocation of ministers
on the matter of the witch-hunt. It seems to have been clear
to everyone that this meeting of important ecclesiastics was
to be largely ceremonial and that the outcome was a foregone
conclusion. Samuel Sewall, one of the Judges, commented in

his diary that "the season and manner of doing it is such that the Court of Oyer and Terminer count themselves thereby dismissed."[55] Governor Phips carried through on this expectation on 29 October and dismissed the Court.

A special court, consisting of many of the members of the defunct Court of Oyer and Terminer, convened in January of 1693 to deal with the remaining cases. Governor Phips had by then specifically forbidden the use of spectral evidence, and the anticipated result of this prohibition materialized: forty-nine people were acquitted outright.[56] Only three people were convicted, two of whom were the "most senseless and ignorant Creatures that could be found."[57] All three were immediately given a reprieve by Governor Phips. In the spring of that year, a general pardon was issued and all remaining prisoners were discharged.

The complex issues of power, self-interest, and social control were especially prominent among the social forces at work during the Salem witch hunt. At the outset, it must be emphasized that the interests and outlooks of the two major social factions in seventeenth-century New England—the ecclesiastical and the commercial—were so fundamentally different by the 1690s that contemporary accounts of the witch-hunt have come down to us in two quite different literary styles. Cotton Mather's celebrated account of the witch-hunt, *The Wonders of the Invisible World* (1692), was written in the metaphorical style of the keepers of the covenant, the Jeremiad. M. Wynn Thomas argues that this book was

> the last important work to use the language of the Chosen people. . . . It was a great Jeremiad, that powerful mixture of lament, rebuke and exhortation so characteristic of the preaching of the second and third generations of the Puritan settlers.[58]

In contrast, Brattle and Calef, along with others of the commercial faction, totally avoided this style. Those in opposition to the witch-hunt, as Moseley puts it, wrote in the "rhetoric of property."[59] These two antagonistic bodies of literature—and particularly Calef's satirical attack on Cotton Mather—have generated the argument that the Salem witch hunt was consciously engineered by the "Clerical Party" to protect their interests.[60] However, when close attention is paid to this episode, there is little to support such a blatantly conspiratorial view of history. Although it is indisputable that members of the ecclesiastical

elite were in forefront of the witch-hunt, it is clear that they
were so because they were genuinely appalled by the beleaguered state of "God's earthly Paradise." And it cannot be ignored that it was members of this same elite, led by Increase
Mather, who brought the witch-hunt to a close. Indeed, some
of the same ecclesiastics who early on signed the published
version of Deodat Lawson's Salem meetinghouse sermon—a
rousing endorsement of the witch hunt—also signed Increase
Mather's Cases of Conscience circulated six months later.

From a theoretical standpoint, it is important to understand
that although dominant actors within powerful groups almost
invariably act in their self-interest, they do not like to be seen
in that light. The appearance of crass expediency, is after all,
unhelpful to the posture of legitimacy.[61] Nor do they like to
see themselves in that light. Stated more directly, people do
not like to perceive themselves as behaving in contradiction
to their own self-concept. Almost universally this potential for
discrepancy between one's self-concept and one's behavior
is mitigated, at the collective level, by the construction of a
world view—a moral landscape if you will—that is self-serving.
Thereby the demands of self-interest and virtue are drawn into
a common course of action. As Marx or, for that matter, Sartre
argue, ideology is not only self-serving, it is self-deluding as
well.[62] However, the immediate problem in this concern is the
imposition of one group's moral landscape upon that of another
group. How is this accomplished?

It is a standard admonition of Durkheimian sociology that
deviance functions to dramatize the configuration of normative
behavior and to outline the boundaries of virtue and wickedness. These "moral boundaries," which are ultimately cognitive,
are the direct result of the labeling and ceremonial punishment of people who engage in particular sorts of behavior
deemed to be deviant. Dealing specifically with this issue, Erikson writes:

> The only material found in society for marking boundaries is the
> behavior of its members—or rather, the networks of interaction
> which link these members together in regular social relations. And
> the interactions which do the most effective job of location and
> publicizing the group's outer edges would seem to be those which
> take place between the deviant persons on one side and and official
> agents of the community on the other. The deviant is a person
> whose activities have moved outside the margins of the group, and

when the community calls him to account for that vagrancy it is
making a statement about the nature and placement of its boundaries. It is declaring how much variability and diversity can be
tolerated within the group before it begins to lose its distinctive
shape, its unique identity.[63]

In actual practice, however, it is very hard to apply this concept to complex societies without abandoning some of the fundamental assumptions of functionalism. In Erikson's view the
Salem Witch-Hunt represents a special dramatization of moral
boundaries that came about because the Puritan community *as
a whole* was threatened. And so it was, by the French and
the Indians about whom the Essex County authorities had been
sufficiently alarmed to order the maintenance of scouts against
possible attack.[64] But the loss of the charter, about which there
was the greatest lamentation, directly threatened only a few—the
ruling class and, in particular, the ecclesiastical elite. Their
depth of concern is amply documented. For instance, on the
day that Samuel Sewall, one of the principal actors on the Court
of Oyer and Terminer, learned of the abrogation of the charter,
he wrote in his diary, "This monday we begin palpably to dye."[65]
The witch-hunt was, in reality, a defense of the eroding social
position and symbolic prestige of the ecclesiastical elite.[66] In
the tradition of the Jeremiads, it demonstrated that the troubles
being visited upon the people of New England were the consequences of their sins—of not heeding their moral leaders. This
is the dominant theme, for example, in Cotton Mather's *Memorable Providences, Relating to Witchcraft and Possessions* (1689).
On the other hand, there is ample evidence that the commercial
segment of Puritan society opposed the witch-hunt soon after
it began. As Hockett has observed, "It was the class least interested in religion which first denounced the persecution."[67]
Taking into account the factionalism and stratification of Puritan society, Erikson's concept of moral boundaries is of utility
in the analysis of the Salem Witch-Hunt only if it is applied
to the actions of the ruling class and not to Puritan society
as a whole. This consideration, which is fundamental, has been
discussed by Morris in a much larger context.

It may be said of Durkheim ... that he assumed a homogeneity
in society, a kind of unified moral community with collective sentiments that was forcefully expressed in the control of deviant behavior. In practice we can observe that there are in fact numerous

moral communities, not all spatially based, and whose collective sentiments may well be conflicting.[68]

During the spring and summer of 1692, the machinery of social control was put to the task of dramatizing moral boundaries that served the interests and reinforced the world view of the Puritan elite. The keepers of the covenant were led by the logic of the reality they lived by into hatching a witch-hunt. In the uncertainty and disquiet that followed the loss of the charter, the leading Puritan divines had prophesied the arrival of Satan's agents and then guided the resulting hunt for them to its fulfillment in the courts. The Salem Witch-Hunt came about because the ecclesiastical elite, in the twilight of their power, had allowed themselves to be "stampeded into barbarism."[69]

Deviance, as Erikson has demonstrated, tends to appear in the form that is most feared.[70] In any society dominated by a religious ideology, the witch-figure constitutes an appalling threat to the established order and, by extension, to the interests
and values of the ruling class. It follows that the witch was the ideal deviant to be used in the public demarcation of the moral boundary that protected their construction of reality. Larner expands on this thesis:

A witch was by identification an abnormal person. The execution of a witch was a demonstration of group solidarity. It removed the provocative deviant and redefined the boundaries of normality to secure the safety of the virtuous community.[71]

From this standpoint, it is obvious that the ecclesiastical elite within Puritan society stood to benefit from a witch trial; but it is equally clear that they got much more than they bargained for. Their frequent cautionary letters and sermons during the spring and summer indicate that the witch-hunt was assuming dimensions they had not anticipated and did not want. By all their past experience it is reasonable to suppose that what they had anticipated and perhaps wanted was a small "boundary maintaining" witch-hunt that would have culminated in the trial and public execution of a few unwholesome (by Puritan lights) and impoverished women. This is exactly what is found in Cotton Mather's *Memorable Providences*, which portrays the mischief, trial, and execution of Goody Glover, a stereotypical witch. The same line of propaganda was attempted in *The Wonders of the Invisible World*, a tract for the times if there ever was one. Its centerpiece is a capsule account of the trials of five of the nineteen people who had been executed at Salem Village. All five were individuals of bad reputation who could easily be represented to an agitated public as believable witches. But as we know, and as Mather undoubtedly knew, they were a very unrepresentative sample.

What the ecclesiastical elite anticipated at the beginning of the Salem Witch-Hunt was, of course, far different from what materialized. What they got, to their astonishment and horror, was a full-blown panic-trial that threatened to destroy the Puritan community. But there is, as I have suggested, little merit in viewing this episode as simply a crass political conspiracy. The actions of the Puritan divines were predictably in their self-interest, but that agenda was hidden to them. There can be no doubt that they were genuinely appalled by the behavior of the "afflicted girls." At the same time, however, it must be emphasized that there were other plausible interpretations of the girls' behavior available to the Puritan leaders. In other situations and at other times—the Great Awakening, for example—exactly the same symptoms were defined as manifestations of the Holy Spirit.[72] But during a period when the ruling class was directly threatened, their conviction that the devil was at work was almost universal.

Nor, given the degree of enmity to be found in Salem Village, is it very surprising that the plague of witches reached such appalling dimensions before it was finally stopped. The factional disputes of Salem Village, in which accusations of witchcraft came to be the accepted weapon, ran so deep that the witch-hunt stood little chance of being contained. In the emotional environment of 1692, the Puritan social control system, which normally would have held the outcome of a spate of witchcraft accusations to the trial and execution of one or two witches, rapidly filled the jails of New England to the bursting point.

By late summer, if not before, it seems to have been recognized in certain circles that it was the witch-hunt itself that threatened Puritan society. When this fact was finally appreciated by powerful men, the hunt was stopped. It is clear that doubt began to be a factor when those legally defined as witches began to diverge markedly from the accepted image of a witch. Just the simple accusation of high-status people was unsettling, and very early on, those jailed, and in some instances executed, were dramatically at odds with the supposed character or status of a witch. The extraordinary effort required to obtain the conviction of Rebecca Nurse was a reflection of this dismay.

Even the frugal statistics of the Salem panic-trial reveal the degree to which the population of officially labeled witches progressively deviated from the recognized "norm." As we know, the first three accused were stereotypical witches. And all those accused in February and March—the first seven people—were women. However, fully one third of those accused in the months of April and May were men.[73] Additionally, the first executions involved women, but five men died in the executions of August and September. When the Court of Oyer and Terminer was finally dissolved in October, the jails were still full, and many more unlikely witches—"considerable persons of unblamable life," according to Governor Phips—were under sentence of death.[74]

Sensing political difficulty, Governor Phips asked Cotton Mather to write an official account of the witch trial, and Mather responded in the only style he knew—the Jeremiad. The *Wonders of the Invisible World* was available to the people of New England by mid-October, 1692. It was written in great haste with Mather galloping off to the printer as each section of the book was completed.[75] Acutely aware of the "various opinions" on the manner in which the witch-hunt was conducted, he argued that the devil can be found in the quarrels of men and called for New England to return to the covenant:

> I have heard it affirmed, That in the late great Flood upon Connecticut, those Creatures which could not but have quarrelled at another time, yet now being driven together, very agreeably stood by one another. I am sure we shall be worse than *Brutes* if we fly upon one another at a time when the Floods of Belial make us afraid.[76]

In the final analysis, the savagery of a full-blown witch-hunt taxed even Cotton Mather's skill at self-deception. It was an obdurate reality that simply could not be made to fit into the world view to which the generation of saints had been socialized. The people of New England, wrote the distressed Mather, had been lured "into a Blind Mans Buffet."[77] On the face of it, *The Wonders* can be read as defense of the Court, which was its political purpose. But it is a very uneven defense, and when Mather's public account of the witch-hunt is contrasted with his private thoughts (his diary), the depth of his personal disquiet become clear. He laments at one point that "the mad people tho' the Country revile me as if I had been the Doer of all the hard things that were done in the Prosecution of witchcraft."[78] "If ever there was a false book produced by a man whose heart was not in it, it is *The Wonders.*"[79]

Even more revealing is the book written by the Reverend John Hale, *A Modest Inquiry into the Nature of Witchcraft* (1702). "It is a sad, troubled, and honest book."[80] It shows clearly how the events of the witch trial had battered his image of reality and his peace of mind. Hale had been one of the major forces in the witch trials. But anguished by the executions and astonished by the high station and good reputation of the people accused, he became profoundly skeptical. It was a wrenching experience:

> A child will not easily forsake the principles he hath been trained up in from his cradle. But observing the Events of that Sad Catastrophe *Anno* 1692, I was brought to a more strict scanning of the principle I had imbibed.[81]

The reasons for Hale's personal crisis of confidence and, by extension, that of the ruling class, are explicitly presented in his book. Hale writes:

> Experience shewed that the more were apprehended, the more were still Afflicted by Satan, and the number of Confessors increasing, but did increase the number of Accused, and the Executing of some made way for the apprehending of others; for still the Afflicted complained of being tormented by new objects as the former were removed. So that those that were concerned, grew amazed at the numbers and quality of the persons accused and feared that Satan by his wiles had inwrapped innocent persons under the imputation of that Crime. And at last it was evidently seen that there must be a stop put, or the Generation of the Children of God would fall under that condemnation.[82]

It is clear that many other leading figures in the hunt for witches were plagued by doubt and, in some instances that we know of, by guilt. For example, fearing the vengeance of his God, Samuel Sewall stood in church and in classic Puritan tradition publicly confessed. "Samuel Sewall," reads his confession, "sensible of the reiterated strokes of God upon himself and family; and being sensible, that as to the Guilt contracted upon the opening of the late commission of Oyer and

Terminer at Salem ... Desire to take the Burden and Shame of it. ...."[83]. While there were exceptions—William Stoughton, the chief justice, remained adamant to his death—the general state of mind among those connected in some fashion with the untimely deaths brought about by the action of the court was that of confusion and dismay. Events had threatened their construction of reality and outstripped their ability to justify their behavior. As Perry Miller notes, one of the principal effects of this tragedy was the corrosion of the self-esteem of many of its principal actors.[84]

The explanation for the Salem panic-trial can be found on the beleaguered moral landscape of the ecclesiastical elite of the Massachusetts Bay Colony. God's chosen saints were threatened; their power and position were beset by dark forces, and the shape of the world as they desired it was eroding. The ecclesiastical elite reacted to the menacing reality of the inter-charter period in the only way that it could and in a way that it had done before—with a moral crusade.

There is no compelling evidence that the political maneuvering of the intercharter period significantly altered the essentially restrained nature of Puritan law. An awkward amalgam of common law and the Old Testament, the Puritan legal system was severe but far from inquisitorial. Above all, a defendant could not be legally tortured into a confession. It is true that after being pitchforked out of Massachusetts, Governor Andros returned to England with tales of legal excesses, but even allowing that some of his charges were accurate, the essential fact is that the most lively abuses recorded during the witch-hunt—the Andover episode, for example–took place after the arrival of Governor Phips and the establishment, on 16 May of the New Charter. In short, the Salem panic-trial simply cannot be explained by a momentary change in the structure of Puritan law. Codified and normally effective organizational restraints were in place during the witch-hunt, and the fundamental question is: Why were these restraints ineffective? The only plausible answer is that the conviction on the part of the ecclesiastical elite that Massachusetts was threatened by agents of the devil was so intense that many of the safeguards of common law were ignored. The comments of Thomas Brattle and Robert Calef, as well as the many petitions to the court, make it abundantly clear that the methods used to produce deviants during this period were extraordinary—and illegal. To suppose, however, that the outraged comments of Brattle and others led directly to public indignation that then brought the trials to a halt is a mistake. There is no evidence to support such a scenario. Statements critical of the witch-hunt stem from the period when the actions of powerful men had already signaled that the hunt was winding down. The body of criticism that circulated in manuscript form took advantage of an, in fact, documents a perceptible shift in the mood of dominant figures.

There can be no doubt that it was very dangerous to publicly oppose the witch-hunt. Those who did so were almost invariably "cried out upon." Of the opposing manuscripts in circulation, only Brattle's is signed; the others, circulated earlier, were initialed, and in all likelihood, even for a person in the position of Brattle, early public opposition would have resulted in accusation. The emotional climate in the summer of 1692 was such that an accused person, even of good reputation, was often stripped of all support. A longstanding friend of John Alden confronted him from the bench saying that he "had always accounted him a good man; but, indeed, now he should be obliged to change his opinion."[85]

It is this emotional climate that is at the base of the witch panic. The momentary lack of effective organizational restraint resulted from a high pitch of *external demand*; and the lack of restraint, in turn, produced evidence (in the form of confessions) that reinforced the menacing construction of reality that argued the necessity of further suborning the law. The pattern of the Salem Witch-Hunt in the spring and early summer clearly demonstrates a deepening spiral of fear on the part of powerful men. It was an infectious (and productive) atmosphere. When Governor Phips arrived in Boston, literally hundreds of people of every station had been accused of witchcraft and every jail within a day's ride from Boston was packed with accused and self-confessed witches. He had two possible courses of action: either let the witches go or begin prosecuting. In the climate of the times, only the latter course of action beckoned, and Phips immediately established a Court of Oyer and Terminer, which began to produce convicted witches within three weeks of his arrival.

It is far from certain that Phips had authority to establish this court.[86] Even more surprising, at the first trail there was simply no law under the New Charter against witchcraft—an oversight fostered by the intellectual climate in England during the 1690s. The willful assumption in New England was that the old 1604 statute of James I was still in force, but it was nevertheless seen as necessary to renew the Old Charter law before the court adjourned following the adjudication of the first case.[87] It would seem, then, that Bridget Bishop was convicted by a court that may have been illegal for a crime that many members of the court suspected was not on the books. The single event that even hints at any outrage over this debasement of the law was the resignation of Saltonstall. In the early going, popular resistance to this court was nil and it was only when the witch-hunt was coming to a close that the legality of the court suddenly became an issue. While the level of external demand was high, criticism of the witch-hunt was both dangerous and ineffective, and, by every indication, the organization of public criticism during the latter part of the witch-hunt seems to have been effective only in the sense that it began to prey upon the doubts already in the minds of central figures.

Put into comparative perspective, the Salem Witch-Hunt falls strictly into pattern, and the several concepts and notions marshalled in the analysis of deviance production in late seventeenth-century New England work well in the much broader context of Europe.

6
Ideology and the European Witchcraze

The European witchcraze, as the rationalist historians have argued, was at least in part an outgrowth of the Counter-Reformation. However, it is not correct to suppose that the witchcraze is explained by the argument that the religions of early modern Europe were killing off their confessional antagonists under the guise of being witches. There is abundant evidence that those on opposite sides of a confessional dispute were perfectly willing to kill one another for what they were—religious enemies. Furthermore, if there is any clearly definable pattern to the various outbreaks of the witchcraze, they would seem to *follow* a religious upheaval. Parker argues:

> A witchcraze normally occurred in areas which had experienced a period of religious upheaval during which Christian teaching was somewhat neglected, especially in outlying regions ... And the persecution tended to coincide with the moment at which one warring Christian church emerged as the victor and was intent on turning mastery into monopoly: Scotland after 1590 in the case of the Calvinists; Southwest Germany after 1625 and Poland after 1650 in the case of the Catholics.[1]

From this standpoint the witchcraze was a by-product of what Delumeau has called "Christianization."[2] The Roman Catholic Church, as it emerged from the Council of Trent (1545–63), was repeatedly confronted with two distressing situations: (1) populations that had been tainted by an opposing Christian religion and (2) a popular culture among the peasantry that never seems to have been anything more than superficially Christian.[3] By the latter part of the sixteenth century, the response of the Catholic Church to this challenge was well organized and thorough. For the first time, the patterns of religious observance were closely monitored among ordinary people: marriages, baptisms, burials, church attendance, and so on were all carefully recorded.[4] Also for the first time, a literate and conforming clergy was established. To this end, and to make the populace more like their social betters, education was emphasized. By 1640 the Jesuits had established more than five hundred colleges across Europe, and at the local level, in innumerable church schools, children recited lessons from books modeled after the catechisms of noted Jesuits.[5] For their part, of course, the Protestants followed suit. The net effect of this process in both Catholic and Protestant Europe was to narrow the limits of acceptable behavior.

There was at the same time a fundamentally political basis to this campaign of Christianization. It was utterly impossible to separate religion and ideology during the sixteenth and seventeenth centuries.[6] The imposition of a particular orthodoxy on peasant and burgher culture was as much a secular control strategy as it was a sacred duty. Larner declares roundly that the witchcraze in Scotland corresponds exactly to the "life-time of Christianity as ideology."[7] In England during this period, church attendance was compulsory. Recusancy (refusal to attend Church of England services) bordered on treason. John Foxe's *Acts and Monuments* (the book of protestant martyrs who were burned in Marian, England) was kept, by law, alongside the Bible in Anglican churches, and, indeed, even the admonitions in the Anglican Prayer Book were subject to Parliamentary approval.[8]

Obviously, the viability of the godly-state and the divine right of the king was dramatically enhanced when the king, and state, could be presented as the enemy of Satan. In this sense the witch-hunt was a "ritual of legitimization," and, accordingly, it can hardly be seen as an accident that the worst witch-hunts on record occurred in the small German ecclesiastical states (Würzberg, Bamberg, Trier, and others) where inquisitorial procedure was the most refined and the legitimization requirements of Christian ideology greatest.[9] And, Christianity aside, this is a process that is very much alive today in regimes (Iran, for example) where matters of state require that revolutionary vigilance and morality be closely guarded. In the context of ideological Christianity, however, the public labeling and punishment of a witch, the embodiment of evil and disorder, was clearly the most efficient method of cloaking a regime in the trappings of virtue and godly legitimacy.[10]

Nothing more clearly exemplifies the pursuit of godly legitimacy than the life and personality of James VI, king of Calvinist

Scotland. Although the Scottish laws against witchcraft date back to 1563, it is clear that Continental demonology had very little impact on Scottish thinking until 1590. Prior to that date, witchcraft was viewed more or less in the English manner—as simple maleficium—and the Calvinist sense of order was oriented towards stamping out a broad spectrum of disorderly pleasures such as "adultery, mass-mongering and abominable and horrid oaths."[11]

The witchcraze came into Scotland at a critical juncture, the coronation of the queen, and by a clearly defined mechanism. In the fall of 1589, James VI sailed to Denmark to claim his bride, Ann. He stayed the winter at the Danish court and was thoroughly indoctrinated with Continental demonology by Lutheran theologians. Naturally, the full bloom of Continental witchcraft theory was introduced into Scotland when James, his bride, and members of the Danish court returned in the spring. The voyage back to Scotland, across the North Sea, was very rough, and one ship was lost. Witchcraft was suspected. By the fall of that year the worst was known: The king, his bride, and the alliance with Denmark had been threatened. The facts behind the ensuing trial are not at all clear from the extant information, but from the perspective of the Scottish king and court, the following had transpired: hundreds of witches had sailed to North Berwick in an armada of sieves, ransacked a graveyard, and entered the local church to hold a standard Continental sabbat. Subsequently, under the direction of the devil, the witches had attempted to raise a storm at sea and sink the king's fleet during his passage back to Scotland. The official belief that this preternatural assault was forestalled by the unusual intensity of the king's faith was widely advertised in the broadsheet "News From Scotland," which preceded James's arrival in England to claim the throne. During the course of the trial it developed that there had been other attempts on the king's life by means of a wax image and by sprinkling magical powder on the royal linen. This ingenious treason was supposedly undertaken at the instigation of James's cousin, the earl of Bothwell, who led the opposition party. The earl was incarcerated and, after unsuccessfully proclaiming his innocence, wisely made his escape. Escape was interpreted as proof of guilt, and a proclamation was issued declaring that the earl had "given himself over altogidder in the handis of Sathan."[12]

It seems safe to say that the image of King James presented in "News From Scotland" (1591), which insists that he was

Satan's principal enemy on earth, became a central feature of his self-concept.[13] It was an image that gradually sharpened into a depiction of the sovereign as God's lieutenant—as James himself so stated in his *Daemonologie*. Indeed, contemporary demonologists went so far as to argue that the power of the devil and his agents diminished in proportion to the virtue and zeal of the Godly magistrate. James, quite naturally, embraced this notion.[14]

The trial of the North Berwick witches was to have massive repercussions. In Denmark, the news of James's encounter with Satan briefly caused the endemic witchcraft of Denmark to flare, and an unknown number of Danish witches were tried in Copenhagen for storm raising. In Scotland, continental notions of witchcraft had been firmly planted in the public mind by the trial, and henceforward, until the end of the seventeenth century, witch-hunts were a major feature of Scottish life.

In the immediate aftermath of the North Berwick trial, standing commissions were established to continue the hunt for witches. These fanned out from Edinburgh to the great peril of anyone of bad reputation.[15] Furthermore, the Privy Council, the secular arm of government, maintained a general commission to expedite the processing of witches. This body does not seem to have had any appellate function whatsoever, and it expressly encouraged the use of torture in a statement that amounted to announcing an open season on isolated and independent-minded women throughout the realm.[16] For six years Scottish witch-hunters were allowed full play, and the hunt continued unabated until the summer of 1597. At that time, reports by the English ambassador, Robert Bowes, indicate that the witch-hunt was getting out of hand and that the king was "pestered and many ways troubled in the examination of witches."[17] According to Bowes, the commissions were generating "many thousands" of witches.

One event in particular seems to have had a key part in bringing the hunt to an end. In the summer of 1597, a woman who had been accused of witchcraft claimed that she could identify witches by looking into their eyes. She was immediately accepted as a witchfinder, and, according to Archbishop Spottiswode in his *History of the Church of Scotland* (1645),

> . . . she was carried from town to town to make discoveries in that kind . . . especially at Glasgow where divers innocent women through the credulity of the minister Mr. John Cowper were con-

demned and put to death. In the end she was found to be a mere deceiver. . . .[18]

It appears that she was tricked by a suspicious magistrate into revealing herself, whereupon she reverted to her former status. At her trial, she confessed that it had all been a scheme to escape death. Spottiswode claims that this incident had a marked impact on the king. It also came to the king's attention, by an unknown avenue, that many of those sitting on witch-hunting commissions were using their positions to settle old scores.

For whatever reason, James seems to have suddenly become receptive to the idea that many people had been falsely accused. He was not alone in this view. Three times during the years 1597 and 1598 the Privy Council had uncharacteristically dismissed cases against accused witches on complaint of their treatment. In the background, tension between secular and ecclesiastical authorities is hinted. There were also complaints from the General Assembly that the civil magistrates were failing to convict standard sorts of "witches," and James is known to have taken legal action against a number of ministers.[19]

The abrupt decision to recall the standing commissions came in 1597, the same year that James published his *Daemonologie*. The resulting Order of Council specifically mentions the execution of innocent people and the credulity of Mr. Cowper. In the order, rules for establishing new and closely controlled commissions were set forth as were the penalties for pursuing witches under the defunct authority of the old commissions. So great was the symbolic importance of witch-hunting to the Crown that anyone who did so without royal permission, whatever his or her status, would be counted as a criminal.[20]

There is nothing at all to indicate that the king lost any of his faith in witchcraft as a result of this experience, but he was clearly less certain about the ability of the legal machinery to detect witches. Under his watchful eye, the new strictures on witch-hunting temporarily shut down the production of witches in Scotland.

When James left for England the twin polities of the Scottish godly-state—the General Assembly of the calvinist divines and the secular Privy Council—replaced him. Throughout the seventeenth century, the prosecution of witches became symbolically important in the turf disputes between these two centers of power. During periods of social strain, each attempted to surpass the other in matters of morality. All three subsequent national hunts were proceeded by official expressions of anxiety and dismay.[21] The massive outbreaks of 1649–50 and 1662 were wholly unrelated to Continental witch-hunts. The 1649 national hunt came at a time when the Covenanting party was strong and during a period of war anxiety. It was, as Larner puts it, "a year for a moral crusade, for it was necessary to demonstrate that the state was a covenanted state."[22] It is hardly surprising that in a year when even the gentry was punished for its pecadillos, the poor were tried as witches by the hundreds. More than 350 commissions for the "Tryal and burning of witches" were issued during the summer of 1649.[23]

The national hunt of 1662 followed the end of the protectorate (in 1659) and, again, took place in the context of the ruling-class anxiety. This anxiety, in combination with the return to home rule, fostered yet another moral crusade. Between April of 1661 and the autumn of 1662, three hundred people were executed for witchcraft.[24] Once again the pace of witch-hunting alarmed the Privy Council, and they grew reticent over the use of torture. And, again, witchfinders were denounced as frauds. The hunt ended abruptly in the late fall of 1662.

Sweden, after the exile of Queen Christina, followed very much the same pattern. By the early 1660s the Lutheran Church of Sweden had broken free of a number of liberal Protestant entanglements and entered into a period of Puritanical orthodoxy. Just as in Scotland, the claim to doctrinal purity in the state required the imposition of moral purity upon the peasantry, and in the same year that the Syncretist movement was branded as heretical by the Church of Sweden, the witchcraze broke out in the province of Dalarna.[25] In 1667 the Swedish church issued a further statement of orthodoxy that was shortly followed, in 1669, by an order of the Council of State that a prayer should be read in all churches in order to bring about the end of "the tyranny of Satan."[26] In that year, the panic-trial at Mora in central Sweden took place, and an even larger trial is reported in the southern province of Bohuslan. This trial saw three hundred people sentenced to death in the span of ten years.[27]

The witch trials held in northern Sweden were similar to the Salem episode in that they were driven by the accusations of children. According to Heikkinen, crowds of children would arrive "at court sessions complaining that they had been taken to the devil's entertainment."[28] Witch beliefs were firmly entrenched among the peasantry, and "excited village communities" continually bombarded the magistrates with requests for investigations. During Queen Christina's reign, these requests were largely ignored, but during the ascendancy of the godly-state, they were acted upon with tragic results. Apparently local authorities—rural police chiefs, priests, and others—were often the recipients of stern orders from the state to eradicate the agents of the devil within their own particular bailwicks.[29] Naturally, an agitated peasantry could produce likely prospects for this status in large numbers.

THE END OF THE WITCHCRAZE

One of the most vexatious problems associated with the European witchcraze is the question of what brought it to a close. The standard explanation provided by the rationalist historians is that the witchcraze was ended by the Enlightenment.[30] On the face of things it is hard to disagree with this assertion. It seems unlikely that the witchcraze would have been sustained by an educated elite that believed in an orderly, mechanistic universe, and it is possible to point to instances where powerful students of Descartes ended the persecution of witches in regions under their control (Queen Christina, for example). Even so, when local and national power brokers are closely examined, it is rare to find evidence that such philosophical transformations were a factor in bringing a particular witch-hunt to an end.[31] Furthermore, it is undeniable that the panic-trials ended long before the laws that upheld them were stricken from the books. It is simply a matter of historical record that the witch-hunts of continental Europe, just as at Salem, were halted by powerful men who still believed in witches.

Midelfort has proposed that the European panic-trials came to a halt when those arrested and executed deviated markedly from the accepted image of a witch.[32] Certainly the sequence of events in a typical panic-trial suggests that the arrest of people of high station or the arrest of men and children—in short, the arrest of anyone who didn't conform to the accepted stereotype of a witch—constituted an assault on the subjective reality maintained by the ruling class. If that practice continued, that is, if large numbers of the wrong sorts of people were accused of witchcraft, the magistrates and town fathers were (evidently) forced into the realization that the witch-hunt had the potential to literally destroy the town. In that sense, Midelfort has argued, "Enlightenment came . . . from the shattering realization that witch hunts could destroy all sense of community and all the inhabitants as well."[33] Midelfort refers to this process as a breakdown of the witch stereotype and argues that "the general breakdown of the stereotype was one of the most common forces that both permitted larger witchcraft trials and ultimately called them into question."[34]

What is being invoked here is the "principle of cognitive consistency," and of the several systematic formulations used to operationalize this notion, the concept of *cognitive dissonance* puts Midelfort's idea on its best footing. The basic idea in the consistency principle is that the mind has a need for consistency and that attitudes are often changed to bring this about.[35] In dissonance theory this principle is formulated with greater precision: people are motivated by the psychological distress brought about by cognitive dissonance to bring discrepant cognitive elements into some degree of consonance.[36] The literature produced by the many practitioners in this area of social psychology is formidable and sometimes contradictory, but, at a minimum, a number of conclusions have a great deal of empirical support. Among these "well-known basics," as Aronson refers to them, is the fact that "dissonance predicts most clearly in situations in which the self is engaged and the person feels responsible for the consequences of his action. . . ."[37] Dissonance theory, in short, links the cognitive and motivational component of attitude to behavior.

As a formal theory, cognitive dissonance has been effectively applied to historical questions; however, in the context of broad historical problems such as the European witchcraze, it is useful only as a sensitizing concept and not as a body of theory.[38] Accepting this limitation, it is still reasonable to argue that during a panic-trial, the realization on the part of those in positions of power that the "witches" being generated by the social control system were radically different (were dissonant) from the sort of people who were supposed to be witches must have been very distressing. Furthermore, when that perception was coupled with the appreciation that the witch-hunt itself was destroying the community, the depth of psychological strain must have been profound.[39] It was, in any event, almost invariably just at that point that key aspects of established procedural law were called into question and the panic-trial stopped.

In his study of southwestern Germany, Midelfort found that

nearly all of the panic-trials for which there is reliable documentation followed roughly the course of events suggested by this sketch.[40] The early stage of a panic-trial typically fed upon the stereotypical witch-figure; it killed old, solitary, and essentially helpless women. However, as the trial progressed, the accusations began to include younger women of good reputation and increasing numbers of men; and, towards the end, children and people of high station were counted among the witches. Often the witch-hunters themselves came under suspicion. The final stages of the mass-trial at Würzburg, for instance, brought about the death of clerics, doctors, city officials, large numbers of children, and, we are told, the most beautiful woman in town.[41] Finally, the prince-bishop and his chancellor were accused; the prince-bishop then stopped the trials and set up regular services to the memory of those executed.[42] In the German southwest alone this same pattern was followed, with only minor variations, in Ellwangen, Schwabish Gmund, Offenburg, Mergentheim, Oberkirch, Oppenau, Esslingen, Reutlinger, and Baden Baden.[43] It would not be fair to conclude that these panic-trials were ended simply because of the immediate threat they posed to dominant personalities, although, in some instances, this was assuredly part of the reason. The primary dimension was cognitive: for the ruling class, the accusation of members of their own station was convincing evidence that the judicial process had gone awry.

Toward the end of the typical panic-trial, the percentage of men executed was substantial. Often more men were being executed than women. In addition, the percentage of children was often very high. For instance, during the Wurzburg panic-trial, in the burnings numbered 16 to 20, 60 percent of those burned were children (seventeen children and eleven adults).[44] It is not hard to see how this sort of brutal reality, which was so at variance with the accepted image of a Satan's conspiracy, undermined the confidence and self-image of those in power. Predictably, the accompanying emotional distress was often associated with expressions of dismay. For example, the town of Ellwangen in southwestern Germany, as I have already noted, suffered a horrendous panic-trial. Midway through this witch-hunt, Johann Fink, a Jesuit Father, wrote:

> Up to now 303 have been burned, mostly from Ellwangen, in addition three more have been caught, and even from the better families, two girls and a boy who was my pupil earlier in Dillingen. I do

not see where this case will lead and what end it will have, for
this evil has so taken over, and like the plague has infected so
many, that if the magistrates continue to exercise their office, in
a few years the city will be in miserable ruins.[45]

And, in a well-known letter dated 1629, the chancellor of the
prince-bishop of Würzburg, soon to be accused himself, wrote:

There are still found four hundred in the city, high and low, of
every rank and sex, nay, even clerics, so strongly accused that they
may be arrested at any hour. . . . There are children of three and
four years, to the number of three hundred, who are said to have
had intercourse with the Devil. I have seen put to death children
of seven, promising students of ten, twelve, fourteen and fifteen.
Of the nobles—but I cannot and must not write of this misery.[46]

Considering that the prince-bishop was himself accused at
the very end of the witch-hunt in Würzburg, it is tempting
to argue that he stopped the hunt in order to save his hide;
but nothing obligated him to establish memorial services to the
hundreds killed. It would seem more realistic to argue that the
course of events had finally driven home the realization that
things had gone terribly wrong.

There were, as suggested, variations on the theme. When the
timing was correct, the occasional inability to extract a confession by torture and/or the public criticism of the magistrates,
although dangerous, often brought a reevaluation by those in
power. Ordinarily, however, the perception of dissonance was
brought about by the killing of unlikely sorts of witches or
by the sheer enormity of the slaughter. The magistrates of Oppenau, a tiny town of 650 people, killed 50 people in the space
of less than a year (from June of 1631 to March of 1632). With
170 people still under direct suspicion, the full dimensions
of the calamity began to sink in, and the town appealed to
the legal faculty of Strasbourg for advice. The lawyers stated
that torture, under the circumstances, was not advisable and
that casual accusations were without legal merit. This opinion
seems to have been almost instantly accepted, and the court
records of the Oppenau tragedy stop in midparagraph.[47]

At Offenburg, a panic-trial raged in the years 1627, 1628,
and 1629. By late 1629 the wives of important officials and,
finally, a member of the town council, had been executed.
Shortly thereafter, a woman was unsuccessfully tortured (i.e.,

she did not confess). The council sent her home. A month later, in January, three confessed witches suddenly declared their innocence. Normally such recalcitrant types were simply tortured; but this time, evidently in self-doubt, the council members entered into a reconsideration and the panic-trial ended.[48]

Overall, this pattern was most pronounced in the regions where witch-hunting was essentially community based and where the witchcraze was most intense—southern Germany. But outside of southern Germany, the major witch-hunts often conformed in considerable degree to this pattern. For instance, in the town of Mora in central Sweden, the accusations of children brought about the execution of something on the order of eighty-five people in the space of a year. It is clear that the trial ended because the jurists began to doubt the evidence provided by children when it became obvious that they could be readily gulled into changing their testimony.[49]

The generally chaotic conditions of French archives make the sort of study accomplished by Larner or Midelfort very difficult.[50] There is, however, a great deal of primary data on the Parlement of Paris, which is accessible to investigation. In a recent study of this body, which functioned as an appeals court for much of northern France, Alfred Soman found that procedural law often became more restrictive following the eruptions of local witch-hunts that brought about the death of large numbers of people.[51]

During the only major witch-hunt in England, the comments generated by the activities of Hopkins and Stearne focused directly on the numbers and quality of those accused as well as on the brutal methods employed by these two men. After the executions at Chelmsford, a contemporary historian, Arthur Wilson, wrote in very typical fashion, "There is nothing so crosse to my temper as putting so many witches to death." "It did not," he insisted, "consist with the infinite goodness of the Almightie God to let Satan loose in so ravenous a way."[52] Midelfort attributes much of Hopkins's success to the fact that he traveled rapidly from county to county, outdistancing the rising skepticism in his wake.[53]

To be sure, there were regions where this pattern did not emerge at all or where there were significant variations. In the Jura, where the restrictions on the use of torture in the Caroline Code were closely adhered to, the panic-trial process seldom got underway, and the stereotype of the witch was rarely challenged. With few exceptions, these small panic-trials ran their course in one or two years after killing a few stereotypical witch-figures. The men killed in these trials were usually drawn in because they were related to the female witches.

In Scotland, according to Larner, the percentage of men held steady or went *down* during the national hunts. Given the manner in which these data are presented (by decades), this assertion is unconvincing; but, that aside, it must be emphasized that Scottish witch-hunting even at its most intense was closely monitored from the highest governmental level. The commissions were always kept on a leash that was quickly reeled in when events showed signs of getting out of hand.[54]

The national hunts in Scotland were very standardized. At the beginning there were expressions of distress on the part of the ruling class. Shortly thereafter, commissions were granted by the hundreds to carefully chosen people (following the experience of 1597); and then, of course, people were tried and burned in very large numbers. In all of these "moral panics," the end followed exclamations of surprise and outrage at the discovery that celebrated witchfinders were out-and-out frauds. As the defrocked witchfinders were being led to their deaths, usually accompanied by well-published statements of contrition, the commissions were canceled and the witch-hunt ended. Larner suggests that Scottish national hunts were so well orchestrated that atypical witches were simply not allowed in significant numbers.

> It looks as though male witches needed time to build up a reputation, and that during a crisis, when an instant supply of witches was required, accusers were more likely to resort to classic stereotypes. It looks as though convicted witches, under pressure to name accomplices, felt they were more likely to convince if they named other women.[55]

In that sense the Scottish national hunts seem to represent the most calculated attempt to dramatize a moral boundary, which naturally could be most effectively accomplished by adhering closely to the accepted stereotype of a witch.

By the latter part of the seventeenth century, news of what panic-trials had done to other towns and regions began to have an impact on the decision-making processes of the powerful. For instance, in the city of Calw on the edge of the Black Forest, a number of children began insisting that they had come under the control of Satan. The execution of two adults brought no abatement of diabolical activity, and by the spring of 1684, the bewitched children, who were rapidly increasing in numbers, had formally accused one hundred people of working for the devil. At this phase of the European witchcraze, the destructive potential to be found in this situation would have been apparent to any informed person. The question of what to do was urgently put to the legal faculty at Tubingen, which made several recommendations and specifically referred to the recent witch-hunts in Sweden. Much alarmed, the district administrators appointed a commission to deal with the charged atmosphere in Calw, which, by this time, showed every sign of spawning a full-fledged witch-panic. The commission immediately acted to quell the impending panic by ordering days of repentance and silence (on the matter of witchcraft) and by banishing several notorious suspects. In the end they resorted to bringing in soldiers to enforce their edicts.

The events of Calw are important because the commissioners stated very explicitly why they took this course of action rather than dealing directly with the witchcraft itself—a phenomenon they emphatically believed in. "If one tried to burn all the witches in Calw and anyone touched by such a vice," they said, "one would sooner run out of wood than such people."[56]

By the end of the seventeenth century, people in positions of power and influence emphasized the deceits of the devil far more than the wicked deeds of his servants. At the very end of the witchcraze, the witch-hunts themselves were often perceived as a manipulation of the devil. This is not to disallow the obvious fact that philosophical changes did occur. The Enlightenment did take place and the transformation that it brought was profound:

> In 1500 educated people in Western Europe believed themselves living at the center of a finite cosmos, at the mercy of (supernatural) forces beyond their control, and certainly continually menaced by Satan and his allies. By 1700 educated people in Western Europe for the most part believed themselves in living in an infinite universe on a tiny planet in (elliptical) orbit about the sun, no longer menaced by Satan, and confident that power over the natural world lay in their grasp.[57]

It is a mistake, however, to automatically assume that the arrival of this cosmology was the single causal agent responsible for the end of the witchcraze. For one thing, the timing is wrong;

the witchcraze ended before the Enlightenment was upon the ruling classes of Europe. In fact, from a strictly materialist stance, it is entirely possible to argue that it was the end of the witchcraze that brought about the Enlightenment. Brian Easlea believes that the acceptance of "anti-demonological" philosophy in the latter part of the seventeenth century was due in major part to the "dramatic upsurge in self-confidence of the western ruling class. . . ."[58]

Even the demonologies of this period express self-confidence. In the last half of the seventeenth century, the reality of witchcraft is argued basically as an academic issue, and the strident sense of peril and holy mission so characteristic of the sixteenth- and early seventeenth-century demonologies is entirely absent. This is particularly true of Joseph Glanvill's *Some Philosophical Considerations Touching Witches and Witchcraft* (1666). The dispute betwen John Webster (*Displaying of Supposed Witchcraft*, 1677) and Glanvill (*Sadducismus Triumphatus*, 1681) was of a dramatically different flavor from the bitter—and dangerous—literary clashes of the sixteenth century. It was essentially a scholarly debate. Glanvill was entirely unafraid of witches (he might as well as have been discussing the existence of elves), and only the hard-pressed Puritan divines of New England seem to have been much influenced by Glanvill's dry, technical arguments.[59]

The whole issue of the end of the witchcraze in Europe, particularly as it relates to the advent of the Enlightenment, is problematical and extremely complex. For our purposes, however, it is clear that the witchcraze ended in an atmosphere of ruling-class confidence. With or without witches, God, in the view of the eighteenth-century ruling class of Europe, had rendered the world safe and controllable.

*   *   *

The witchcraze was advantageous to those groups and individuals whose self-interest and self-concept were tied to the state and, in that respect, was a part of the process by which the state came into existence.[60] In the minds of dominant secular and ecclesiastical personalities, the very existence of diabolical witchcraft justified the development of an apparatus of social control that was a major factor in the emergence of the early modern state. More fundamentally, it was the sudden and contrived appearance of the "new cult of witches" that provided the state with much of its ideological charter; the role of the prince in combatting the enemies of God is a central theme in the demonologies of this period.[61] A statement issued by the Privy Council of Scotland (1623) in anticipation of a witch-hunt could not have been more explicit. Witch-hunts, said the Privy Council, were "necessary for the Grace of God and the purging his land of such heinous offenses and for avoiding the heavy judgment of God."[62] In view of this attitude, it is hardly unexpected that Donaldson can argue, "One of the most important and enduring achievements of the seventeenth century was the transformation of Scotland from a country in which the law had often been ill-enforced to one in which the law was generally obeyed."[63]. Much the same statement could be applied to other regions of Europe.

The geography and history of the witchcraze reveals that the hunt for witches was most virulent at those times and in those places where the established order was threatened. The suppression of the most visible and accessible manifestation of the diabolical conspiracy that menaced the Christian states of Europe, the witch, was a means by which the ruling classes of Europe could mantle themselves in Godly legitimacy and was fundamentally important to the imposition of the moral landscape of the ruling classes upon the populations they controlled. Witch-hunts were, then, eminently practical undertakings made all the more tempting by the heartfelt belief among monarchs and church leaders that the devil did, indeed, recruit human servants. The fact that witch-hunting often escaped the bounds of practicality, became disruptive, and killed far too many of the wrong sorts of people does not undermine the conclusion that witch-hunting was a purposeful activity, a control strategy, put to the service of church and state.

And regardless of the nature of the social control system, whether inquisitorial or not, God's enemies were produced at the demand of powerful factions. So the history of witch-hunting in both England and Massachusetts would seem to argue. It may be suggested that accountability and organizational restraint operated to cut short the panic-trials that took place in those areas, but, clearly, in the presence of overwhelming external demand, normal restriants were rendered temporarily impotent; they did not prevent panic-trials from occurring. At the same time, in the context of the unrestrained inquisitorial systems of the continent, expressions of ruling-class alarm (here taken to be evidence of high external demand) often preceded the production of extraordinary numbers of officially defined witches. On this basis, which is proposition (3.0), southwestern Germany emerges as a worst-case scenario. That is, the slaughter of people defined as witches in this region followed from the frequently very high level of external demand for the public punishment of Satan's servants and from the near absence of accountability and organizational restraint.

It was in Bamberg, perhaps, that this process can be seen in purest form. There, during the reign of Prince-Bishop Joahann George II Fuchs von Dornheim, the infamous *Hexenbischof* (1623–33), six hundred witches were destroyed by fire, according to contemporary reports. It does not seem credible that the true slaughter falls far short of this mark because it is known that the prince-bishop constructed in 1627 an elaborate "witch-house" that was capable of producing confessed witches with unparalleled efficiency. Often only a few weeks separated arrest and execution. And when, as happened on repeated occasions, the emperor ordered the prince-bishop to release highly placed witches, the order was simply ignored. The Bamberg Witch-Hunt finally ended only with the approach of a foreign army (that of King Gustavus of Sweden) and the death of the prince-bishop.[64]

I take it that the propositions presented in chapter one—especially (1.0) through (4.1)—accurately describe the impact of critical social forces during the witchcraze at a level of abstraction sufficient to allow prediction. Naturally, any formal claim on the basis of the history of the witchcraze that these propositions have "evaded falsification" would be entirely unremarkable since they were, in fact, derived from that history. The true test lies in the fit of these relational statements, and the patterns they describe, to events of this century. That evidence remains to be presented. It would, however, be difficult to deny that magnified and elaborated to a degree that would have been unimaginable to the most zealous inquisitor, the same horrors and processes that characterized the witch-hunt in Bamberg have also shaped this century.

7

The Red Scare

America's entrance into the First World War sparked a spirited and innovative denial of German culture. Wagner, for example, was not performed, sauerkraut became "liberty cabbage," and towns with German names frequently established new identities. These quaint and well-known measures, however, masked a fundamental erosion of liberty to which most Americans acquiesced as a wartime necessity. Anyone critical of America's participation in the conflict ran considerable risk of being beaten or fired. German-Americans were categorically suspect. Teachers were summarily dismissed for comments that were taken to be unpatriotic. Political opponents of war were jailed and conscientious objectors were singled out for special torments. The few lawyers who tried to defend such people were disciplined by their bar association.[1]

Federal management of the moral landscape that justified this repression began immediately after the declaration of war. The Committee on Public Information was formed in April of 1917 and quickly taken in hand by the journalist George Creel, who saw his mission with great clarity: sell the war. It was, in Creel's words, "The world's greatest adventure in advertising."[2] Under Creel's proddings, the publishing industry accepted a policy of "self-censorship," and unleashed a flood of anti-German propaganda. The committee also encouraged Americans to report those who criticized the war, urged peace, or were simply pessimistic.[3]

A vast and unorthodox surveillance apparatus sprang up almost overnight. Wartime legislation empowered the Justice Department to undertake security activities on an unparalleled scale. Information streamed into this agency through a chaotic network of "loyalty leagues" made up largely of small businessmen, executives, and professionals. Issuing their own badges, identity cards, and a variety of other junior G-Man paraphernalia, these sodalities could too easily be dismissed as harmless; but, in fact, they were largely unsupervised and anything but harmless.

First among the loyalty leagues was the American Protective League, which had direct links with the Justice Department and semiofficial status. This amazing organization of amateur sleuths grew by means of a loose network of business cronies to have a membership of two hundred fifty thousand and became proficient at protecting industry from the inroads of organized labor. It also assisted local and federal authorities in conducting "slacker raids," a practice that ultimately detained tens of thousands of draft-age men. Anyone rounded up in a slacker raid was held in the station house or county jail until a response from his draft board confirmed his status. This often took weeks. Little attention was paid to the illegality of such activities until after the manpower needs of the army had been met.[4]

There were other national organizations with similar objectives and much the same constituency as the American Protective League, including the American Defense League and the National Security League, the latter of which was heavily supported by big business.[5] In addition, there was a host of state and local patriotic societies. Together with official agencies, the loyalty leagues amounted to an all-pervasive apparatus of social control. Ellis Hawley notes of this establishment:

> As in other areas of war administration, the [surveillance] machinery that evolved tended to collapse distinctions between the public and private sectors, which meant in practice that "disloyalty" was defined and punished not only by legally constituted bodies but by what amounted to vigilante groups. Supplementing the prosecutions were organized lynchings, floggings, tarrings, and other extralegal acts of vengeance, all a part of a behavior pattern that would reappear in the postwar Ku Klux Klan.[6]

In this atmosphere, state legislatures and city councils passed sedition laws by the hundreds. At the federal level, three such pieces of legislation were passed: the Espionage Act (1917) and two broadly phrased sedition acts (1918). The last of this series, which became law in October of 1918, is of special concern. Its focus was the nonconforming alien who was taken by Anglo-Saxon America to be the principal seedbed of disloyal ideas. The law provided that

> any alien who, at any time after entering the United States, is found to have been at the time of entry or to have become thereafter, a member of any one of the classes of aliens . . . shall upon warrant of the Secretary of Labor, be taken into custody and deported. . . .[7]

The Red Scare flourished in the social environment created by the First World War, but its taproot went much deeper. It should not be overlooked that the preceding decades were periods of enormous social change in the United States during which the lines of social conflict hardened.[8] The wartime economy exacerbated economic and social tensions.

Following the armistice, it was argued that the economy should be returned to the control of "natural forces" and, as a result, an already high rate of inflation went even higher. In New York the cost of living shot up 28 percent between 1919 and 1920.[9] Organized labor, the salaried middle class, and big business were once again in hostile camps. The American Federation of Labor, under the government-dictated truce with management, had increased its membership and had generally made great strides. During the war, wages were allowed to rise slightly faster than the rate of inflation. The middle class, by contrast, lost ground. By 1919 the purchasing power of the 1913 dollar had been reduced by half, and the position of professional and salaried people had deteriorated in measure; or at best, salaries had increased by 5 or 10 percent. Compounding matters, in March of 1919, Congress, under pressure from business, curtailed funds to the federal agencies charged with the task of demobilization. The demobilization was therefore very rapid. By November of 1919 almost the whole of the military establishment had been discharged, pitchforking four million men onto an already crowded job market.[10] In the upshot, by the Fall of 1919, labor and big business had squared off; labor was organized and on the crest of past successes while business, after demobilization, was in a buyer's market.

Many of the ethnic cleavages within the American society were obscured by the larger confrontation between business and labor, but this did not hold true for the fundamental separation between black and white. The race riot that took place in East St. Louis in 1917 was a precursor of events to come. During the war, manpower requirements increased the northern migration of black Americans. Following the end of the war, the competition for jobs increased with the predictable result that blacks were either crowded out of their jobs or used as strike breakers.

In the context of heightened black expectations, 1919 became the scene for dozens of race riots.[11]

THE IMPACT OF THE BOLSHEVIK REVOLUTION

The Bolshevik Revolution was a profound shock to most Americans and the subject of lurid speculation. Reports on the conditions within Russia, which even had they been accurate would have been deeply alarming, were largely comprised of gory fantasy, and, without noticeable interruption, stories of Bolshevik atrocities replaced stories of German atrocities. The revolution in Russia was seen as a German plot by many high officials, and the Overman Committee in the Senate, which had been investigating a supposed link between German propaganda and the American brewing industry, shifted its attention to Bolshevik propaganda.[12] Public apprehensions were exaggerated all the more by the fact that an American expeditionary unit was now actually fighting the Bolsheviks in Siberia.

Conditions throughout postwar Europe were ominous. The Third International was founded in the early part of 1919 and by every indication was prospering: Hungary had actually established a soviet, and Germany was in revolt; Italy and France seemed about to follow. Karl Radek, executive secretary of the Third International, stated that the funds sent to Russia were nothing compared to those sent to New York.[13] Radical groups at home publicly rejoiced at these developments.

The American Communist movement emerged largely from ethnic chapters of the Socialist party, primarily those in eastern cities, since these groups had not been crushed by the loyalty apparatus during the First World War.[14] In many respects their membership conformed to the stereotype—foreign-born, bitter, alienated, and doctrinaire. Many did not speak English. They identified with the Bolshevik revolution and, to the limit of their capabilities, they trumpeted the coming revolution. However, it is indisputable that their capabilities were very limited indeed. They were, with few exceptions, devoid of any understanding of the American political scene, and, taken together, both the Communist party and the smaller Communist Labor party, which had some native-born leadership, had no more than seventy thousand members. Both parties were riddled with dissension and poorly organized. By any realistic assessment, the Communist movement in the United States was not a threat to the established government; nor, at this juncture, was it taking orders from Russia.[15]

In the wartime atmosphere that lingered after the armistice, the public refocused its fears, and the hobgoblin of middle-class America, the unassimilated alien, was seen anew as the alien radical who plotted the overthrow of the United States. Faced with a new and possibly welcome menace, many of the moribund wartime loyalty leagues rejuvenated themselves, and the most powerful loyalty league of all, the newly formed American Legion, undertook a full-fledged crusade. Legionnaires were in the forefront of the many antisocialist riots of the postwar period, and it is entirely reasonable to suggest that the American Legion took on the dimensions of a Freikorps during the Red Scare.[16]

THE ORCHESTRATION OF THE RED SCARE

Public opinion followed the vanguard of powerful interests. The imaginary threat to the well-being of the United States stemmed largely from the intense efforts of big business and federal agencies to identify all activities left of center as radical and alien. Stated more in the abstract, the Red Scare derived from a successful effort on the part of a coalition of powerful interests to undermine the moral capital of their enemies.

A constant stream of alarming press releases from a variety of authorities linked threatening international events with developments at home. As an example of the nature of this information, it can be noted that the Immigration Service gravely reported to an investigating official, "Anarchists are flocking here from Mexico at a rate of 100 a day."[17] Most federal agencies quickly developed a capacity to generate and to believe such statements.

THE SEATTLE GENERAL STRIKE

In January of 1919 a series of events began which, given the inflammatory interpretation of the national press, served to convince the general public that revolution was indeed in the wind. On 21 January, thirty-five thousand shipyard workers in Seattle walked off the job amid calls for a general strike. In all, some sixty thousand workmen in Seattle went out, and nonessential services ground to a halt. In this environment the distribution of Industrial Workers of the World (IWW) literature and the convenient misinterpretation of the seasonal migration of western labor served to bring about a general state of alarm. The Mayor of Seattle, Ole Hanson, was an implacable foe of the IWW and, despite the fact that the strike was by any objective reckoning over wages and hours, managed to convince himself and the public that it was a Wobbly attempt to establish a soviet.[18]

Mayor Hanson called for federal troops and instantaneously received them in battalion strength. Riding in a flag-draped automobile, Mayor Hanson met the incoming column of soldiers, pronounced himself their leader, and led them into the city during the early morning hours of 6 February, the same day that the general strike came into effect. Within a matter of days, federal and state agents rounded up the few foreign-born activists they could lay hands on and shipped them east on a train dubbed the "Red Special" by the press. In all, some fifty-four men were transported under heavy guard to Ellis Island and slated for deportation under the October 1918 sedition law. However, at this stage of events such high-handed behavior on the part of federal authorities aroused considerable public opposition, and the attorney general's office, stung by criticism, backed off.[19]

The Seattle general strike was doomed from the beginning. The press had a field day and consistently presented the strike as a bold attempt to establish "One Big Union." Conservative national labor leaders were dismayed; they correctly regarded the general strike as a dangerous and counterproductive tactic and brought pressure against the local strike leaders.[20] In the total absence of middle-class support and, indeed, in the face of open hostility from conservative labor, it rapidly became clear to the Seattle unions that a continuation of the strike was folly. Mayor Hanson, elated and victorious, soon resigned his office to go on the lecture circuit.

THE BOMB PLOTS

Alleged conspiracies to blow up public officials kept the topic of bombing on the front pages during the spring months. On 29 April, this line of speculation produced dividends. A plot to mail package-bombs to an odd assortment of liberal and conservative dignitaries was revealed when one of the bombs ex-

ploded in the house of Senator Thomas Hardwick, injuring two
people. An ambitious but poorly organized bomb plot was soon
revealed when sixteen parcels identical to that containing the
device that exploded in the Hardwick household were discovered, sidelined for insufficient postage, in a New York City post
office. Eighteen other such bombs were soon intercepted.[21] No
other people were injured, and the culprits were never found.

The timing of the plot was clear to everyone. Attorney General
Palmer and a host of others correctly predicted that May Day
would bring a frenzy of radical activity. There were mass meetings and "Red Flag" parades in most major cities. In New York,
Boston, Cleveland, Chicago, and Detroit such displays were
followed by riots, some of epic proportions.[22] Naturally, all of
this was advertised by public officials and the media as a dress
rehearsal for an attempted revolution.

In early June a second bomb plot materialized when timed
explosions took place in eight separate cities. Again, a curious
collection of public officials and industrialists had been targeted;
one of them was the attorney general. On the evening of 2
June, a large bomb nearly blew the front off the Palmer residence
in Washington, D.C. Neither the attorney general nor his family
were injured, but they were all badly shaken. As would be
expected, the attempt on the attorney general's life produced
banner headlines. Those of the *New York Times* blared:

MIDNIGHT BOMBS FOR OFFICIALS IN 8 CITIES: BOMBER DIES AT ATTORNEY GENERAL'S HOUSE

RED LITERATURE FOUND

The "Red Literature" consisted of copies of a broadsheet found
drifting about the attorney general's front yard. The *Times* saw
fit to plaster every single word of it on the front page.

A time has come when the social question's solution can be delayed
no longer; class war is on, and cannot cease but with a complete
victory for the international proletariat. . . . We are not many, perhaps more than you dream of though, but all are determined to
fight to the last. . . . There will have to be bloodshed; we will not
dodge; there will have to be murder; we will kill. . . .

And so on for many paragraphs.

The second bomb plot proved to be a catalyst. Two days

later Palmer announced the appointment of a new assistant attorney general, Francis P. Garvan, who had formerly been chief investigator in the Alien Property Bureau, to oversee the Justice Department's campaign against the radical menace. William J. Flynn, in times past chief of the Secret Service, became the director of the Bureau of Investigation and brought with him into the inner circle Franke Burke, the director of the Secret Services's New York office and head of its Russian division. According to Richard Powers, the decision to implement a program of mass deportation of offending aliens was made by Palmer and his close advisors on 17 June.[23] To facilitate his ambitious program of public hygiene, Palmer requested and quickly received an appropriation of $500,000 from Congress.

The most fundamental organizational change fostered by the political climate of the summer of 1919 was the formation of the General Intelligence Division (initially more straightforwardly identified as the "Radical Division"), which under its director, J. Edgar Hoover, was to become the headquarters and the driving force behind the government's hunt for politically undesirable aliens. In appointing Hoover to direct the General Intelligence Division (GID), Palmer drew upon attitudes and expertise that derived from wartime experience. Hoover had previously been a ranking functionary within the Justice Department's Alien Enemy Bureau and was thoroughly familiar with the Immigration Bureau's deportation statutes. From his perspective, the crusade was a matter of paperwork, liaison, organization, and the substitution of a new alien enemy for an old one.

Knowledge of the enemy was the key. Hoover, who had worked his way through law school as a clerk in the Library of Congress, promptly instituted a system of index cards to keep track of suspected radicals.[24] This clerical innovation is the direct ancestor of the vast data bank that is presently maintained by the FBI. Under Hoover's energetic leadership, the GID's efforts to keep tabs on the new alien menace were comprehensive and relentless. The GID soon established an office of some forty readers and translators to monitor more than four hundred radical periodicals; and in brief time the division had an extensive library of radical literature in which its new director immersed himself only to emerge with a construction of reality as delusional as that of the Communist Left. Thus prompted, the GID busied itself dispensing information on radicals and the threatened revolution to the press, corporate officials, and the local police. This operation rapidly took on the dimensions

of a major advertising campaign, and Robert Murray asserts
that it was a central element in the genesis of the Red Scare
"hysteria" that gripped the nation in the fall of 1919.[25]

Two official investigations conducted by the Overman Judiciary Subcommittee of the United States Senate and the Lusk
Committee of the New York State Legislature served to amplify
the events of 1919 and lend credence to the need for dramatic
federal action. Witness after witness came before the Overman
Committee and regaled Senators and reporters with hair-raising
speculation about the nature of communism in Russia and what
it would mean in the United States. It provided good copy
and enormously supplemented industrial propaganda. The final
report of the Overman Committee came out in mid-June and
served to confirm the fears of an alarmed public. Many papers,
as did the New York Times, carried substantial portions of the
report.

The Senate investigation slightly overlapped that of the Lusk
Committee, which held the public eye on and off for almost
a year and a half. Its final report, which ran an astonishing
4,456 pages, was issued far too late to have had any major
impact on the course of the Red Scare; but the frequent public
hearings and the constant leaks combined to create an ongoing
national morality play. Much of the information available to
the Lusk Committee was obtained through raids on radical organizations in New York City. Several such operations were sponsored by the committee and carried out by agents of the Justice
Department and the state police.[26] There was very little criticism
of these activities and they appear to have occupied a place
in the public mind as merely a triumphant scene in a continuing
drama of good and evil.

The Lusk Committee was, among other things, also responsible for a purge of the public schools, an activity that occupied the New York Legislature throughout the Red Scare and
for long after. Actually, the committee was responding to an
already long-standing concern. As early as February, the New
York Times had printed an article under the heading "Bolshevism in the Schools."

> 'Down with everybody who wears a collar or a clean shirt.' That
> is the pemmican of Bolshevism. It is not only meat for strong men,
> it is milk for babes. Our high school boys are to be fed on it. . . .[27]

Much of higher education was thought to be "parlor pink,"

and noted educators were castigated as radicals. In New York and in many other states, the accepted remedy for this situation was an out-and-out purge and the imposition of loyalty oaths within the school system.

Establishment America was also convinced that the black anger so much in evidence during the fall of 1919 was entirely inspired by radicals. Such was the message of the Lusk Committee. All evidence points to another motive force. The experience of the First World War had raised the hopes of black people only to have the postwar period destroy them. Race riots, all of which were brutally suppressed, were a major feature of this period. Using lynchings as an overall index of suppression, it can be noted that the number of lynchings doubled from 1917 to 1920 and then declined.[28]

ORGANIZED LABOR

Although the tag of radical activity was useful in the suppression of blacks, it was far from essential since blacks could always be suppressed merely for being black. This was not true of white labor. There had to be a "reason" for the suppression of white labor, and the identification of the American labor movement with the radical community was an essential ingredient in the crippling of American labor in the post war period. This aspect of the Red Scare seems to have been carefully engineered.[29]

THE FALL STRIKES

A period of dramatic labor unrest began in early September of 1919 when Boston blundered into a police strike. During the summer the Boston Police Force threatened to affiliate with the A F of L. The national press viewed this prospect with alarm and presented the entire episode as a Bolshevik plot. When the strike began in earnest on 9 September, chaos and anarchy were predicted. There were, in fact, some disturbances, but the "Bolshevik nightmare" predicted by the press never materialized.[30] A volunteer force of students (many from Harvard), businessmen, and legionnaires guarded the city under the direction of the nonstriking police. All of the strikers, two thirds of the entire force, were fired within a matter of days, and a new force composed largely of veterans was recruited. The strike was crushed within weeks and would now be forgotten except that it set the tone for the great fall strikes and because it raised Calvin Coolidge to the status of a national celebrity on the strength of his role in the destruction of the police union.

The Boston police strike overlapped two events of major importance. On 22 September, the steelworkers went on strike, and by the end of the week 365,000 steelworkers had left their jobs. It was the largest strike in U.S. history, and it crippled the industry. The striking steelworkers were soon joined by over 300,000 United Mine Workers under John L. Lewis.

The reasons for the strikes of 1919 were not very mysterious and would have been readily apparent to anyone who cared to look for them. The average work week for a steelworker in 1919 was sixty-nine hours, and one half of the work force typically worked a twelve-hour day, often seven days a week. The income for an unskilled worker was below the subsistence level for a family of five.[31] The situation in the coal fields was worse.

By the end of 1919, there had been hundreds of strikes involving millions of men and women. Only a few of these strikes were successful. In great measure, this record was due to the fact that the American labor movement had been successfully painted Red by opposing interests. There was little basis for this identification. The dominant force in American labor was the A F of L (consisting mostly of craft unions), led by Samuel Gompers, who had carefully manicured its conservative image. Particular care was lavished on the maintenance of a clear separation from the IWW. The same could be said of the United Mine Workers. John L. Lewis was a bitter anti-Communist, and the official strike literature in the coal fields talked of little but wages, hours, and working conditions—all of which were deplorable. But in the context of a constant barrage of business and government propaganda, this counted for little in the realm of public opinion. Both the coal strike and the steel strike were seen by the typical middle- and upper-class American as little short of insurrection. In this climate, both federal and state troops were used to break strikes and the UMW was permanently enjoined.[32]

The companies never deviated from the assumption and the message that the activities of organized labor reflected the influence of alien radicals. They went to extreme lengths to demonstrate such influence. As a matter of routine, companies hired detective agencies to sniff out dissatisfaction within the plant and to infiltrate unions. The information gathered in this manner not only went to the company, it went to the Justice Department as well.[33] Evidently, many of the people arrested in the Palmer Raids were identified by this process.[34]

Murray Levin quotes testimony given before the Senate Committee on Education and Labor by Lt. C. Van Buren, who was in charge of military intelligence for Gary, Indiana. His testimony reveals how information was gathered at the local level and then piped to the Justice Department.

> Information comes to us from various sources, all sorts of information, and we try to file, index it, and give it to the proper authorities. Information of that sort came to us from Gary . . . away back in March or April at which time the so-called Reds were planning a nationwide strike in order to free political prisoners. . . .
>
> When we arrived in Gary, we found that the Sheriff had sworn in a great many deputies and that he was running a little intelligence office of his own; the police chief had sworn in a great many policemen, and he was running a little intelligence office of his own; and the Loyal Americans League composed of citizens who were largely either deputy sheriffs or special policemen—I believe to a man—also had a little intelligence service of its own. So did the American Legion. They were all of them lined up on this Red proposition and had a mass of information.[35]

There is overwhelming evidence of deliberate manipulation of the press by the steel companies. Corporate officials, for example, actually printed radical documents and then distributed them as proof of a radical conspiracy.[36] To the business spy, radical activity was a valuable commodity, and when none could be found, they were receptive to broad hints that they should organize it on their own.

Strike breaking was something of a growth industry during this period. There is every reason to believe that a substantial percentage of the business of detective agencies consisted of providing company spies, and, indeed, there were "labor detective" agencies that so specialized. The manager of one such operation volunteered to the investigators of the Commission of Inquiry of the Interchurch World Movement that he had five hundred men working for him during the steel strike.[37]

In the end, the steel strike was a complete failure. The National Committee voted to end the strike on 8 January 1920 after having gained nothing. The reason for failure is clear: it was the almost total lack of outside support from establishment interest groups. This denial stemmed directly from the public image of the steel strike as a Bolshevik ploy to take over the country. The report by the Interchurch World Movement states this thesis directly:

> A stranger in America reading the newspapers during the strike and talking with the steel masters both in and out of steel communities must have concluded that the strike represented a serious outbreak of Bolshevism red hot from Russia.[38]

The United Mine Workers fared little better. Almost none of the wholesale bullying and intimidation employed by the companies got into the papers, but anything that smacked of radical activity was given full play. As a result, public sentiment was solidly against the strikers, and Lewis, in the face of so much public hostility and a restraining order, canceled the strike.

In the upshot, the efforts by big business to tar the image of its rival were successful. The union shop became "sovietism in disguise" and the open shop became the "American Plan."[39]

NATIONAL HYSTERIA

It is hard to appreciate the depth of public fear during this period. One English journalist wrote, "No one who was in the United States . . . in the Autumn of 1919 will forget the feverish condition of the public mind at that time. *It was hag-ridden by the spectre of Bolshevism.*"[40]

The level of apprehension in the United States was matched by the intensity of jingoism. An astonishing number of people were shot out of hand by indignant patriots for such things as refusing to stand for the Star Spangled Banner, or yelling, "To hell with the United States." One U.S. Senator, McKeller of Tennessee, proposed that native-born radicals—who after all could not be deported—be sent to a penal colony on the island of Guam. William Gibbs McAdoo noted "a strange poison in the air."[41] Many states passed "red flag laws" during this period, and the American Legion, which now numbered more than a million men, demanded that enemy aliens buried at Arlington Cemetery be removed. All Legionnaires were to be ready at a moment's notice to repel the Bolsheviks. Coben argues that the general state of mind was akin to that which accompanies a revitalization movement and quotes an editorial from The Saturday Evening Post: "History will see our present state of mind as one with that preceding the burning of witches, the children's crusade, the great tulip craze and other examples of softening of the world brain."[42]

DEPORTATION

The propaganda barrage, the race riots, and the fall strikes had a predictable effect in Washington. On 19 October the Senate unanimously adopted a resolution that the Justice Department take legal action against radicals in this country. The Justice Department readily accepted the senatorial nod and jumped headlong into a program of political hygiene.

The apparatus to sweep aliens out of the country was already in place in the form of wartime sedition laws, and it is quite apparent from events to follow that what Palmer and Hoover were planning was a production line. William Preston had exactly that imagery in mind when he suggested this:

> Government officials were planning to introduce a scientific speed-up into the deportation process. Like a pig in a Chicago packing plant, the immigrant would be caught in a moving assembly line, stripped of all his rights, and packaged for shipment overseas—all in one efficient and uninterrupted operation. American know-how was going to put an administrative procedure on a mass production basis.[43]

The Justice Department and the Labor Department had established close ties during the war, most notably in the Alien Enemy Bureau. The continuation of these ties was important. Although in most instances the leg work involved in deporting an alien was accomplished by the Justice Department, the co-operation of the Department of Labor was essential since the authority to deport was vested in the secretary of labor. Deportation was accomplished by means of what was (and remains) basically administrative procedure. It was recognized that aliens, in theory, did have some rights; but in practice, everything was weighted in favor of the apparatus of social control during the deportation process. Accordingly, the Justice Department did not prosecute actual crimes since this would have resulted in

hundreds of court cases, which was the last thing the Justice
Department wanted. Instead, the attorney general's office focused its energies on the public display of ideological pariahs
who could be dealt with administratively.

Deportation proceedings were simple, direct, and, when the
bureaucracy was unfettered, very swift. Assistant Secretary
Louis Post describes the bureaucratic routine:

> Upon information that a resident is unlawfully in the country, the
> Secretary of Labor issues his warrant of arrest, a subordinate arrests
> the alien, and giving him an informal hearing, reports to the Secre-
> tary, who governed by it, passes upon the aliens residential rights.[44]

The detained alien could, if knowledgeable, challenge deportation through a writ of habeus corpus; however, if there was
any evidence to support the contention that the deportation
was at all justified, the court had to dismiss the writ.[45]

On 7 November 1919 the Justice Department staged a series
of coordinated raids on radical organizations in twelve cities.
The heaviest blow fell on the Union of Russian Workers in
New York City. Two hundred people were arrested in the Russian People's House, the headquarters of the Union of Russian
Workers, and fifty people were arrested in other cities. In New
York, anyone around or in the Russian People's House was taken
into custody, transported to Justice Department headquarters,
and given the "third degree"—a common practice at that time.
All in all, the treatment was about what could be expected
from an overzealous constabulary. Of much greater concern is
the fact that some men were ultimately held as long as five
months without charge.[46] The federal raids opened flood gates,
and local authorities of every variety joined in. On 8 November
the Lusk Committee, aided by seven hundred police, raided
seventy-three so-called radical centers in New York City, arrested five hundred people, and carted away a great amount
of literature. Likewise in other cities, hundreds of radicals were
taken into custody.[47]

Out of the total federal and state catch of aliens, 246 were
slated for deportation. Most were members of the Union of Russian Workers.[48] Public approval was boundless, and Attorney
General Palmer, now the "Fighting Quaker," replaced Ole Hanson as the nation's leading plague saint. Congress gave rapt
attention to Palmer's report to the Senate, which detailed the
radical menace that was facing the country and stressed the

need for a peacetime sedition law of an unbelievably comprehensive nature. Anyone even loosely affiliated with an organization that advocated sedition, an activity that was defined
in the broadest possible terms (such as a attempt to "hinder"
the "free performance" of the "United States Government or
anyone of its officers, agents or employees . . ."), would have
been deemed guilty of sedition. The November raids were in
part designed to advertise the need for such draconian measures.[49] Palmer's testimony, much of it the handiwork of J. Edgar
Hoover, provides insight into the dimensions the "alien conspiracy" was assuming in the minds of control agents:

> If there be any doubt of the general character of the active leaders
> and agitators amongst these avowed revolutionists, a visit to the
> Department of Justice and an examination of their photographs there
> collected would dispel it. Out of the sly and crafty eyes of many
> of them leap cupidity, cruelty, insanity, and crime; from their lop-
> sided faces, sloping brows, and misshapen features may be recog-
> nized the unmistakable criminal type.[50]

THE BUFORD

The conclusion to this stage of the Red Scare was very swift
in coming: on 21 December the U.S.S. Buford steamed for Fin-
land with 249 aliens aboard. It would be very hard to imagine
within the context of an industrial society a more strict enact-
ment of the traditional ritual of the scapegoat.

The press gave the impression that the aliens aboard the
Buford were all criminals of the wildest sort. In fact, only a
few had criminal records, and there is little to indicate that
very many of those deported fell within the purview of the
sedition laws.[51] Most of the prisoners aboard the Buford, the
"Soviet Ark," had been arrested without warrant and held
without benefit of counsel until their departure. Furthermore,
according to official sources, twelve men on board the Buford left wives and children behind (unofficial estimates are
much higher). The New York Times (22 December) took care
to note in its headlines that when the Buford sailed with its
"Cargo of Sedition" those on board carried with them a "Great
Quantity of Baggage and a Quarter of a Million Dollars in
Cash."

The November raids by the Justice Department established

the fact that close cooperation with the Department of Labor was essential. Inevitably, there was pressure to streamline procedure and to disregard individual rights.[52] Under existing guidelines, the attorney general could apply to the Department of Labor for warrants *if there was probable cause*. In practice, this meant that an application for warrant to arrest a particular person was filed with an "information and belief affidavit" that often represented nothing more than the imagination of a Justice Department functionary. According to Louis Post, affidavits of probable cause were run off in "job lots." They were literally mimeographed forms filled in by supervisory detectives on the strength of information given to them by a subordinate who was probably just passing on information provided by a business spy. Many affidavits were defective, some were not sworn to, some were not signed by the affiant, and some were blank except for the name of their victim.[53] Resident aliens were sometimes arrested on the strength of the fact that they had the same surname as was listed in the membership book of a proscribed organization. Nevertheless, the Labor Department did little about this because of the public clamor, the size of the GID operation, and the "aggressive nature" of the detectives. The result was that such "affidavits" would be delivered to the Bureau of Immigration (part of the Department of Labor) where "an obedient clerical force" drafted warrants to be perfunctorily signed by the secretary of labor. On one occasion the Justice Department demanded that the Immigration Bureau provide signed blank warrants.[54]

THE PALMER RAIDS

The prelude to the next stage in the Red Scare, the "Palmer Raids," was a blanket request from the Justice Department for three thousand warrants. Neither the secretary of labor, William B. Wilson, nor the majority of his assistants wanted to approve them, but as the solicitor for the department of labor, John W. Abercrombie, noted in his testimony before the judiciary committee, "The country was wild on suppression of anarchy, every paper was full of it."[55] Thus pressured, and on the assurance of the attorney general that aliens in large numbers were engaged in a conspiracy to overthrow the government, acting Secretary of Labor Abercrombie signed the warrants. Abercrombie, who as solicitor was actually an employee of the Justice Department, also altered departmental procedure (Rule 22) so that aliens did not have to be apprised of their right to counsel at the beginning of their hearing. This naturally meant that in practice aliens would not be told of their rights.[56]

January 1920 marked the height of the Red Scare. On the second of that month, more than four thousand aliens were arrested as a result of closely coordinated raids in thirty-three cities. The methods used in these roundups were even more outrageous than those of November. Agents infiltrated organizations and often encouraged illegal activities. The emphasis throughout was clearly on volume since agents were urged to schedule meetings to coincide with the raids.[57] Most of those swept up in the "inquiry dragnet," as the Justice Department officially referred to this operation, were captured at organization rallies, business meetings, and social functions. Others, individually targeted, were seized in their homes.[58]

Alien and American-born radicals, altogether something in the neighborhood of eight to ten thousand people, were taken with or without warrant to local jails or make-shift holding centers in federal buildings (or even warehouses) to be sorted out. Those aliens summarily categorized as radicals were quickly moved to "concentration points." (As always the figures are vague, but there seems to have been around three thousand such people.) American radicals, and there were an equal number of these people caught up in the raids, were bound over to local authorities to be prosecuted under the syndicalist laws.[59]

Each section of the country had a concentration point. In Boston, of the eight to twelve hundred people arrested, some four hundred were taken to the Deer Island retention center in Boston Harbor. During the early morning hours of 3 January, these people were marched in chains through the streets of Boston, a drama portrayed in the press as evidence of the violent nature of radical aliens.[60]

Practices varied: in Pittsburgh there was no illegal incarceration "apparently because the prison warden would not receive anyone without a lawful commitment."[61] But in other sections of the country, people were held incommunicado for long periods and in the most marginal conditions.[62] In Hartford the authorities also jailed the visitors who came to see those arrested in the raids on the assumption that they too must have been radicals.[63] The worst sins of this aspect of the Red Scare came about because the system was simply not capable of handling the massive influx of "detainees" generated by the attorney general's office. Prisoners were held for long periods—often months.

Treatment at the hands of federal and local agents was generally rough. Captives were interrogated, sometimes brutally, by immigration inspectors who were under orders to "get results." Statements derived in this manner were written "categorically into mimeographed question blanks," and then the "radical" was required to swear to the authenticity of this information.[64] Often these people spoke no English, and it is clear from transcripts of these "hearings" that the translator provided often had at best a limited command of the language.[65]

For several days following the raids, the nation's press carried blaring headlines, and on each successive day more of the imaginary alien plot unfolded. The 3 January *New York Times:*

REDS RAIDED IN SCORES OF CITIES: 2,600 ARRESTS, 700 IN NEW YORK; DEPORTATION HEARINGS BEGIN TODAY

Excerpts made public from a manifesto of the Communist Party revealed that the organization contemplates the overthrow of the American system of government and its replacement by a "workers industrial republic" or Soviet system. It was said tonight at the Department of Justice that the Communist Party and the Communist Labor Party . . . supported the Third International—which was formed under the auspices of Lenin and Trotsky at Moscow, May 6, 1919.

On 4 January the *Times* revealed this:

REDS PLOTTED COUNTRY-WIDE STRIKE: ARRESTS EXCEED 5,000, 2,635 HELD; THREE TRANSPORTS READY FOR THEM

Radical leaders planned to develop the recent steel and coal strikes into a general strike and ultimately into a revolution to overthrow the government, according to information gathered by Federal agents in Friday's round-up of members of the Communist Party and Communist Labor Party.

Offering a typical sentiment, Billy Sunday was quoted by the *Times* (4 January) as saying, "I would stand everyone of those ornery wild-eyed, anarchists, crazy socialists and other types before a firing squad and save space in our ships."

If one ignores the propaganda confiscated in the raids, the haul of incriminating evidence was astonishingly small. The really remarkable thing about the raids was the almost complete lack of weapons turned up in a search of several thousand men. Apart from a stock of arms taken from an amateur theatrical group, agents both federal and local found only four pistols. The raids also produced four iron balls that were naturally assumed to be bombs. These objects were dumped in a pail of water for safety's sake and at various times displayed to the press as infernal devices. But, as Louis Post reasoned, "Those four iron balls must have melted in that pail of water for they were never heard of again."[66] In another instance, plans for "various types of bombs" were, in due time, revealed to be diagrams for an improved phonograph.[67] Despite the fact that the arsenal of revolution never materialized, the raids served to renew the interest of Congress in a peacetime sedition law. Had this legislation passed, it would have been the first such law since 1798.

THE END OF THE RED SCARE

By the spring of 1920, the country was no longer on a war footing and Europe was perceived as being out of the clutches of the Bolsheviks. This perception, along with the growing appreciation that the radical community at home was actually quite small, served to take the edge off the hysteria. Added to this was the fact that the great strikes of the fall had ended and labor was clearly in the process of cutting its losses. In sum, the world was far less threatening to establishment America than it had been in the fall of 1919.

In this altered, less meancing environment, internal restraints began to reassert themselves. In particular, the administrative agreement by which aliens could be rapidly and conveniently deported began to break down. The assembly line by which Palmer and Hoover intended to spirit aliens out of the country depended, in the last analysis, upon an agreement between cronies. In the months following the raids, Secretary Wilson revoked John Abercrombie's decision on Rule 22, and from that point forward, aliens had to be informed of their rights to counsel at the outset of a hearing.[68] More and more, during the spring and summer of 1920, aliens were exercising those rights. In the same week of late January, Justice Holmes announced the decision of the Supreme Court in the case of *Silverthorne Lumber Company vs. the United States* that set the principle that evidence obtained illegally could not be used to incriminate. The impact of this decision on the deportation process was felt almost immediately; the pace of deportations slowed and the system began to clog with detainees.[69]

In the main, however, the Red Scare wound down because the social control machinery set in motion by the attorney general out-stripped the public perception of the danger it faced and because it began to threaten powerful interests. The New York State Assembly led the way by voting to expel five duly elected socialist members after a bitter and well-publicized political battle. Far from being alarmed at the prospect of socialists sitting on the legislature, the public looked upon the effort to bar these meek and idealistic officials as a species of vaudeville. La Guardia summed up the public mood when he remarked, "If we keep up at this rate we will build up a radical party in this country."[70]

Equally important, the peacetime sedition bill that was noisily making its way through Congress was beginning to frighten powerful groups. The newspapers, not surprisingly, balked at the prospect of censorship. Organized labor took the position that the bill could (and therefore would) be interpreted to disallow the right to strike.

In March, the gentlemen's agreement between the Justice Department and the Department of Labor completely broke down. Secretary Wilson was ill, and Solicitor Abercrombie, with his eye on the Senate, gave notice that he would temporarily leave the department. These departures left Louis Post in charge of the Labor Department at a time when thousands of deportations were pending.

Attorney General Palmer's most reliable ally in the Labor Department was the commissioner general of the Bureau of Immigration, Anthony J. Caminetti. Caminetti had kept the deportation process as closely under his control as possible, maintaining the records of thousands of deportation cases at Ellis Island— not Washington. Acting Secretary Post promptly withdrew deportation authority from the Bureau of Immigration—over Caminetti's strident objections—and ordered that Caminetti "transmit not less than 100 records per day [to Washington] until all warrant cases are disposed of."[71]

On the basis of these records, Post found the situation to be even more appalling than he had suspected, and in consultation with Wilson he dramatically reimposed internal restraints. With Wilson's blessing he established that membership in the Communist Labor party was *not* a deportable offense since this organization, unlike the Communist party, did not advocate violent overthrow of the government. Post also took special pains to note cases in which the alien had joined an innocuous local labor group that, without his knowledge, was transferred to the Communist Party. He was also alive to the fact that the Communist party inflated its membership by claiming long inactive members. Post cancelled the arrest warrants in all such cases of "automatic" membership. In addition, he canceled warrants in cases where the Justice Department did not present proof of illegal intent, in cases where evidence had been initially seized without warrant, and in cases where men had been denied counsel.[72] Working literally night and day, Post decided altogether some sixteen hundred cases by the middle of April, and in about two-thirds of the cases he found cause to cancel the warrant. The alien was then released.

Only after a close reading of some of Post's decisions is the magnitude of his accomplishment appreciated. His decisions are always faultlessly reasoned. Some amount to full-fledged legal briefs. Moreover, despite the fact that Post's decision to cancel often exceeded the letter of the law, his efficient prose and ruthless logic left little room for attack. Consider Post's decision to release an alien arrested on 7 January 1920 and subsequently charged by the Justice Department with being *both* a Communist and an Anarchist on the basis of his alleged membership within proscribed organizations. After a review of the alien's past affiliations, Post writes, "Examination of this record makes it evident that alien is not a communist. Neither is he an anarchist. He is the opposite of an anarchist, namely, a socialist. . . . The warrant is cancelled."[73]

The attorney general and most of the nation were furious. Palmer, an ambitious man, was running for president, and the slim chance that he would be elected hinged on keeping his image as protector of the faith in the public eye. This prospect was being torpedoed by a functionary in the Department of Labor.

The efforts of the Justice Department to protect its crusade followed two principal courses of action. First, on the basis of an intensive investigation of Post's background, it fed Congress with information that rapidly led to a movement to impeach him.[74] Second, it predicted widespread disturbances and sabotage for the forthcoming May Day. The public was provided with reports of impending general strikes, bombings, and plots to assassinate top officials.

The nation, naturally, fully anticipated a repeat of May Day 1919, and precautionary measures were massive: federal troops were put on standby, in some states the National Guard was called up, and patriotic organizations everywhere marshaled their membership. Along with other cities, New York put its entire police force, eleven thousand men, on twenty-four-hour alert, and Boston equipped its constabulary with machine guns mounted on automobiles.[75]

May Day 1920 proved to be absolutely quiet. Thoroughly intimidated, radical groups were silent, and nothing whatsoever in the way of radical activity took place. The Justice Department could do nothing but observe this tranquility with egg on its face. Moreover, on that same day, the House Committee on Rules merely decided to offer a resolution censuring Post's "leniency." There was simply no evidence to support impeachment. But far from being pleased by this development, Post was incensed, and the committee obligingly offered to extend the hearing so that Post could testify on his own behalf.

On 7 May the acting secretary made his defense. He proved to be an articulate spokesman and was able to recount the sins of the Justice Department in specifics, noting among other things that the arsenal of the supposed revolution, so far as the Justice Department was able to detect, consisted of only four handguns. He defended the character of the aliens, insisting in plenum style that "nearly all the 'conspirators' were wage workers, useful in industry, and good natured in their dispositions, unconscious of having given offense."[76] Both the committee and observing reporters were impressed by Post's testimony, which amounted to a public airing of the obdurate reality underlying the Red Scare. It cut the legs out from under the attorney general.

Louis Post had powerful liberal connections and had not gone to face the Judiciary Committee unprepared. On word that a number of Congressmen were out to "get" Post, a benefactor had given him $10,000 to hire the best available legal talent. Post hired a friend, an established Washington Lawyer, Jackson

Ralston, who was the attorney for the National Popular Government League (NPGL). Ralston was able to accomplish a number of things that not only aided Post but were very instrumental in debunking the Red Scare. Together with the resources of the NPGL and other organizations, Ralston was able to amass a vast amount of documentation to support Post's claims that the Justice Department was out of control.[77] And on the strength of this information, Ralston was able to use his connections to encourage a number of national figures to publicly support the actions of the acting secretary of labor.

Three weeks to the day after Post's brilliant defense, Ralston published under the auspices of the NPGL *A Report Upon the Illegal Practices of the United States Department of Justice*. It carried the endorsement of and is likely to have been in large part written by many of the top men in the legal profession, including Zechariah Chafee, Felix Frankfurter, and Dean Roscoe Pound of the Harvard Law School. Described by the secretary of the NPGL as "bomb proof," the report was superbly documented and was impossible to discredit. It listed in graphic detail the activities of the Justice Department, which clearly involved, among other things, cruel and unusual punishment, arrest without warrant, unreasonable search, agents provocateurs, and violations of the Fifth Amendment. Included in this litany were a number of carefully documented horror stories of large groups of aliens incarcerated under very harsh conditions.

Shortly after Post's appearance before the Rules Committee, the attorney general was "invited" to testify before that same body to answer charges of misconduct. Palmer presented himself on the first of June and was an unconvincing witness. He was by this time very much on the defensive, and his task was not made any easier by the timely publication of the NPGL's *Report* on 28 May.

The attorney general's difficulties came as a direct consequence of making powerful enemies. In the spring of 1920, a small but influential group of conservatives led by Charles Evans Hughes organized in response to the activities of the attorney general's office.[78] This "Counter Community," as Levin refers to it, called attention to the self-serving nature of Palmer's activities—a charge he found hard to deny. To add to Palmer's desolation, this criticism came at a time when the support of big business was beginning to wane now that organized labor had been cowed. Industry spokesmen expressed concern over the curtailment of cheap labor that resulted from the Red Scare.[79]

The final blow to the deportation assembly line came on 23 June when Judge George W. Anderson ruled that even membership in the Communist party was not necessarily a deportable offense. This single act, above all others, signaled that the use of administrative gambits to shovel aliens out of the country was no longer acceptable. The restraints of procedural law were officially reimposed.

*   *   *

Such as they are, the figures on the deportations are revealing. From 1 July 1919 to 1 January 1921, 6,328 warrants were issued by the Labor Department. Louis Post states that 4,038 arrests were made on the basis of these warrants and that of these, 2,919 were ultimately canceled while 1,119 were sustained.[80] In just the period from November 1919 through January 1920, about 5,000 warrants were issued. Something on the order of 3,000 were used, of which 2,202 were canceled by Louis Post.[81]

Post notes that according to official records, from 1 January 1920 to 13 June 1921, 556 people were deported. He states, "This figure is probably not far wrong. It may be exactly right although I should guess the number to be at least 100 more."[82] Murray notes that 35 people left over from Buford's departure can be added to the official figure of 556, making a total of 591.[83]

It is obvious that the figures available for the Red Scare deportations simply don't add up. They don't even come close, and it is quite apparent that neither the Justice Department nor the Department of Labor had any clear idea of how many people they had under lock and key. Some aliens were ultimately held for as long as eighteen months.[84]

There is no summary information at all on the fate of the several thousand native-born Americans who were caught up in the raids. The majority were probably released as soon as they could establish their citizenship; however, a large but unknown number were charged under the manifold syndicalist laws of this era.

It is also important to emphasize that once the perception of a vast and malevolent Bolshevik presence finally broke down, it proved highly resistant to resurrection. At noon on 16 September 1920, a huge bomb exploded in New York City at the corner of Wall and Broad Streets. Twenty-nine people died immediately and over two hundred were hospitalized. It was a sensational event and nothing could have been better calculated to renew public faith in the Jeremiads of Palmer and Hoover. Instead, both men were ridiculed by the press for asserting that this was the beginning of another Bolshevik plot.[85]

*   *   *

The Red Scare left in its wake a durable undercurrent of fear and nativism that manifested itself in isolationism, distrust of organized labor, and the reemergence of the KKK, which had an estimated membership of 4,500,000 in 1924.[86] Patriotic organizations continued to flourish, and a variety of national patriotic observances were concocted (Flag Day, for example). Military intelligence became actively involved in antiradical surveillance and a "war plan" was developed to cope with internal uprisings. The FBI disseminated lists of subversives and enthusiastically infiltrated reform movements. Smearing individuals, ideas, and groups as "Communist" became a familiar and effective tactic. During the twenties and thirties everything from criticism of prohibition to advocacy of birth control was so tagged.[87]

DISCUSSION

Following the First World War, the Justice Department, the Department of Labor, patriotic organizations, and big business pumped life into the bogus reality of a vast Bolshevik underground and then joined to spirit offending aliens out of the country. The watchword was cooperation. The Immigration Bureau and the Justice Department's Alien Enemy Bureau, in which Hoover had been a leading light, had all but fused during the war. Hoover's past connections and familiarity with the Labor Department's deportation statutes made him the logical choice to manage the Justice Department's crusade against radicals.[88] Throughout the Red Scare the Bureau of Investigation had less than six hundred agents, and the Palmer Raids necessarily drew heavily on state and local authorities. Even the resources of local patriotic groups were utilized. Without that broad support, the Palmer Raids would have been impossible.[89] And when the Red Scare is examined at the ground level, it is clear that both big business and government agencies dipped into a common pool of private detectives.[90]

The press fundamentally influenced the construction of public reality during the Red Scare, and the Justice Department attempted, with much success, to orchestrate the press's presentation of events. So long as the public was convinced that an alien underground was in the process of hatching a revolt, the antics of the Justice Department were tolerated—in fact, encouraged. In the end, however, the Justice Department was unable to control the press in the face of obdurate reality that was flatly in contradiction to what it had advertised. Many influential papers turned on Palmer and the Justice Department after the uneventful May Day of 1920. It was a public fiasco, and those interests opposing the Justice Department's policies exploited the attorney general's miscue to the hilt; he was increasingly presented to the public as an ideological hysteric.

It is apparent that flagging support of big business was a major factor in the decay of the Red Scare. Big business was a major source of pressure on Congress and a conduit of antiradical information, much of it imaginary, to the Justice Department. In the atmosphere of fall strikes, Congress and the press, with the enthusiastic support of big business, badgered Palmer into undertaking the November raids and then bathed him in adulation for the remainder of the year. By the spring of 1920, however, the labor movement was back in the bottle, and big business no longer perceived red baiting to be in its interests; indeed, some business leaders were beginning to see it as a liability since it was drying up the source of cheap labor. Palmer's downfall was, therefore, precipitious.[91]

CORRESPONDENCES

It seems reasonable to argue that propositions (1.0) through (6.0) in the explanatory scheme presented above have been upheld. The specific nature of this support is worth reviewing:

(1.0); (1.1); (1.2)—The circumstances leading up to the Red Scare argue for a solid connection between an increase in the level of social strain among members of powerful groups and an increase in the level of external demand. According to Gengarelly, "Political hysteria grew fat on national discontent, and its promoters, both self-serving and sincere continued to wreak public suspicion and hate against the specter of an international conspiracy."[92]
(2.0); (2.1); (2.2); (3.0)—The Red Scare was axed long before the objectives of the Justice Department had been reached. Hoover's innu-

merable memorandums betray a constant battle to stave off normal organizational restraints as well as frenzied efforts to undermine the credibility of those who would call the Justice Department to account.[93] The Red Scare, however intense, was brief because the normal account-abilities and organizational restraints could not be held at bay for long in the absence of a persuasive conspiracy.

(4.0); (4.1)—The attitudes, procedures, personnel, and legislation that allowed the Red Scare to take place all hail back to the social environ-ment of the First World War. It seems indisputable that one conse-quence of the dramatically elevated level of external demand during the Red Scare was the relaxation of normal organizational restraints. Hoover later acknowledged that the Justice Department's antiradical activities had "no authority under the law."[94] Deportation was defined as administrative procedure and not as punishment for a crime. The Justice Department was empowered only to investigate crime and tech-nically should not have been involved in deportation proceedings. Jurisdictional issues were "only technicalities" during the Red Scare.

(5.0); (5.1); (5.2)—It is an easy task to identify the several interest groups that encouraged and carried out the Red Scare. So long as these groups acted in concert, the exercise of effective accountability was essentially impossible. The November raids and the swift depar-ture of the Buford provide an example of just how effective this coali-tion was.

(6.0)—But the January raids frightened many people and put pressure on the coalition. The Labor Department began to have second thoughts and would soon reinstitute organizational restraints; big business, more secure, withdrew its support. Furthermore, the menace of the Third International had by the spring of 1920 diminished, and at the same time the feeble nature of the radical community at home became the accepted wisdom. Very much related to these events was the rise of the influential "counter community," which actively opposed Palm-er's methods as a threat to liberty. The discordant nature of the activi-ties of the Justice Department was the dominant theme of Palmer's critics. He had, they said, "overreacted" and was in the process of riding roughshod over the Bill of Rights.

WHAT IF?

One possible sticking point in the analysis of the Red Scare hinges on the incapacity of President Wilson. In other words, would the Red Scare have taken place had Wilson been healthy? Naturally, speculation about "what if," the stock in trade of the Sunday supplement ("What if the South had won the Civil War?"), gives rise to doubts, but in the instance of the Red Scare such uncertainty is largely foreclosed by the parallel occurrence of the McCarthy Era a generation later. The assertion that the excesses of the Red Scare were due to the interruption of normal political authority falls flat for the simple reason that after World War II there was no interruption of authority, and yet the course of events was essentially the same. In both instances the response of dominant groups to threats to their values and interests was the mass production of deviance. Indeed, President Truman was a leading, if not entirely willing, actor in the establishment of the apparatus of repression following the Second World War.[95]

8

The McCarthy Era

The apocalyptic view of international communism reemerged full-blown with the cold war and reached its zenith during the Korean War. Just as during the Red Scare, the danger was exaggerated by the social strains of postwar life and manipulated to the advantage of powerful groups that perceived their interests to be threatened.

Within two years of the end of World War II, the two major political parties in the United States were in headlong competition to impose absolute loyalty and ideological purity on the nation. This is the dominant theme of the McCarthy Era, and it calls to mind the politics of seventeenth-century Scotland when the Privy Council and the General Assembly periodically competed for political legitimacy by laying claim to the status of religious purity. As the reader will recall, burned witches were the principal index of success in this competition, and it is interesting to note that some three hundred years later one of the highlights of the early Eisenhower administration was an intense debate between Republicans and Democrats over which party had fired the greatest number of civil servants.[1]

From the late forties to the middle fifties, the engine driving the production of ideological devience was the political rivalry between Republican and Democrat.[2] Each goaded the other to extremes. Nothing more clearly exemplifies this process than the passage of the Internal Security Act (the McCarran Bill) by the eighty-first Congress. This legislation, passed in the early months of the Korean War, required the registration of "Communist organizations," broadened the espionage laws, and allowed the detention of "potential" spies and saboteurs.[3] The "liberal" retort was the Emergency Detention Bill, which recognized the right to simply round up and hold in detention camps all individuals the attorney general "had reason to believe" might be a threat during an "internal security emergency." Initially

155

intended as a counter proposal to the McCarran Bill, it was enthusiastically incorporated into the final form of the Internal
Security Act and passed (in less than an hour) over a presidential
veto.[4] Criticism of this legislation was minimal and chiefly focused on matters of practicality—would it work? This mood
did not abate until after the war in Korea had ended. In 1952,
for example, Congress appropriated $775,000 to establish and
maintain six detention camps.[5]

The Internal Security Act must be taken as the culmination
of a conservative legislative thrust that flourished in the political
environment of the Second World War. Richard Fried writes
that "by the time Joe McCarthy reached national prominence,
most of the paraphernalia of witch hunting—the lists, letter-
heads, even the vocabulary—had been in use for years."[6] In
fact, by the beginning of the war a number of bills had been
passed (i.e., the McCormack Act in 1938 and the Smith Act
in 1940) that contained in embryonic form the various measures
of the Internal Security Act.[7]

It was the high level of anxiety over the international political
situation that enabled these measures to pass. Roosevelt, for
example, fended off critics of the Smith Act, which stipulated
the registration of all aliens and encouraged the repression of
pacifist activity, by saying that it could "hardly be considered
to constitute an improper encroachment on civil liberties in
the light of present world conditions."[8] Wartime security measures were even more severe and left a potent legacy. Richard
Freeland notes:

> The Attorney General's list, the deportation drive, the new controls
> on official information and on access of the press and public to
> it, the new controls upon alien visitors—all had a common origin
> in the policies that had been developed during war-time emergencies
> to protect national security by assuring public support of the military
> effort.[9]

Throughout the thirties and forties, New Deal liberalism was
consistently presented as a stalking horse for Communism. Postwar realities and the consequences of a genuinely lax attitude
towards security prior to the war gave credence to the charge
that Communist agents and "fellow travelers" riddled much of
the executive branch of government. A running series of spy
cases (such as the Amerasia exposé) and repeated congressional
investigations maintained this perception in the public mind.[10]

The pivotal year was 1946. The Congressional elections in which the Republicans gained control over both houses drove home to the Truman administration the fact that all foreign aid proposals would face very difficult Republican opposition if they were not linked to the overarching issue of anti-Communism. It is clear that the Truman Doctrine speech, delivered to a joint session of Congress on 12 March 1947, was written with this in mind.[11] Truman's speech was, in the words of Bernard Baruch, "tantamount to a declaration of . . . an ideological or religious war."[12]

Nine days after the Truman Doctrine was announced, Truman issued an executive order establishing the Federal Employee Loyalty Program. Here again, there is every reason to believe that domestic political considerations were at work.[13] Under the dictates of the Federal Employee Loyalty Program, present and potential employees of the federal government were subject to a background investigation that included a check of information held by the FBI, the House Committee on Un-American Activities (HUAC), military intelligence, and local authorities.[14] Applicants or employees found to have "derogatory information" (often derived from anonymous sources) were subjected to a very detailed field investigation. Suspect employees were required to appear before a "loyalty" board and answer charges. By and large, this program brought few changes to the basic procedures established in wartime; but in the climate of ideological war, the pressure to produce deviants was great, and, therefore, the damage to lives and reputation pervasive. Thousands lost their job and many others were intimidated into resignation.

In the face of Republican pressure, the Truman administration's efforts to display itself in the trappings of ideological purity were extravagant. In the spring of 1947, J. Edgar Hoover and Attorney General Clark decided that a national program to rally the public against the Communist menace was needed.[15] Featured in this campaign was the "Freedom Train," which carried patriotic displays and was a platform for oratory all around the country. In November, the administration staged a "Week of Rededication" in Washington. Included in the agenda were several carefully orchestrated demonstrations during which massed federal employees took the "freedom pledge" and sang "God Bless America." It goes without saying that one of these demonstrations was the occasion for the arrival of the Freedom Train.[16] This week of theater was timed to coincide with the congressional debate on the question of interim aid, and temporarily forestalled effective criticism of the Truman administration and its policies.

In addition to the two major political parties, there were many other interest groups that enthusiastically supported the Red baiting of the forties and fifties. Among these were the American Legion and the Veterans of Foreign Wars, the Catholic Church, the Knights of Columbus and the Catholic War Veterans, the DAR, the A F of L, much of the business community, many organizations representing eastern block ethnic groups, and the relatively small, but zealous, political right wing.[17] These groups, spurred on by the conservative press, comprised a large portion of the electorate and were especially effective at lobbying and propagandizing.

Very likely the single most influential interest group was the United States Chamber of Commerce. Certainly the community of interests represented by this group was a major political force during this period. During the war, and for a short time afterwards, the economic potential of east-west trade spawned considerable goodwill towards the Russians among the business community, but increasing Soviet intransigence coupled with the extreme militance of labor during the winter of 1945–46 drove much of the business community into the embrace of the right wing.[18]

If anything, the strikes of the period immediately following the Second World War were more widespread and more crippling to the economy than those following the First World War.[19] Peter Irons notes of this period:

> American workers suffered from inflation during the war while they watched corporation profits soar, and in frustration they chafed against the no-strike pledge during the war and then unleashed the greatest strike wave in the country's history.[20]

Businessmen responded to union militancy with shock and surprise and once again leveled the charge that labor was infiltrated and dominated by Communists. In the increasingly threatening postwar environment, this charge became credible. Irons argues that the passage of the Taft-Hartley Act was greatly facilitated by the general perception that the Kremlin lurked somewhere in the background of the labor movement and specifically by charges from the business community that major unions were under Communist influence.[21]

It would seem to be difficult to overestimate the political impact of the United States Chamber of Commerce and the National Association of Manufacturers during this period. These organizations were the principal swordbearers of the business community and worked in close concert with other anti-Communist organizations. The National Association of Manufacturers spent millions in an effort to undermine the Wagner Act and the union shop.[22] And, according to Irons:

> The Chamber served as the nexus of an alliance of disparate groups: its Cold War propaganda was primarily written by Father Cronin of the Catholic Church, drawing upon information and files supplied by right-wing forces in labor, the FBI and the Un-American Activities Committee; distributed in the hundreds of thousands by both Catholic and Protestant and anti-union businessmen; given a national forum by the HCUA and serialized in a number of newspapers; and even utilized by the FBI in the internal struggle within the Employee Loyalty Commission. Primarily directed against labor, the Chamber's campaign was a broad-brush attack on liberal and left-wing groups in general, and was directly aimed at the Truman administration.[23]

From the very beginning, the chamber's well-funded campaign was controlled by zealots. For example, the chamber's Permanent Committee on Socialism and Communism published an anti-Communist handbook (Program for Community Anti-Communist Action) which, among other things, gave detailed advice on how to set up a file on local Communists. Under the direction of professional Red-baiters, the chamber unleashed a flood of propaganda keynoted by two booklets: Communists in the Labor Movement and Communist Infiltration of the United States, which was sent to every Catholic bishop in the country and to about eighty thousand Protestant clergy. Published in 1946 and 1947, these two epistles alone were eventually distributed by the hundreds of thousands.[24]

Within another political context, much of the chamber's propaganda would have been taken as the work of crackpots of the wildest sort; but during the cold war the tales spun by the chamber's propagandists were often taken to be genuine and greatly influenced the construction of political reality. The fact that the structure of the Federal Employee Loyalty Program conformed in most particulars to the demands of the chamber argues the influence of this group. Indeed, the chamber saw nearly all of its anti-Communist program embodied in the Mundt-Nixon Bill and, ultimately, in the McCarran Bill, its successor.[25]

In the final analysis, the efforts of the Truman administration to deflate the issue of a Communist fifth column were doomed to failure by a series of threatening events that could be presented by the political opposition as the handiwork of the international Communist conspiracy. The litany of these events includes the Communist coup in Prague (which was followed by the reinstatement of the draft), the "loss" of China, the explosion of a Russian atomic bomb, the Klaus Fuchs spy case, the operatic trials of Alger Hiss, the "Atomic Spies," and above all, the outbreak of the Korean War.[26]

It is hard to overstate the political impact of the Korean War. Freeland writes:

> Had a mischievous deity determined to produce an event that would bring to a fever pitch the already heated political situation in the United States, he could have succeeded no better than did the North Koreans in this bold attack upon an Asian area that only six months before the American Secretary of State had indicated would not be defined by American arms.[27]

AMERICA'S WITCHFINDER GENERAL

The amazing career of Joseph McCarthy closely brackets this conflict. A mountebank, he was product of the times, and most of its sins were not his handiwork.[28] All the same, McCarthy's vicious and reckless antics kept him constantly in the news, and his name justifiably identifies the second Red Scare. From 1950 to 1954, McCarthy skated rapidly from one exposé to another, often leaving his critics in the lurch. By the time they caught up with him on one set of bogus charges, another was already in the news; just as Matthew Hopkins did not tarry too long in one place, McCarthy did not dwell overlong on any one nest of Communists.

An epiphany can be found in the circumstances surrounding McCarthy's vault to power. On 9 February 1950 he was in Wheeling, West Virginia, dutifully giving a Lincoln Day speech on Communists in the State Department; eleven days later he was defending his outlandish accusations before the Senate and the national press. No one was more surprised by this turn of events than Joseph McCarthy. The GOP had assigned him a journeyman schedule of Lincoln Day speeches—Wheeling, Salt Lake City, Reno, Las Vegas, and Huron (South Dakota)—and in anticipation of this drudgery, McCarthy ordered his staff to prepare speeches on public housing and Communists in government. Upon his arrival in Wheeling, McCarthy learned that his speech would be carried by the local radio station and was very much alive to the suggestion that the "Communist fifth column" was the more interesting issue. The speech, as prepared by his press secretary, contains the celebrated paragraph:

> And ladies and gentlemen, while I cannot take the time to name all the men in the State Department who have been named as active members of the Communist Party and members of a spy ring, I have here in my hand a list of 205—a list of names that were made known to the Secretary of State as being members of the Communist Party and who nevertheless are still working and shaping policy in the State Department.[29]

It is unlikely that McCarthy strictly followed his prepared text—he seldom did—but several people remember him mentioning a list of 205 "known Communists." However that may be, McCarthy's oratory, which immediately followed a group sing, does not seem to have created much of a stir among the 275 people assembled in the Colonnade room of the McClure Hotel, but his accusations, appearing in an AP wire, soon reached a wider and more receptive audience. When McCarthy landed at Denver on his way to Salt Lake City, reporters were waiting, and the Denver Post ran a front-page story accompanied by a picture of McCarthy peering intently into his briefcase. "Left Commie List in Other Bag," explained the caption.[30] As McCarthy hopscotched across the West, the story snowballed into front page news.

As always, the credibility of McCarthy's charges derived entirely from the desire of many Americans to believe them. During his Lincoln Day sojourn the "list" was comprised variously of 205 "known communists," 207 "bad risks," and 57 "card carrying communists." Before the Senate, McCarthy talked of 81 "loyalty risks." All of these figures can be derived (allowing for a little bad arithmetic) from routine and, by 1950, dated security checks. The information in these files, all hearsay, includes such items as "A bit leftist" and "She entertains both Negroes and whites, both men and women, in her apartment."[31]

McCarthy was bold, ambitious, and consummately skilled at the game of national politics (and it was something of a game to him). Wanting notoriety as much as power, he achieved both by providing an image of a massive internal conspiracy at a time when the world menaced and bewildered most Americans. Communists in government explained the shape of things. Long out of power and stung by the election of 1948, the Republicans were perfectly willing to make use of him providing they could put some distance between themselves and his tactics.[32] Senator Taft, in a well known bit of advice, suggested to McCarthy, "If one case doesn't work, try another."[33] However, with the Republican success of 1952, McCarthy came to be seen by the party leadership as a loose cannon.

The immediate cause for the elimination of McCarthy—but not McCarthyism—was the opposition of the U.S. Army and the Senate (both institutions had been directly attacked by Mc-Carthy). However, at base, McCarthy's political career foundered because the end of the Korean hostilities took the edge off the menacing construction of reality that had given him license. In this altered context, just as with Attorney General Palmer a generation before, McCarthy's actions were deemed excessive and "out of place." A series of media events (most notably Edward R. Murrow's "See It Now," which aired on 9 March 1954, and the celebrated Army-McCarthy Hearings) presented McCarthy in an unfavorable light and left him open for censure (actually "condemnation") by the Senate.[34]

It is important to recognize that the media exposés and the censure *followed* a significant loss of support for McCarthy. Many prominent businessmen, leaders of the right-wing press, and the entire leadership of the Republican party had by this time turned against him.[35] In many ways the army acted as a surrogate for the White House when it filed charges against McCarthy. Discussing the "See It Now" program, Bayley argues:

> In some ways the most remarkable thing about the program was that it was so late. Even the conservative Republican newspapers had begun to turn on McCarthy as it became apparent that he was willing to fight President Eisenhower in the same way he had fought President Truman.[36]

The censure of McCarthy by the Senate was effective largely because of its timing. Other men had been censured—Robert LaFollette, for example—and gone on to greater accomplishments; but this was not to be the case with McCarthy, who was a creature of collective anxiety. In 1954 the high level of external demand that had provided support to his fictitious crusades no longer existed; the censure simply signaled that he was without political leverage. McCarthy, who had received two thousand requests for speaking engagements just prior to the 1950 congressional elections, was now consigned to isolation.[37] Rovere describes the setting of McCarthy's decline:

> When he got the floor, Senators would drift from the chamber to the cloakroom or to other business. The Vice-President would summon some freshman Senator to take his place in the chair, and Lyndon Johnson, the new majority leader, would leave some junior Democrat behind to observe the proceedings and be on guard against a sneak play. At the announcement of a McCarthy speech, the reporters in the press gallery would see a chance to catch a bite, to exchange gossip or find out what Lyndon Johnson was up to. Handouts from McCarthy's office would land in the wastebaskets. . . .[38]

The McCarthy Era was by far the most corrosive of America's purges. The Red Scare was a brief (albeit violent) interlude that was aimed primarily at a "foreign element" and directly touched relatively few American citizens.[39] But the social impact of McCarthyism was pervasive.

State governments enthusiastically aped federal measures. By 1954, thirteen states had laws against the advocation of violent change or membership within a group that advocated violent change. In Tennessee, seeking to overthrow the *state* government was punishable by death.[40] At the local level, ideological hygiene became a fetish. Municipal police departments often maintained anti-subversion units ("Red Squads") and free-lance anti-Communist organizations sprouted like mushrooms. The political clout of these groups vastly exceeded their size; for example, the politics of Houston—and, for that matter, all of Texas—was dominated throughout the early fifties by a powerful coalition comprised of the Americanism Committee of the American Legion, the Committee for the Preservation of Methodism, and a chapter of the Minute Women of the USA Inc. As in many other cities, the principal arena for conflict in Houston was the educational system.[41] State and local school systems routinely demanded loyalty oaths, and, in fact, in no occupation could one assume to be entirely free of this obligation. The state of Indiana, for example, required professional wrestlers to take a loyalty oath.[42]

The cost of this "great fear" is hard to calculate. Probably tens of thousands lost their jobs and had careers destroyed for failure to sign a loyalty oath or for nebulous past connections (Caute calculates that 379 teachers suffered expulsion in the New York school system; the casualty rate in other states was comparable). The threat of incarceration for contempt of court or for failure to register as a member of a "Communist Front" organization (a very broad category) was real for a great many people, and at least one individual—Oscar Smilack, the "angel" of the Franklin County, Ohio, Communist party—was committed to a state hospital for the criminally insane.[43] Once again, there was talk of establishing an American Devil's Island.

Nothing is more emblematic of this period than the House Committee on Un-American Activities. Often portrayed by its critics as inquisitorial theater, the many hearings of this committee (more than four hundred during this period) did indeed function, by design, to label and degrade. The pretense that HUAC was an investigatory body was largely a fiction. The information uncovered by the committee in open session had often already been made known to committee members in executive sessions that were, in fact, rehearsals. In HUAC's long career, little if anything was revealed by the committee that was not previously known to the FBI.[44] HUAC hearings were entirely degradation ceremonies that served to establish a moral boundary. Hoover very clearly saw the committee in this role and entered into an enthusiastic and very supportive alliance. At one point, more than three hundred FBI agents were assigned to the task of proving that Alger Hiss had perjured himself.[45]

The degree of emphasis placed on this symbolic process is not usually appreciated. As a practical matter, HUAC did not have anything like a normal legislative function, and very few bills were ever referred to it. Nevertheless, during the decade following the Second World War, this single committee employed roughly 10 percent of all house committee staff and 12 percent of all committee funds. Since 1945 and until its demise, the committee entertained testimony from more than five thousand witnesses.[46]

"Names,"as Walter Goodman insists, "were the food of the second [1951] Hollywood investigation."[47] Indeed, throughout all of the hearings of this committee, the principal test of virtue was the willingness of the witness to incriminate others. Only those witnesses who had "named names" were granted the saving words, "Thank you," from the committee chairman.[48] These words meant that the witness had been at last touched by the hand of redemption and would not be blacklisted.

Blacklists were a fundamental part of the moral boundary erected during this period. Many—very likely most—conservative organizations compiled lists of ideological pariahs. In Hollywood, for instance, the rabidly conservative Motion Pictures Alliance for the Preservation of American Ideals cooperated with gossip columnists to publicize the names of errant filmworkers.[49] Apart from the federal government, which must be regarded as the keeper of the master blacklist, the American Legion was the most powerful organization maintaining a blacklist, and to be mentioned as a party member or fellow traveler in its national magazine was an anathema.

Some blacklists were concocted purely as business ventures. The most successful operation of this type was American Business Consultants, established by three ex-FBI agents in 1947 with the aid of China Lobby money. Their first product was a newsletter, Counterattack, which was available to subscribers (and there were many) for $24.00 a year. American Business Consultants also published Red Channels, the blacklisters bible for radio and T.V. There were other entrepreneurs, many of whom relied heavily on unofficial connections with HUAC staffers who had access to committee files.[50] About fifteen hundred people were directly affected in radio and T.V.

Having manufactured a viable threat, the private blacklisters soon expanded into the business of "clearing people." Aware Inc. actually published a clearance handbook, The Road Back (Self Clearance): A Provisional Statement of View on the Problem of the Communist and Communist-Helper in Entertainment Who Seeks to Clear Himself.[51] Such organizations prospered in a unique and enviable niche within the apparatus of social control: they manufactured both deviance and redemption and made money from both processes.

There were, however, legitimate practitioners in the clearance industry. Typically, specialists in the art of political redemption, especially those who defended federal workers called before a loyalty board, emphasized their client's abiding loyalty to capitalism and deep sense of contrition for having allowed themselves to be ensnared in ideological wickedness.[52] It can be argued that the entire entertainment industry was intimidated into collective demonstrations of loyalty. During the late forties and fifties, Hollywood produced more than four hundred anti-Communist films, nearly all of which—it is worth mentioning—lost money.[53]

* * *

No one would argue that the cost of the McCarthy Era is in any way directly comparable to the cost of the Great Purge or to the raw and monstrous tragedy of the Holocaust. But all the same, the cost of the McCarthy Era was not small. It was not small in that many thousands lost their livelihoods, and many times that number lived in fear of that private calamity. Beyond that, the imposition of the narrow moral boundaries of the fifties fostered an era of political and intellectual conformity at a time when wisdom and flexibility were required. The State Department suffered a crippling purge of its wisest and most experienced Asian hands at the precise point in time when such qualities were urgently needed. Ignorance and fear and consequent rigidity of thought led directly to that vast and futile expenditure of life and treasure known as Vietnam and to an arms race of such unusual insanity as to defy the drawing of historical parallel.

DISCUSSION

Nothing in the history of the McCarthy Era offers any serious challenge to the scheme presented in Chapter 1. Overall and in the realm of many particulars, the course of events following the Second World War parallels that following the First World War.

It would seem beyond dispute that the perception of a Communist underground of fantastic size was preceded by the appearance of a menacing reality that directly threatened the status and resources of powerful groups. This perception was quickly followed by a demand for large numbers of ideological pariahs, which HUAC was admirably designed to produce. Institutions and interest groups that in normal times would have hindered the production of deviants now saw it in their interest to support the mass production of deviance, and the established restraints of procedural law were frequently overlooked; they became, as before, mere technicalities. The FBI routinely operated at the fringe of established law during the cold war with little prospect of being called to account.

During both the world wars, laws were enacted that dramatically enhanced the ability of the apparatus of social control to produce deviants. Similarly, during both periods, the specter of the International Communist Conspiracy fostered a broad coalition of interest groups, which raised the level of external demand. The cold war coalition, similar in constituency to its Red Scare predecessor, also followed a similar pattern of decay.

Opinions regarding the disappearance of the virulent McCarthyism of the Korean War have focused on an astonishing variety of causal factors. Among these are the removal of McCarthy from the political scene, a reduction in the political impact of the "red" issue, the opposition of the press, McCarthy's exposure on national television, a hitch in the normal cycling of conservative and liberal dominance in Washington, and, according to Norman Thomas, "A saving common sense about our democracy."[54] Other "causes" have been suggested.

Obviously, some of these explanations are not subject to falsification in any meaningful sense; others seem to evade the issue. Unless the "great man" McCarthy is assumed to be the prime cause for the repression of the late forties and fifties—which would seem unlikely since he was not even indirectly associated with the worse legislative evils of the period—there is no basis for seeing in his disappearance the reason for the pronounced reduction in the level of repression.

During the fifties, as before, the mass production of deviance began to taper off when the menacing reality that threatened dominant groups began to decay. The relatively brief period spanning the years 1953 to 1955 saw the end of the Korean War, the death of Stalin, the clear success of the Marshall Plan in Europe, and a more conciliatory attitude on the part of the Russians at Geneva. In short, the "holy war" atmosphere so characteristic of the crest of the McCarthy Era had subsided.[55]

9

The Great Purge

French history fascinated the Bolsheviks. After the Civil War, the fear that the French Revolution and the Bolshevik Revolution shared a common reactionary path began to nag the architects of the new Soviet State, and exchanges between party factions were colored by accusations of "Thermidorian degeneracy" and "Bonapartist" ambition. Trotsky resigned his position as war commissar in the face of such a charge and was for the remainder of his life haunted by the specter of "Russian Thermidor."[1] But the grip of French history should not be exaggerated; Russian revolutionary leaders were highly selective in their perception of historical analogy. Trotsky's rhetoric could have explored another parallel: both revolutions embraced similar principles of social control. As Saint Just, one of Robespierre's colleagues on the Committee for Public Safety and a prime mover during the terror of revolutionary France, once advised, "You must punish not merely traitors, but the indifferent as well."[2]

THE CIVIL WAR

Soviet history prior to the Second World War is traditionally broken into three periods: 1917–21, the period of revolution, civil war, and War Communism; 1921–28, the period of economic retrenchment known as the New Economic Policy (NEP); and 1928–39, Russia's "Iron Age," the period of industrialization and collectivization.[3] The first and third periods were equally periods of social revolution; the second was a period of economic recovery. It is often claimed that the Soviet State was "forged" during the Civil War. This is certainly true of the fundamental institution of Soviet social control, the political police.

The Russian Civil War was devastating. Famine, disease, and

168

occupation by the brutal soldiery typical of all participating armies were routine evils. Throughout, the Communist party had only nominal hegemony over a vast and predominantly rural landscape. The party—and hence Soviet Russia—survived because its army prevailed over the armies of its principal opponents, the counterrevolutionary "White Russians," and over no less than a dozen foreign expeditionary units. In addition, the party defeated or simply endured nationalistic movements, peasant uprisings, guerrilla bands, and endemic banditry.

The party's response to this upheaval was War Communism. The tsarist judiciary was dismantled and replaced by people's courts, which dealt with ordinary crime, and the more explicitly political revolutionary tribunals.[4] Banks were nationalized, industry placed under the control of workers' committees, and the peasantry officially encouraged to do what it had already largely accomplished—confiscate the land and eliminate the land owners. These measures were a reflection of ideology, but subsequent measures were survival tactics. By and large, the party did not dictate events during the Civil War; it merely trotted after them, and in many respects the central party apparatus became an appendage of the organizations that protected it: the army and the political police.

Erratic communication, work stoppages, and the lack of raw material quickly combined to curtail the production of consumable goods; this, in turn, isolated the cities from the countryside since the Russian peasantry was not inclined to provide urban residents with grain in return for nothing. Officially, rationing and government distribution replaced private trade, but by 1918 there was often little to distribute; areas under Soviet control sank predictably into a black market economy. Paper currency, printed in abundance, soon had no value and payment in kind became standard.

Communist control over the countryside and the peasantry was everywhere limited and directly proportional to the distance from urban centers.[5] As the flow of grain to the cities and, most alarmingly, to the Red Army fell to starvation levels, the party resorted to outright confiscation (officially termed a food levy). Decrees issued in May and August of 1918 allowed trade unions and workers committees to organize paramilitary "food detachments" to requisition agricultural products, principally grain, from the peasants. Half the grain was to be kept by the organization that sponsored the detachment and half was to be given over to general distribution.[6] The impact of this policy was entirely predictable: the peasants responded by concealing stores of grain and in following years by reverting to subsistence agriculture (grain not grown cannot be confiscated). Peasants often resisted violently, and here and there the countryside erupted into wholesale uprisings.

THE CHEKA

In addition to its military and economic woes, the Communist party considered itself beset by internal ideological enemies in the form of opposition parties (one of which, the Socialist Revolutionaries, tried to assassinate Lenin) and "class enemies." This front was manned by a remarkably ruthless police force— the Cheka—which, although it served the interests of the central party, became a law unto itself.[7]

Where the party was in power, social control was savage. Within two months of the October Revolution, the All Russian Commission for Combatting Counterrevolution and Sabotage (acronym Cheka, which means linchpin in Russian) was established. There is little reason to dispute the claim by a ranking Chekist that "the existence of the chekas was not provided for by any legal basis. . . . Life itself dictated that they should be organized."[8]

On 19 December 1917 the Council of People's Commissars, chaired by Lenin, was confronted with the threat of a general strike by state employees. The council turned instinctively to the reliable personnel of the Military Revolutionary Committee (MRC), which at the boot level had engineered and protected the revolution. A provisional organization, the MRC had been officially disbanded only the day before.

One of the MRC's leading lights, Feliks Dzerzhinski, was charged with the task of examining methods of combatting the anticipated strike by "the most energetic measures." The following day, Dzerzhinski advocated policies that the Council soon implemented. "We need," he said,

to send to that front—the most dangerous and cruel of fronts— determined, hard dedicated comrades ready to do anything in defense of the Revolution. Do not think that I seek forms of revolutionary justice; we are not now in need of justice. It is war now—face to face, a fight to the finish. Life or death! I propose, I demand an organ for the revolutionary settlement of accounts with the counter-revolutionaries. And we must act not tomorrow, but today, now . . .⁹

The resulting embryonic organization, the Cheka, an "organ for the settlement of revolutionary accounts," was in every way a creature of expedience. The Cheka's heritage in the provisional MRC is unmistakable: six members of the MRC's "liquidation commission" were on the ten-member Vecheka Collegium. Under Dzerzhinski, a fanatic of Cromwellian intensity, the Cheka became the embodiment of what Lenin referred to as "revolutionary consciousness." Idealistic and in his personal life puritanical, Dzerzhinski harbored a ferocious hatred for all party enemies; as chairman of the central administrative bureaucracy of the Cheka (the Vecheka), his impact on the organization was enormous.

Originally conceived as an investigative commission (one of a number) that would hand evildoers over to the Revolutionary Tribunals, the Cheka rapidly acquired the right to hold secret trials by troika (three-judge panels) and to arrest, fine, incarcerate, and execute. Summary execution was a primary responsibility. By the summer of 1918 the Cheka routinely carried out mass reprisals (the White Russians were no less murderous), and since terror was now an official party policy these activities were widely advertised. *Isvestia* frequently carried detailed reports of Cheka activities, and the aptly-titled Cheka periodical, *Krasny Terror* (Red Terror), regularly vilified class enemies and advocated their liquidation.¹⁰ As an agency of reprisal, the Cheka relied upon the principle of "class morality," and opponents to the regime were defined by class origins, professions, and education as well as by actual misdeeds.

Organized into regional chekas, the number of political police exceeded one hundred thousand by 1921. An early organizational innovation was the establishment of Cheka troops; these soon developed into heavily armed, battalion-sized units that were self-contained and mobile. By March of 1919 the Cheka military corps numbered thirty thousand, and it served at the front with the Red Army and against internal insurrections.

Much of the linchpin function of the Cheka derived from its hostage policy, which guaranteed the reliability of key personnel. Misbehavior could (and often did) lead to the execution of one's family at the hands of the Cheka. This tactic was especially important in ensuring the dependability of the Red Army, which under Trotsky's reorganization relied heavily on former tsarist officers and NCOs.

The Cheka was popularly perceived to be, and indeed had become, an oprichnina—a terrorist government within a government.[11] By the latter part of 1921, the unpopularity of the Cheka became burdensome to the central government and in February of 1922 it was officially abolished.[12] In fact, the personnel, the organizational structure, and most of the functions of the Cheka were taken over by its successor organization, the State Political Administration (Russian initials, GPU). Ostensibly, the GPU was now integrated with the sprawling Commissariat for Internal Affairs—the NKVD—but in actual practice it answered directly to the Politburo of the Communist party. Feliks Dzerzhinski retained his former position and maintained a close association with Lenin.

At the beginning of the New Economic Policy there was a fleeting attempt at restricting the power of the political police. However, as early as March of 1922, Lenin was complaining of the untimely reorganization of the Cheka. By August of 1922, many of the extra-judicial powers enjoyed by the Cheka were granted the GPU.

THE OGPU

The ratification of the Constitution of the USSR in January of 1924 put an end to the fiction that the political police were an integral part of the NKVD. The GPU was lofted to the status of a separate commissariat and renamed the Unified State Political Administration—the OGPU. In the end result, the Soviet political police, which began as a creature of the Civil War, was "enshrined in the constitution."[13] By law its authority permeated every aspect of Soviet society, and any pretense that it was a provisional institution was completely abandoned. The mission of the OGPU is expressly stated in Article 61 of the Soviet Constitution: "To unite revolutionary efforts of the Union Republics in the struggle against political and economic counterrevolution, espionage and banditism."[14]

The OGPU period of Soviet political police history (1924–34) represents a period of consolidation. Under the New Economic Policy the political police focused their efforts on controlling those social elements that most preoccupied the leadership of the party, such as religious groups, individuals with the wrong ethnic profile, and, above all, those connected in any manner with the Trotsky "opposition."[15] During the collectivization and industrialization drive under Stalin, the OGPU was the final and most reliable agent of repression and control. The dictatorship (Stalin) came to depend on it more and more; as it did so, the status and privileges of OGPU officials and operatives increased in measure.[16] The OGPU came to be a privileged elite and has been compared to the Prussian officer corps.[17] The military forces under its control were given preferential access to equipment, training, and personnel, and their numbers increased substantially.

THAT "HUGE PILE"

By 1921 party membership had increased to roughly half a million, but the party remained an urban apparatus; its control over Russia's vast and restless peasantry was, therefore, fragile. It was virtually an army of occupation (Fainsod's characterization), and a relatively small one at that, whose leadership faced the frustrations of trying to exert their will through the agency of an inefficient, corrupt, and increasingly ponderous bureaucracy—that "colossal ballast" Bukharin once called it. At the Eleventh Party Congress (March 1922), Lenin observed:

> Suppose we take Moscow with its 4,700 responsible Communists, and suppose we take that huge bureaucratic machine, that huge pile–who is directing whom? I doubt very much whether it can be truthfully said that the Communists are directing this pile. To tell the truth, they are not doing the directing, they are being directed.[18]

Although candid, Lenin's comments do not tell half the story. In fact, the party center could control its regional organization with only the greatest difficulty. Unwelcome directives from the central party hierarchy were often simply ignored. Factionalism and localism flourished. Party membership had grown like topsy during the Civil War and was cluttered with corrupt and inefficient opportunists. But identifying such people, however numerous, was a problem since party membership records were so chaotic that the central hierarchy had only the sketchiest notion of who comprised its membership at the local level. In other words, the bureaucracy within the bureaucracy was also beyond effective control.

Two long-term remedies were applied to the problem of bureaucratic inertia. First, the use of political police surveillance and intimidation was increasingly perceived as the path to administrative efficiency. "Threaten to shoot the idiot who is in charge of telecommunications," an aroused Lenin once advised.[19] On Lenin's principle that the "Cheka must become an instrument of discipline," especially urgent tasks were placed under the aegis of the political police. Dzerzhinsky at various times headed commissions overseeing rail transport, aid to homeless children (a monumental problem in the years after the Civil War), the Soviet film industry, and, briefly, the Extraordinary Commission for the Struggle Against Snowdrifts.[20] In 1924 Dzerzhinsky became chairman of the Supreme Economic Council, and thereafter the institution of the political police was intertwined with Soviet industry. Predictably, the political police fostered and maintained a comprehensive system of informants, and OGPU agents were routinely slotted into administrative offices.

Second, the party resorted to a policy of periodically purging its membership of undesirables. As early as May of 1918, the Central Committee decreed that the party would shed itself of "idlers, hooligans, adventurers and thieves."[21] Foreshadowing a surprisingly durable pattern, this edict produced very little response from the regional party structure (practically none, in fact), and the following year another purge was ordered. By the end of the Civil War the problem had grown so acute that the party, with great urgency, introduced another purge, and within months 25 percent of its membership had been expelled. Judging from the Smolensk archives, most of those expelled were expelled for cause—that is, any administrative apparatus would have been well rid of such people. Others, of course, succumbed to faulty class origins.

MEMBERSHIP PURGES

Two purge strategies—the chistka, a "comb out" or "cleaning" of membership, and the proverka, a verification of membership—were regularly employed to cope with the fact that (1) the party was "cluttered" with undesirable people, and (2) the party did not know, even as late as the 1930s just who was in the party.[22]

From 1919 until 1936 (when the central party finally resorted to calling in all cards and reissuing them), any membership drive would be followed by either a proverka or a chistka. Each successive effort proved to be a source of dismay and frustration to the party leadership. Taking the 1929 chistka as a typical example, character defects, criminal offenses, violations of party discipline, and "passivity" (nonparticipation in party activities or ideological ignorance) account for 61 percent of those expelled. The Smolensk archives[23] indicate that drunkenness, evidently chronic, figured in no less than 37 percent of the expulsions. Nationally, only 19 percent were expelled for class background or connections with the opposition. Twenty-two percent were expelled for "other" reasons. Among the rank and file, there was a disturbing level of total ideological ignorance. Even in the realm of platitudes, some of the membership could not separate Marxism from capitalism, and the party, quite naturally, insisted on the ability to make that distinction.[24]

Party records provide a classic example of bureaucratic chaos. Spot checks of cards revealed that a near majority were in some way faulty–cards that were altered or forged or did not belong to the presenting person. Cards were often stolen, and it was discovered that during membership drives some party offices simply handed out blank cards to all comers. Registry checks also disclosed large numbers (more than fifty-five thousand in 1934) of "dead souls"—people officially on the party rolls who could not be found because they had evidently died, moved away, or assumed a new identity. For whatever reason, the party could not find them.

Turnover was high. In addition to the normal organizational attrition resulting from death and disenchantment, five of the twelve purges conducted from 1919 to 1936 pruned more than 10 percent of the party membership (the chistkas of 1921 and 1933 expelled 25 percent and 18.5 percent respectively). In every instance, ideological expulsions were the minority, and it is obvious that an unavoidable consequence of the party's periodic membership drives was a sizable influx of exactly the sort of "ballast" that the Central Committee had been trying to eject as early as 1918.[25]

Nothing indicates that this almost continual cleansing in any way diminished the disorder within the party ranks. It was, instead, a holding operation, an attempt to maintain at least minimal standards. As late as 1935, N. I. Ezhov, then in charge of the verification of documents of that year, was forced to admit to the Central Committee: "We are currently beginning only now to find out the composition of the leading party workers in the *oblasts* and *raions* (regions and districts)."[26]

Even under the hard-driving Ezhov, who was soon to direct the political police, the proverka of 1935 provided party leaders with an epic of regional bureaucratic sulkiness and ineptitude; and to Stalin's fury, a project that should have taken three months dragged on for ten months only to be canceled before it was completed. Unsurprisingly, "fulfillment of decisions" came to be a preoccupation of the party leadership.[27]

The NEP

The New Economic Policy introduced by Lenin at the Tenth Party Congress in 1921 amounted to a partial return to a market economy and was accepted as a necessary ideological retreat. By the spring of 1921 the Civil War was over, but three years of War Communism had virtually destroyed the economy and infuriated the peasantry. Drought and then famine soon added to the country's desolation.

At the core of the NEP was a new agricultural policy. The hated and much-abused food levy was replaced by a graduated tax in kind (a percentage of the harvest) geared to fall heavily on the Kulaks—the most prosperous peasants, who were the most likely, in the party's calculation, to be withholding grain. Peasants were assured tenure over their land and were allowed to dispose of any surplus on the market. Agricultural productivity soon rose. Within the urban industrial base, the party retained the "commanding heights" of finance, transport, foreign trade, and heavy industry; and during all of the NEP, most industrial workers were employed by the state.[28] Small industry, under private ownership or leased from the state, was encouraged and soon prospered.

With the implementation of the several policies that made up the NEP, the Soviet economy rapidly recovered and began to approach the productivity levels of 1913. In the words of E. H. Carr, the NEP threatened to "overwhelm its creators."[29] Legalizing private trade brought Russia's vast black market economy into the open, and the NEP-man, equally adept at manipulating the market and state agencies, became a ubiquitous feature of Soviet urban life. "The exchange of goods broke loose," bemoaned Lenin. "It broke loose in the sense that it turned into buying and selling."[30]

In the countryside the Kulaks (Russian for "fist," read "tight-fisted") and the clergy, both fundamental class enemies, began to reassert their former position of social leadership. The peasantry as a whole demonstrated little interest in collectivization, and their celebrated reproductive efficiency showed every sign of swamping the efforts of the minority urban proletariat. Realizing that it must temporarily suffer these economic and ideological peccadillos, the party hierarchy gritted its teeth and focused its attention on solidifying its administrative apparatus and expanding its political influence over the countryside.

THE FIRST FIVE-YEAR PLAN

The first Five-Year Plan, beginning in 1928, is a watershed in Soviet history. Stalin proposed that the USSR, an undeveloped country with a literacy rate of only about 30 percent (roughly that of revolutionary France), propel itself into the industrial age in five years time. In this ambition Stalin was relentless, and at great cost he was successful. Raisanovsky defines 1928 and 1929 as the true revolutionary years in Russia.[31] Heavy industry was emphasized, and wildly unrealistic goals were established. Steel production was to increase from 4 million tons to 10.4 million, coal from 35 million tons to 75 million, chemical fertilizer from 175,000 tons to 8 million tons, and electricity from 500 million kilowatt hours to 22 billion! And so forth. The actual achievements, although far short of these goals, were nevertheless remarkable and could be accomplished only by organizing the industrial work force along pharaonic lines under the watchful OGPU. All the same, it would be idle to entirely discount Soviet claims of a "veritable upsurge of labor enthusiasm." The excitement of participating in great events and the willing sacrifice of many urban workers, especially the young, was often genuine.[32]

Soviet leaders imposed a nearly wartime reality complete with iron and coal "fronts" and "shock brigades" of workers. It was also at this time that Soviet factory managers emphasized the virtues of piece work. In Stalin's design, the agricultural base was to support this expansion, and by the hardest of measures it did. Collectivization was the key. It was assumed to be more efficient and would therefore ensure the investment capital to support the increase in Russia's industrial plants. It was ideologically pure in that by gathering the peasants into state farms (literally agricultural factories in which the workers are paid directly by the state) and collective farms (cooperatives), the peasantry could be transformed into something like a haystack proletariat—more like workers than peasants. Finally, and most important, placing the peasant on state farms and collectives had the undeniable political advantage of rendering them more controllable.[33]

The Smolensk archives make it clear just how feeble the party was in the countryside. In 1930 only 12 percent of the 6,500,000 people of the western region—the territory covered by the archives—resided in urban areas. Total party membership for the region, including candidate members, was 45,610, of which only 32 percent were peasants, indicating that the rural party apparatus within the western region consisted of roughly 14,000 members. Most, but probably not all, of these people lived among 5,500,000 peasants. Their influence cannot have been great.[34] The achives also suggest that rural party members were less than fanatical communists. The tugs of kinship and village, as well as the opportunities of power, often overrode party loyalty. Many rural Communist officials hobnobbed with the hated Kulaks and with the clergy. OGPU records routinely complain of bribery, of favoritism to relatives and friends, and, in one instance, of an important official who drank openly with members of the local banditry—evidently his former companions.[35]

The First Five-Year Plan (October 1928 to December 1932) was a party crusade. It was also an urban invasion. Initially, upwards of a quarter of a million factory workers and party officials were dispatched into the countryside to advise, badger, and bully the peasants into collectivization. Army units and OGPU troops backed up the effort. A corps of twenty-five thousand plus urban zealots (the "Twenty-Five Thousanders"), many of them party members, were selected from some seventy thousand applicants, provided with two weeks of training, and parcelled out to collective farms to provide proletarian inspiration.[36]

Machine-tractor stations (MTS)—centralized depots of agricultural machinery—soon began to ideologically garrison the countryside and played a key role in the collectivization drive. The *History of the Communist Party of the Soviet Union* (1950) emphasized the largely unfulfilled hope that the peasants could be proselytized through these institutions.

The peasant masses definitely began to turn to collective farming. In this a great part was played by the state farms and the machine and tractor stations. The peasants would come in crowds to the state farms and machine and tractor stations to watch the operation of the tractors and other agricultural machines, admire their performance and then and there resolve: "Let's join the collective farm."[37]

The MTS political section was staffed by selected party workers and was charged with the political reorganization of the peasantry. The head of the political section was often coequal with the MTS director and in no way subordinate in political matters. He answered only to the Commissariat of Agriculture and would often report unfavorably on the activities of the MTS director. By design and in practice, the MTS political sections bypassed the regional party apparatus, which was regarded as untrustworthy or, at best, weak. All MTS political sections contained a "deputy for special work" who was an OGPU agent.[38]

Officially the collectivization drive was an instantaneous success. In reality, it was an economic catastrophe, and for the peasant it was an agony that soon had all the earmarks of War Communism. Stalin always clung to the belief that the Kulaks were hoarding unlimited amounts of grain. Confiscation, therefore, became utterly rapacious, and only those peasants who had voluntarily joined a collective were spared. As the number of collectives increased, so did the size of the levy against them. The peasants resisted as they had before. Planting was limited, and rather than see their animals confiscated, the peasants ate them. Once again, organized violence became commonplace: there were two hundred guerrilla groups in the Moscow region alone.[39] Russian peasant women especially loathed collectivization and often fiercely defended their animals, upon which the welfare of their children depended. Robert Conquest cites a typical Soviet press report: ". . . A great crowd of women came, armed with clubs and other things, and began demanding that the horses be returned. They also tried to beat up representatives of the District Executive Committee and the District Party Committee. . . ." This pattern of resistance was so consistent that Soviet historians have coined the term "Womens' Rebellions" (Babsky Bunty).[40]

In the end, the peasantry was dragooned onto collective farms, and all organized resistance was ferreted out and crushed by the OGPU. This time the Kulaks were destroyed. The class enemy was subdivided into three groups, according to the danger each supposedly represented to the state, and assigned a corresponding fate: *Active Counter-revolutionaries*—heads of families to suffer the "highest measure of punishment" and families to be exiled to "distant regions"; *Counter-revolutionary Elements*—confiscation of property and resettlement out of the region; and a third, presumably residual category, to be relocated within the district on marginal land.[41]

Careful calculation on the part of the central party apparatus established set quotas for each Kulak category. Invariably, in actual practice, these quotas were exceeded. The Smolensk archives reveal that "dekulakization brigades," which in organization, personnel, and tendency to brigandage were reminiscent of the food detachments of the Civil War, often engaged in activities that can be best described as search and destroy missions.[42]

All evidence points to a bureaucracy run amok. The *History of the Communist Party* admits to "excessive zeal" by the party apparatus of the Moscow region and elsewhere but makes no mention of the western region covered by the Smolensk archives, which is replete with horror stories.[43] By all indications, "excessive zeal" was standard. In some regions, collectivization goals that were to be achieved in four years were attempted in one. Stalin's article "Dizzy with Success" (printed in March of 1930) chastised those party officials who had been carried away by the "success" of collectivization.

"Dekulakization" removed from the best agricultural land precisely those peasants who were the most productive. Soviet sources, which can be taken as exceedingly conservative, indicate that three hundred thousand Kulak families were exiled. Lacking in motivation, organizational skill, and equipment, the peasants confined to collective farms produced little. Nevertheless, even as agricultural production dropped, agricultural exports were increased to support Russia's burgeoning industrial plant. An entirely man-made famine fell upon the Ukraine, one of the world's richest grain-producing regions, taking the lives of four million people.[44] Stalin persisted.

By the end of the First Five-Year Plan, 71 percent of all peasant households and 87 percent of the arable land was collectivized.[45]

PROLETARIAN CATEGORIES OF DEVIANCE

During the period of the five-year plans, Soviet manufacture of deviance showed an astonishing ability to keep pace with the changing times. A peasant could be a Kulak for objective reasons—controlling too much land, owning too much live-stock, and hiring labor—but often it was the act of offering resistance to collectivization that brought the tag Kulak. It was here that the new and infinitely expandable category of "subk-ulak" or "subsidiary kulak" (podkulachniki) was so useful.[46] A peasant who hired no one, who controlled little land, and who owned no livestock is not easily defined as an exploiter of his fellow peasants—as a Kulak—but virtually anyone who had the economic wherewithall to survive could be labeled a subkulak. The sin lay in the peasant's attitude; ideological Ku-laks abounded during the First Five-Year Plan.[47]

Soviet planners hoped to drive a wedge between the Kulak and the middle peasant[48]—something that Lenin had tried to do during the period of War Communism. This time they were successful in that peasants who resisted collectivization were redefined as Kulaks and suffered the standard fate, and those who accepted the inevitable became enlightened collective farm-ers. This process did not escape local observers. The OGPU reports in the Smolensk archives present us with this perceptive comment by a state bookkeeper:

> Even if they take away all the Kulaks, and there are no more to be taken, there will soon be new Kulaks. It seems that there will have to be new Kulaks until the time when everybody will be herded into Kolkhozes (collective farms).[49]

On the industrial front a new category of deviant emerged, that of "wreckers." Rapid industrialization and centralized con-trol, in combination with a dearth of managerial skills, brought about an astonishing amount of chaos and inefficiency. The record is full of delays, snafus, impossibly poor products, and major accidents. Expensive equipment was repeatedly allowed to rust for months in the open, delicate machine tools were set up on unleveled floors, and so forth. "Wrecking" was the universal explanation for such ocurrences.

Factory managers attempting to meet impossible quotas re-sorted to all manner of expedients. Bribes were offered to obtain necessary raw materials or to lure skilled personnel from other factories. Skilled people with nebulous (i.e., probably class en-emy) backgrounds were hired with no questions asked. Such activities were routine. Indeed, industrial managers were some-times more like freebooters than bureaucrats and were not above "commandeering" (hijacking) necessary supplies.[50] All this rendered the industrial expansion even more chaotic and when revealed to party officials, became further evidence of wrecking. Attempting to set realistic production goals was defined as "limiting."

The campaign against wrecking organizations was coterminous with the period of industrial expansion and gave rise to a new form of political theater, the "show trial." The first of these stemmed from the Shakhty case, which resulted from a series of problems experienced in the coal mines of the Shakhty region in the Donets basin. Flooding and breakdown of new machinery that had been ordered from abroad without spare parts curtailed production. Wrecking was of course suspected, and in due time an organization of fifty-three wreckers in the employ of capitalistic elements was revealed to be the source of this long string of misfortunes.

All of the features of the show trials of the purge of 1936 to 1938 appear embryonically in the trial of the Shakhty wrecking organization. Entirely an OGPU production, the trial, held in Moscow, was given enormous publicity in a press campaign that urged "Death to the Wreckers," and the evidence consisted entirely of rehearsed confessions. Andrei Vyshinsky, soon to be the procurator-general of the USSR, presided over the trial and ensured its outcome.[51] The Shakhty trial, all the same, was a pioneering attempt and not an entire success in that not all of the defendants confessed. This problem would not recur at subsequent show trials.

Wrecking organizations were soon discovered, as Stalin had predicted, in all key industries as well as on the collective farms.[52] These phantom conspiracies took on vast and improbable dimensions. At the second full-fledged show trial, that of the "Industrial party," a wrecking organization of some two thousand was alleged to exist. Its eight leaders were accused of carrying out the orders of the president of France, a Dutch oil magnate, and Lawrence of Arabia.[53] Wreckers were perceived to be everywhere and required the utmost vigilance to detect. "A real wrecker," observed Stalin, "will from time to time do good work, because it is the only way for him to gain confidence and to continue wrecking."[54]

Wreckers in Soviet society were in time counterbalanced by exemplars of virtue produced by the Stakhanov movement, named after Alexei Stakhanov, a coal miner who in a single day produced a heroic 102 tons of coal (fourteen times the established output). Rate-busting soon became an organizational fetish and all other major industries quickly and necessarily produced their own Stakhanov. Such hagiography was highly contrived and was intended to justify an increase in production norms. Proletarian production saints were given preferential treatment, glorified in the press, and were perhaps modestly inspirational. *The History of the CPSU* (1950) tells us that Stakhanov's example produced a mass movement of workers bent on raising standards of output but fails to mention that Stakhanovites were often attacked by their fellow workers.[55]

THE NKVD

In 1934 the OGPU was formally merged with the Peoples' Commissariat of Internal Affairs (the NKVD), which had long been responsible for routine police duties. The new head of the NKVD, Genrikh Yagoda, was an experienced Chekist who had presided over the expansion of the OGPU's Main Administration of Corrective Camps (GULAG)—a by-product of the First Five-Year Plan. It would be accurate to say that under Yagoda the political police engulfed the NKVD. The new-model NKVD incorporated all of the enormous political police apparatus of the old OGPU and retained its control over the fire brigades, ordinary police, and forced labor camps.[56] The reorganized NKVD, the "unsheathed sword of the revolution," is described by Adam Ulam as having the combined powers of the ordinary police, the FBI, IRS, and the Holy Inquisition.[57] This characterization, if anything, understates its comprehensive powers. By the beginning of 1935, the NKVD was entirely impregnable to all efforts at outside control, save those coming directly from Stalin; and Stalin, for his part, receded deep within the protective envelope of a massive personal security apparatus.[58]

THE ASSASSINATION OF KIROV

On the face of things, the statute authorizing the reorganization of the NKVD seemed to limit the arbitrary authority of the political police. If such was actually the intention of the party hierarchy, events would intervene: in December 1934, the popular Sergi Kirov, a member of the Politburo and head of the party organization in Leningrad, was assassinated. Stalin reacted savagely; the assassin, who was personally interrogated by Stalin, and thirteen others who had been tenuously implicated in the crime were tried and immediately shot. More than one hundred people already in jail for "counterrevolutionary activity" were also executed. In the spring of 1935, thousands of Leningraders suspected of "oppositionist sentiments" were dispatched to workcamps. This development was accompanied by repeated calls for vigilance and, in a letter from the Central Committee, by an out-an-out declaration of war against all "Oppositionists." Anyone with even the remotest connection with Trotsky, who was by now a satanic figure in the mind of Stalin, was numbered among the oppositionists.[59]

It was during this period that Stalin first demonstrated his willingness to move against the "Old Bolsheviks," who had until that point been relatively immune to criminal accusations. In January of 1935, G. E. Zinoviev and L. B. Kamenev, both formerly members of the Politburo, were brought to trial along with seventeen associates. The principal defendants accepted "moral responsibility" for the Kirov murder, finally agreeing that their political attitudes had no doubt contributed to the criminal degeneration of Kirov's assassins.[60] In sharp contrast to the Purge years, little publicity was accorded these proceedings, and the sentences handed out were ridiculously light—five to ten years. Both men were retried in 1936 in the first of the Great Show Trials and executed.

THE PURGE YEARS

The Great Purge began in the spring of 1936 and was over by the early months of 1939. Bringing the greatest destruction to the party hierarchy, the purge reached out to include (certainly) hundreds of thousands (and, by many accounts, millions) of people—people who learned only as they disappeared into the labyrinthian network of NKVD prisons and camps that they were members of a Trotskyite conspiracy. Many, possibly most, Soviet citizens were directly and profoundly affected by the purge, suffering the loss of friends or relatives. Everyone in Soviet Russia was at least indirectly affected.

Victims of the Great Purge were arrested on a variety of standard charges, including being a member of the right or left opposion, wrecking, and being an agent of a foreign power. Very often an individual would be comprehensively charged with being an "enemy of the people," a very broad and therefore bureaucratically useful concept originated by Stalin.[61] Typically these various sins were linked in some unlikely manner to the archvillain Trotsky.

The Great Show Trials were the iceberg and public tip of the Great Purge. They justified—provided a "reason"–for the increasingly ferocious pace of political police arrests in a series of performances that many Russians (and many foreign observers) accepted as reality. All three show trials—of the Trotskyite-Zinovievite Terrorist Center (August 1936), of the Anti-Soviet Trotskyite Center (January 1937), and of the Anti-Soviet Bloc of Rights and Trotskyites (March 1938)—carried exactly the same message: "We have internal enemies," and they were in every way the proletarian equivalent of an auto da fé. Held in the ornate ballrooms of what in tsarist times had been the Nobles Club and was now the Trade Union House, the show trials represent the final perfection of the art of judicial theater. The audience was limited to about two hundred selected spectators, including some thirty foreign journalists, and the performance was placed in the responsibility of two men with long experience in this realm, V. V. Ulrikh, who presided, and Andrei Vyshinsky, procurator-general, a man who literally believed that the fundamental purpose of a trial was political education. Overall control was in the hands of the NKVD, which left nothing to chance. Interrogations were, among other things, rehearsals; the defendants were not only told what to confess, they were provided scripts. Prolonged and brutal interrogation accompanied by threats to family satisfactorily explains why the defendants faithfully played their roles. Death was the usual sentence.[62]

Since the verdicts were predetermined, the purpose of the show trials was entirely educational and largely successful. Everything—the collectivization calamity, the industrial failures, the shortages, the murder of Kirov—was explained by the performances given by the accused. The confessions of the old guard Bolsheviks allowed the public to "see" the evil that Soviet society was facing.[63] The emerging social reality was of an insidious, hostile world

of long-drawn-out conspiratorial cold war for the purpose of destroying the Soviet State and the Revolution it embodies. It is a world dominated by the machinations of external and especially internal "enemies" who are diabolically cunning as well as totally vicious and evil. . . . Abroad . . . their chief arm is the secretly functioning intelligence services of the major powers. But inside the Soviet Union they do all their nefarious work by stealth and devious means, practicing deception as their primary technique of political warfare. They wear "masks" of loyal citizens and prominent party and governmental leaders until they are finally exposed as persons who, in the words of Vyshinky's summing up speech in the Bukharian trial, "spent the whole of their lives behind masks. . . ."[64]

Wrecking at the highest level and in ingenious forms was the principal accusation (the plot) in all of the show trials and served to explain the multifaceted economic misfortunes of the five-year plans. The defendants confessed to inspiring peasant uprisings and undermining Soviet industry, finance, distribution, and agriculture. In short, they confessed to attempting to wreck everything. Specific wrecking tactics included, among many other activities, upsetting the order of crop rotation on collective farms, raising anemic horses in Byelorussia, infecting pigs and cattle with diseases (i.e., in a "wrecking" manner), shipping too much coal to one generating plant and not enough to another, selling timber too cheaply, and seeing to it that Soviet citizens "encountered endless unpleasantness, insolence, rudeness and lack of attention" at savings banks.[65]

The morning-long confession of Isaak Zelensky, who from 1931 to 1937 was the Chairman of Consumer Cooperatives and subsequently one of the Anti-Soviet Bloc of Rights and Trotskyites, is typical.[66] Asked by the president if he wishes to confirm the testimony he gave at his preliminary investigation, Zelensky answers that he does and requests permission "to recount the incriminating episodes of my treacherous and criminal activity as a member of the counter-revolutionary traitorous bloc of Rights and Trotskyites whose aim it was to restore capitalism in the Land of the Soviets."

He is allowed to do so. In addition to disrupting the collectivization process, Zelensky enthusiastically confesses to systematically interrupting the supply of bread, sugar, and salt to Soviet shops in order to "provoke discontent against the government." Having seen that established, the procurator-general passes on to another commodity.

Vyshinsky. And how did matters stand with butter?

After some confusion, Zelensky admits that people within his organization of wreckers "threw" nails and glass into shipments of butter. And then Vyshinsky goes on to discuss eggs.

Vyshinsky. Was there a case in 1936 when Moscow was left without eggs through your fault?

Zelensky. There was.

More prompting.

Zelensky. In 1936 fifty carloads of eggs were allowed to spoil from wrecking motives.

Zelensky's confession then begins to run ahead of Vyshinsky's interrogation.

Zelensky. I consider overcharging, short measure and short weight to be wrecking in no less degree.

Vyshinsky can only agree. In the ensuing monologue Zelensky confesses to defrauding Soviet citizens in thirteen thousand shops in order "to arouse discontent among the population" and then goes on to describe his method of "freezing trade" through an organizational policy of deliberately dispatching the wrong goods to the wrong districts at the wrong time.

Vyshinsky. That is, the public was offered felt boots in the summer and summer shoes in the winter.

Zelensky. Yes.

Zelensky next describes his highly effective method of encouraging embezzlement and theft and then provides specifics on the vast extent of his wrecking organization. He identifies his confederates, metaphorically including among them "interdepartmental friction" and "bureaucratic red tape."

Many of Zelensky's theatrical sins have been omitted in this recounting but his entire performance is easily summarized: Zelensky confessed to causing mischief in every area of Soviet society where it would have been humanly possible for him to do so. This was the norm. Zelensky was executed.

Using a logic that would have been entirely accessible to Stalin, Vyshinsky, in his summation, argued that the existence of shortages proves the guilt of the Old Bolshevik wreckers.

> In our country, rich in resources of all kinds, there could not have been and cannot be a situation in which a shortage of any product should exist. . . . It is now clear why there are interruptions of supplies here and there, why, with our riches and abundance of products, there is a shortage first of one thing, then of another. It is these traitors who are responsible for it.[67]

The objective reality was that from the early part of 1936 until the end of 1938, the NKVD behaved as though the Soviet Union was confronted with a gigantic internal conspiracy. In cruder form, and with much swifter results, the purge operated at every level within Soviet society: in very large numbers, people were denounced, arrested, forced into implausible confessions, and then either sent to the camps or executed. Usually this took only a matter of weeks.

THE EZHOVSHCHINA

In late September of 1936, Stalin indicated to other Politburo members that Yagoda was "unequal to the task of exposing the Trotskyite-Zenoviet Bloc."[68] Yagoda was removed and briefly took the position of commissar of communications; shortly thereafter he was arrested and would appear as a member of the Anti-Soviet Bloc of Rights and Trotskyites charged with organizing a series of "medical murders" (a theme that would crop up again in the 1950s when Stalin was in his dotage).

The new head of the NKVD, N. I. Ezhov, owed much to Stalin and was not a Chekist except by inclination. Ezhov joined the party prior to the October Revolution and served as a Red Army officer during the Civil War. There is a record of Ezhov's brief suspension for "excessive" brutality while working as a local party secretary—a rare occurrence. Ezhov joined the staff of the Central Committee in 1927 and after service as a dekulakization specialist became the director of the Central Committees Cadres Department, which supplied dedicated proletarians to the industrialization and collectivization fronts. In 1935, he became the head of the Party Control Commission (KPK) and with much publicity waged war against economic corruption and mismanagement, a duty that was carried on simultaneously with his administration of the verification of party membership documents.[69] Thus, Ezhov emerges from sparse biographical data fundamentally as a personnel specialist, and as such, he was a dedicated enemy of bureaucratization, corruption, and bourgeois specialists. He does not seem to have been intelligent. He was a fanatic. While head of the KPK, Ezhov's cadres of inspectors imperiously scrutinized all aspects of the Soviet's economy and provoked howls of indignation from harassed party leaders and factory managers.[70]

Ezhov brought many of his Central Committee entourage to the NKVD, and a more or less equivalent number of Yagoda's men were fired and subsequently arrested. The consequences of putting a dull-witted zealot in charge of the NKVD should have been obvious to everyone and cannot have escaped Stalin: every aspect of Soviet society was now exposed to Ezhov's baleful eye. Under Ezhov's demanding guidance, the purge process soon snowballed, and his tenure as the head of the political police is remembered as the Ezhovshchina—"the time of Ezhov."

By the latter part of 1937, physical coercion was standard. This materially cut down on the processing time since interrogation simply took the form of beating a confession out of a prisoner. Always there was the standard inquisitorial preoccupation with "naming names," which, coupled with the practice of issuing quotas of "enemies of the people," ensured an almost geometric increase in the number of deviants produced. Conquest writes:

> The snowball system had reached a stage where half of the urban population were down on NKVD lists. They could not all be arrested and there was no particular reason to take one rather than another. . . . The first substantial question an interrogator asked was "Who are your accomplices?" So, from each arrest several other arrests more or less automatically followed.[71]

The overall cost in lives is hard to gauge; estimates of the number of executions range from the tens of thousands to the millions. It is, however, possible to greatly narrow this bracket. Available data suggests that most of those swept up by the purge were males between the age of thirty-five to fifty and that most lived in urban areas. This dramatically restricts the size of the population that was at risk. Relying on a study of the age cohort born in 1906, Hough and Fainsod argue for an execution figure in the "low hundreds of thousands," and Ulam suggests a figure of about 500,000 executed.[72] Other demographic studies (see Horowitze 1982, appendix I) have produced a figure of 4.4 million deaths (plus or minus 200,000) from all causes.[73]

The Smolensk archives provide some indication of what the purge was like at the local level. Anticipating, with little difficulty, the outcome of the trial of the Trotskyite-Zinoviet Terrorist Center, the Central Committee sent a top secret letter to all western region party committees explaining that such "monsters" still remained in the bosom of the party as a consequence of an "absence of Bolshevik vigilance." Advice on party morality then followed: "The inalienable quality of every Bolshevik under present conditions should be the ability to recognize an enemy of the party, no matter how well he may be masked."[74]

Party records document a storm of accusations within the local party apparatus. Evidence of internal enemies began to materialize throughout the region: in one district, for example, a portrait of Trotsky was discovered in the quarters of the collective farmer Afranasiya Uromova. . . . Uromova carries on subversive work and should be brought to trial; there has been an influx of outsiders attracted by the reduced level of Bolshevik vigilance within the region; there have been irregularities in railroad construction; the director of the Red Combine State Farm once gave a favorable description of Trotsky's character but has never publicly admitted his mistake—"now Lyustenberg is always silent and never speaks."[75]

There is a certain amount of pattern to be found within this whirlwind. "Arrest Chains" were a prominent feature of the Ezhovshchina and were a logical consequence of the bitter factionalism found at every level within the party. The purge provided a setting wherein ideological disputes and personal animosity could bring fatal results. Equally, there could be benefits. An ideological enemy or a superior could be removed through denunciation. The arrest and final destruction of the Old Bolsheviks, Kamenev, and Zinoviev signaled that everyone, except Stalin, was liable to this hazard. The fall of a central figure infallibly included his organizational allies and NKVD zeal ensured that all those in connection with even peripheral figures suffered the same fate. Very often this included family members for "lack of vigilance." Eventually, at some distance from the central figure, the linkages in this network weakened and the cycle of arrests came to a halt. In this manner, an entire stratum of Soviet society, the "Old Elite" was virtually swept away.[76]

The impact of the purge on the central party hierarchy was staggering. Of the 1,966 delegates to the seventeenth Party Congress in 1934, 1,108 were dead by the year's end in 1938—the vast majority evidently victims of the purge; similarly, 98 of the 139 members of the Central Committee had died. Eighty percent of the Council of People's Commissars was purged as was an even higher percentage of regional secretaries.[77] Stalin also paid attention to the military, the only organization that had any potential to oppose him. According to the tabulation provided by Medvedev, three of five marshalls, three of four first-rank army commanders, and sixty of sixty-seven corps commanders were purged.[78] Such attrition extended through all levels of the officers corps. Army commissars suffered comparably and ranking naval officers even worse—apparently, there were no Soviet admirals at the beginning of the Second World War.

The slaughter of regional party secretaries points to Stalin's preoccupation with "fulfillment of decisions" or, more accurately, the lack of it within the regional party apparatus. As with any political machine, the regional party apparatus had given itself over to patronage and had become thoroughly entrenched. Repeated attempts at reform from below had failed to dislodge it or to render it capable of efficiently carrying out central party directives. At some point during the latter part of 1937, Stalin seems to have decided that the regional party secretaries and their immediate cronies were beyond redemption.

Again the Smolensk archives illuminate this process. Within the western region, the cycle of accusations unleashed by the Ezhovshchina crept up the party hierarchy and soon involved the top leadership, including Ivan Rumyantsev, the first secretary. It may be that First Secretary Rumyantsev dominated the western region in too grand a fashion. He allowed factories to be named after him, and his picture was nearly as common in the region as those of the Bolshevik trinity. It was said that he scattered kopecks to the peasantry as he traveled the countryside, and there was talk of loose living. More concretely, he had installed his followers in important positions, and the region had performed poorly on the collectivization and industrialization fronts. He had, in short, left himself open to denunciation. All the same, Rumyantsev and those about him had shown a surprising ability to deflect such criticism and retain their power.

The immediate circumstances surrounding the downfall of Rumyantsev and his entourage involved Stalin's purge of Marshall Tukhachevsky and seven other prominent generals, among them the commander of the western military district, General Uborevich. Rumyantsev had worked closely with Uborevich and so fell with him. Denounced as spies and as members of the "Right-Trotsky Band of Enemies," Rumyantsev and his followers disappeared from view.

Rumyantsev's successor hailed from the Moscow party apparatus and fared better. He continued the purge of the local party leadership with enthusiasm and could soon report that about one thousand new people had been promoted to party positions.[79] It is reasonable to suggest that many others had departed the party roles to assume a new status provided by the NKVD.

The regional base of the Soviet Army provided a convenient link with the regional party structure, and with only minor variations the same scenario was played out in nearly all regions of the country. Getty describes:

> An important official arrived on the spot (L. M. Kaganovich in Smolensk, for example), convened an emergency meeting . . . and invited rank and file denunciation from the floor. This sanction from above unleased a torrent of abuse against the helpless Obkom [Regional] Commitee leaders who were removed from office on the spot and usually arrested in short order.[80]

The enhanced authority of the central party as a result of these maneuvers is documented by the change in the constituency of the Central Committee. In 1934, twenty-three members of the Central Committee were provincial party secretaries; in 1939, only nine were.[81]

The emphasis on the activities of the wreckers found in the show trials is reflected in the pattern of arrests found among the top party leadership. An inspection of the small sample of Old Bolsheviks for whom there are significant biographical data shows that of the seventy-six who were alive at the beginning of the purge, thirty-eight were executed. This is not by the standards of the time an unusually high rate of attrition for high party officials. But all in the sample whose principal responsibility lay in the area of economics (fourteen people) were swept up by the political police and perished.[82] Their value as scapegoats had placed an inescapable bounty on their heads.

It must also be appreciated that the NKVD was impregnable to all other Soviet institutions and was by every indication devoid of internal restraint. Indeed, the merest hint of diminished enthusiasm on the part of an NKVD officer would have ensured his arrest. The political police listened only to Stalin, and the single organization that could have exerted pressure against the NKVD (and Stalin) was the military. The political commissar system, which Stalin reinstated, effectively prevented that course of action, and the purge of the officer corps provided further insurance against this eventuality. There is, in any case, nothing to indicate that the military had any such designs: the charge that the ranking generals of the Red Army were in league with Germany was a fabrication.

Driven by the relentless Ezhov, the NKVD maintained its pace of arrests until the purge showed every sign of crippling the Soviet economy. By the latter part of 1937, the political police hit full stride. If the estimate of the processing time—the period from arrest to execution or incarceration in a labor camp, usually only a matter of weeks—is at all correct, then a sizable percentage, 5 to 15 percent, of the population would have been incarcerated had the Purge continued; and indeed, by some estimates the 5 percent figure had already been realized. It is certain that unknown tens of thousands were arrested simply on the basis of "objective characteristics" such as being a foreign-born Communist, having been abroad, having contacts with foreigners, and having been a Red partisan. Many arrests seem to have been motivated only by a desire to fulfill an established "target figure" specifying that so many hidden thousands of Trotskyites, wreckers, and enemies of the people lurked within this or that jurisdiction.[83]

The terror was widespread, savage, . . . and bungled. "The Unsheathed Sword of the Revolution" is not an apt description of the NKVD during the Ezhovshchina; it was more like a perversely animated bludgeon that could in time be expected to smash everything. All of the bureaucratic pathologies so characteristic of Soviet society during the twenties and thirties seem to have been magnified within the vast organization of the NKVD. At the very same time that Stalin was complaining publicly of the high-handed manner in which party members were being expelled, the NKVD was beating thousands of party members into giving confessions of the most fantastic nature. With much publicity people would be promoted to high position and then arrested; nor is there the slightest indication that any consideration was given to the economic cost of arresting key personnel. It seems quite certain that Stalin approved lists of ranking purge victims, but there is no reason to suppose that the quotas of "enemies of the people" to which local NKVD offices responded so slavishly orginated with Stalin. It is just as likely that they were established by Ezhov or, indeed, at a lower level.

A predictable and often effective survival tactic was to denounce everyone around you. During the Ezhovshchina a few individuals became reservoirs of denunciations that NKVD men, hard against a quota, presumably welcomed. There is also evidence that, once denounced, some would deliver themselves of accusations of the wildest nature in an effort to render the purge absurd and so bring it to a close.[84] Dully and mechanically, the NKVD acted upon such improbabilities.

At the same time, individuals sometimes escaped arrest by the simple device of going on vacation or relocating. J. Arch Getty, relying on primary sources, provides examples of the purge being "just local stuff."[85] Upon learning that he had been denounced to the NKVD, a Red Army colonel, then stationed in Minsk, boarded the train to Moscow, presented himself to the Main Personnel Administration of the Red Army and requested reassignment to "anywhere but Minsk." The request was granted, and he survived. Pavel Kuznetsov, a newspaper editor, learned of his denunciation and immediately moved to Kazakhstan. He managed to escape detection long enough to get his translations of "Odes to Father Ezhov" published in Pravda and so redemmed himself.

Towards the end, Stalin and his lieutenants became distressed by the administrative and economic cost of the purge. The comprehensive predations of the NKVD showed every potential of stripping the country of the talent that it required to maintain itself. In December of 1937, two of Ezhov's deputies were pulled out from under him and assigned to minor and materially dead-end positions. The following January, notes Getty, the Central Committee saw fit to chide ". . . certain careerist Communists who are striving to become prominent and to be promoted by recommending expulsions from the party." This sort of person, cautioned the committee, "indiscriminately spreads panic about enemies of the people [and] is willing to expel dozens of members from the party on false grounds just to appear vigilant himself."[86]

This should not be interpreted as a blunt attempt to shut

down the political police. The activities of the NKVD were not directly criticized, and the glorification of the NKVD in the press continued. Furthermore, the final and greatest of the show trials was not staged until march of 1938. Getty suggests that Stalin was not trying to halt the purge, but rather he was trying to render it less chaotic and more useful to his purposes. That is, Stalin wanted the NKVD to smash the bureaucracy, not everything.[87]

Peevish complaints on the part of the Central Committee, it seems, did not foster the desired level of precision within the NKVD operation, and, in any case, much of the damage had already been done. Brzezinsky lists some of the specific concerns that brought a halt to the purge.[88] He notes that loyalty to the regime had been reduced due, in no little part, to the general perception that the party was a tool of the political police. Probably of immediate concern, the industrial machine was slowing down due to a lack of trained personnel, and, at a time when the external situation was looking very dangerous, the military was becoming increasingly demoralized and incapacitated (as it was, the destruction of the officer corps nearly sealed the fate of the regime).

In May of 1938, Ezhov was appointed Commissar of Water Transport but retained his position as head of the NKVD. In July, Ezhov was provided with a new deputy, Lavrenti Beria, an important man who had performed yeoman service in the destruction of the regional secretaries, and Ezhov could not have failed to realize that Beria was likely to replace him. Working side by side, both men continued the purge into the latter part of 1938, focusing on ranking enemies of the people. During this uneasy transitional period, the NKVD began to slowly feed upon itself. NKVD interrogators were executed for extracting false confessions, which was, of course, their job, and the regional prosecutor of Omsk was tried and sentenced to prison for false arrests.[89]

Ezhov's fated downfall was not long in coming. On 8 December it was publicly announced that he had been relieved of his duties as head of the NKVD. Ezhov was seen in January of 1939 at a public ceremony and thereafter not at all. His name does not again appear in print during Stalin's lifetime.

In the days immediately following Ezhov's official departure from the NKVD, it was announced that the Moscow Regional Court had reversed the convictions of five engineers who, it seems, had actually been trying to block the activities of "real enemies."[90] Beria reinforced this change in policy when he released—surely with Stalin's permission—all those who had not yet signed confessions. Such people were allowed to return to their former positions. In the established pattern, Beria's people replaced those of his predecessor; this time, however, the turnover was wholesale and cut deeply into the ranks. Gulag residents knew that the purge had ended when their former captors began to join them in large numbers. Although arrests continued, the purge was essentially over by 1939.

Who Gained?

The literature abounds with elaborate attempts to identify the forces behind the Great Purge. It has been argued that because of the calamities associated with collectivization and industrialization, Stalin feared a coup at the hands of the party "golden boy," Sergi Kirov, secretary of the Central Committee and the head of the party organization in Leningrad.[91] For this reason, it is often suggested that Stalin was responsible for Kirov's assassination. Not everyone agrees, and given the available documentation, the truth cannot be established. The most reasonable view is that Stalin did not fear Kirov, had little to gain from having him murdered, and quite rightly feared the precedent of political assassination. Stalin is unlikely to have survived had this practice come into vogue.

George Kennan has reasoned that in part, the purge resulted from Stalin's desire to obtain a free hand for his foreign policy.[92] But then why did he decimate the military? It has also been argued that the Great Purge was prompted in part by the "growing generational problem" created when the graduates of the higher educational system began to flood an administrative and managerial apparatus already staffed by an older and less educated group.[93] Other explanatory notions, more inventive, insist that Stalin feared that his link with the Okhrana (the tsarist secret police) would be exposed and so destroyed all who had any recollection of this indiscretion; that Stalin was certifiably paranoid, and the whole thing, from beginning to end, was a complicated plot; or that the Great Purge resulted, in the final analysis, from Stalin's "inordinate vanity and lust for power."[94] Some of these may provide partial explanation, some beg supporting data, and some are simply not open to falsification. In his classic treatment of Russian history, Raisanovsky simply

states that there "was madness in Stalin's method." This characterization is probably true.

The voluminous émigré literature and the writings of historians and political scientists generaly agree on a number of
essential points. We may, for instance, accept without serious
reservation the description of Stalin as a "sickly suspicious
man." Khrushchev in his speech before the Twentieth Congress,
states that

> Stalin was a very distrustful man, sickly suspicious; we know this
> from our work with him. . . . The sickly suspicion created in him
> a general distrust even toward eminent Party workers whom he
> had known for years. Everywhere and in everything he saw enemies,
> two-faces and spies.[95]

Others close to Stalin have described him in a similar fashion,
and we may suppose that such perceptions of the world were
not rare among ranking party members of this era. Stalin's savage
treatment of his political enemies and of the military hierarchy,
which he evidently distrusted, was a reflection of Stalin the
"sickly suspicious man." But that is as far as we can take this
line of speculation; Stalin functioned far too well to be a full-
fledged schizophrenic.

Also, it should not be supposed that the purge was universally
unpopular. Apart from the fact that many Soviet citizens had
taken the lesson of the show trials to heart, it is undeniable
that a new class of educated administrators benefitted directly
from the purge. The Great Purge had the effect (never mind
what it may have been intended to do) of clearing the decks
for the new educated elite. The turnover of upper-level administrators during this period was astonishing, and for all intents
and purposes, the political and administrative generation that
preceded the new elite was wiped out. The combined effect
of rapid industrialization and the Great Purge was a burgeoning
of opportunities for the new educated elite. In that sense, the
Great Purge had a "quasi-populist" aspect to it that tended to
tie those who were young, ambitious, and capable to the Stalinist
Regime.[96] For a great many who received their higher education
during the First Five-Year Plan and graduated between 1932
and 1936, the purge years brought lightning advancement.

> Generally those who were to prosper the most were first assigned
> to low-level posts in industry (foreman, shop head, or the like)

and enjoyed fairly rapid but orderly promotion in the period up to 1937. From 1937 to 1939, however, there was nothing orderly about most of the promotions. A young engineer in a major Leningrad artillery plant could travel to Moscow with the gloomy director of his plant and suddenly, totally unexpectedly, find himself named as the director's successor. A minor Central Committee functionary, who had finished graduate school in 1937, could be named first secretary of the Stalingrad regional party committee so suddenly in early 1938 that he did not have time to go home for a suitcase and had to phone his wife on the way to the station.[97]

Not only did the members of this group tend to prosper during the purge, they also displayed an astonishing immunity against its effects; they nearly all survived.[98] In sum, the numberless vacancies left in the wake of the Great Purge were also opportunities. Many profited. "They inherited the positions, apartments, possessions and sometimes the wives of the vanished. Generations built lives upon a holocaust."[99] Everything indicates that such fortunate people embraced the slaughterous regime that provided them with prosperity.

It should also be emphasized that Stalin's status at this time was "just short of technical deification," and that there can be little doubt that he both instigated and ensured the continuation of the purge.[100] But it does not follow that every facet of the purge was part of a comprehensive conspiratorial design. Getty argues that Stalin need only have intervened at three critical points to ensure that the purge would take its course—(1) 1936, when he brought Kamenev and Zinoviev to trial for a second time upon the strength of "new evidence obtained by the NKVD" in the Kirov investigation; (2) when he unleashed the fanatical Ezhov upon the nation; and (3) when he chose to continue the show trials.[101] Surely, the degree of Stalin's guidance over the purge was more extensive than that (Krushchev states that it was much more extensive); Getty's point is that it need not have been great to explain the whirlwind. Given the nature of Soviet bureaucracy, especially the NKVD, and the warlike atmosphere of the five-year plans, Soviet society lacked only a catalyst to produce a Great Purge. There can be no doubt that it suited Stalin's purposes to provide that ingredient.

The matter of Stalin's deification is compelling and has repeatedly fostered the argument that if Stalin's status was godlike, then his control over the bureaucracy must have been absolute.

Therefore, the purge could not have taken the form that it did except at his design. Such reasoning is false. History is full of deities who were unable to control the bureaucracies that supposedly served them. The plight of the later Roman emperors comes to mind, but the bureaucracy they wrestled with was in some respects more responsive, and certainly better educated, than the Soviet bureaucracy of the twenties and thirties. Everything known of the Soviet bureaucracy of this era argues that Stalin could not have closely controlled the course of the Great Purge. He seems to have directly involved himself only in the destruction of the upper echelons of the bureaucracy—in itself a massive operation that took the lives of thousands. His personal involvement in the show trials and in the destruction of the regional secretaries and the military leadership is indisputable. If we are to believe Khrushchev, Stalin personally reviewed 383 lists of victims during the height of the Ezhovshchina. There were evidently thousands of names on these lists. Furthermore, Stalin must have realized that putting Ezhov in charge of the political police assured that the purge would be conducted with numbing ruthlessness. This quality Ezhov delivered, but it is far from certain that Stalin anticipated, much less wanted, the Ezhovshchina. All the same, he was perfectly willing to tolerate the ghastly consequences of a police bureaucracy run amok so long as his objectives were met—just as he had tolerated them during the collectivization drive. Only when Ezhovshchina assumed its final, monstrous dimension and threatened to destroy the Soviet economy did Stalin move to shut it down. This he could do only with difficulty; it proved far easier to initiate the purge than it did to bring it to a halt.

Still, despite its monumental cost, the purge served Stalin's purpose. Even allowing a certain "madness in his method," Stalin's reason for generating the Great Purge can be judged from the results. The period of Stalin's absolutism and the full bloom of his deification *followed* the purge. The purge destroyed the old bureaucracy and installed a new and subservient apparatus. Its ranking members largely replaced, the role of the party dwindled, and its several deliberative bodies, reduced to impotence, seldom met.[102]

Whatever Stalin's private motivation may have been, the public role of the show trial defendants is obvious. All the hardships, privations, and shortages, and even the needling inconveniences suffered by the Soviet people during the five-year plans, originated by official and public accounting in the crimes of these men. Their public stain spread to include the many thousands who disappeared; they too had been part of the conspiracy.

DISCUSSION

The destruction of anyone who resisted collectivization (Kulaks and subkulaks), or during the Great Purge practically anyone at all (wreckers, enemies of the people, and those deficient in revolutionary vigilance), brought Stalin finally to a position of impregnable power. At the beginning of the Great Purge, Stalin stood securely at the pinnacle of a vast and centralized police force; after the purge, after Stalin had decimated and cowed the party and imposed unquestioning obedience on all segments of the Russian population, he surmounted everything.

That Stalin, ruthless, vindictive, and suspicious, desired this outcome and was all but indifferent to the cost cannot be doubted; but such qualities, which are not rare, do not provide a fundamental explanation for the Great Purge. It is all too easy to lose sight of the fact that the machinery of social control that Stalin had at his disposal was the product of the imperatives of the Civil War and the many crash programs of the Soviet state. The structure of the NKVD and the tactics and resources legally afforded it must be seen as the end result of long-term threats to the beleaguered party. Stalin did not create the political police; it was already there to serve him.

The Great Purge closely followed the fevered atmosphere of the First Five-Year Plan, and the emergence of the Nationalist Socialist Germany further reinforced the entirely reasonable view that the world was a very dangerous place for the young Soviet state. The degree to which Stalin really believed that the Soviet Union was also menaced from within–that, true to his prediction, conspiratorial resistance would increase as the Soviet Union moved toward socialism—can never be known, but it is significant that Trotsky maintained many political contacts within the Soviet Union after his exile. It is not hard to imagine what the political police made of these communications, and it is plausible that Stalin accepted some or all of their confections as the truth. However that may be, it is certain that Trotsky's letters doomed their recipients.

The essential thing about the assassination of Kirov is that it took place. If Stalin was behind Kirov's murder, it was the act of a fearful and insecure man; if he was not, his subsequent behavior reveals a man terrorized by an assassination that reached high into the party hierarchy. That many others also saw a conspiracy cannot be doubted.

Stalin lavished great attention on generating the appearance of a menacing reality through the device of the show trials. He clearly considered it necessary to establish the fiction that the activities of the NKVD were in harmony with the prevailing danger to the state. The show trials, which destroyed Stalin's political enemies and explained his economic failures, were therefore a multifaceted success. Many Russians were convinced by this theater, and, needless to say, those who benefitted from the purge—the new elite—were the most willing to believe. It is entirely likely that the principal beneficiary of the Great Purge also believed that somewhere beneath the slaughter a genuine conspiracy was being rooted out.

The preoccupation among the upper reaches of the party—and most especially of Stalin—with a lack of "fulfillment of decision" is also manifested in the purge. For nearly two decades the elephantine Soviet bureaucracy had demonstrated an astonishing immunity to the acquisition of efficiency.[103] Soviet decision makers were repeatedly presented with no results or, now and again, with the spectacle of a bureaucracy run amok. The outcome of a party decision was always uncertain. In the midst of such frustrations, method can be found in Stalin's policy of destroying the indifferent, inefficient, and potentially disloyal and making pariahs of them in the process. Madness can be found in the ghastly organization that he employed. Getty has persuasively argued that the comprehensive scope of the Great Purge was due in great measure to the nature of the NKVD bureaucracy—that as with any other Soviet bureaucracy, it could reliably be expected to do either far too little or far too much. Putting the fanatical Ezhov in charge meant that it would unfailingly do too much.

It did far too much. The NKVD was devoid of organizational restraint, and its personnel at every level manifested—if only out of fear of death—a very high degree of internal demand. It was accountable only to Stalin. But once set in motion, even Stalin found it difficult to stop. That Stalin had to stop the purge when he did is clear: industrial production was threatened, and the military was profoundly, almost fatally, weakened. Ezhov's replacement, the intelligent and efficient Beria, suggests the shape of the purge that Stalin may have preferred.

At all events, Beria continued to prune the independent, inefficient, and potentially disloyal from Soviet society until his master's death.

Nothing in the history of the Great Purge nor in the events
leading up to it offers any serious challenge to propositions
1.0 through 6.0.

1.0; 1.1; 1.2 - The atmosphere during both the five-year plans was
in every way reminiscent of War Communism, and the cost in life
and suffering, if anything, was even greater than during the Civil
War. Stalin seems to have harkened back to this environment, and
everything that is known of his behavior during this period argues
that he was a deeply threatened man.

2.0; 2.1; 2.2; 3.0 - The destructive activities of the NKVD during
the Great Purge conform to the potential of a social control system
devoid of organizational restraint in the context of very high external
demand. After Yagoda's removal, the NKVD was accountable only
to Stalin and, once unleashed by Stalin, seems to have rapidly
outstripped even his expectations.

4.0; 4.1 - The Soviet Union, of course, never had a restrained social
control system, but at the same time it is clear that the institution
of the political police was forged during the experience of the Civil
War. The ever beleaguered party chose, with only modest interrup-
tions, to continually enhance this institution. The political police
were there, full powers untested, for Stalin to use.

5.1; 5.2; 6.0 - The Soviet Union at this time was not by any stretch
of the imagination a pluralistic society, and it is pointless to seek
for such processes within the oligarchical factions at the top of
the party. Even Politburo membership provided no safety. All of
us around Stalin, says Krushchev, "were temporary men."[104]

All the same, Stalin did not, and probably could not, just have
his enemies murdered by his lethal police. During the purge, however, it was an easy matter to define them as enemies of the people
and then destroy them. One of the consequences of the Great Purge—
and likely part of its design—was the near absence of any potential
for factional interests (whether high in the party hierarchy or region-
ally based) to withdraw their support from the official (Stalin's)
goals of the state.

Stalin's purposes during the purge were self-serving; that is,
he used the purge to destroy his enemies—real and imaginary.
But such "practicality," from Stalin's point of view, does not
undermine the explanatory scheme above. Palmer's crusade, although heartfelt, was no less practical to his ambitions. The
crucial point is that from the perspective of those with power,

the mass production of deviance is a practical undertaking; it establishes a moral boundary. It cannot be thought an accident of history that the cult of Stalin's infallibility blossomed during the Great Purge. All who opposed "Great Stalin," the "Greatest Man of All Times," the "Driver of the Locomotive of History," must have been evil.[105]

10

The Holocaust

From September of 1939 until early May of 1945, the calculated attrition of camp and ghetto life, as well as refined techniques of mass murder, brought about the death of between six and seven million Jews. The discussion below emphasizes the nature of the ideology that made a virtue of this slaughter and the history and organizational structure of the bureaucracy that accomplished it.

HITLER

"Anxiety was the permanent emotion of the time," writes Joachim Fest of the period following the First World War. Hitler the master politician—with his oratorical powers (so puzzling to contemporary Germans) and above all his ability to dramatize a myth—can be understood only in the context of what Fest calls "The Great Dread" (Die Grosse Angst).[1] Hitler wove his mythical biology into a comprehensive explanation for defeat, chaos, and economic deprivation. Few Germans accepted all of this, but a great many accepted some of it. A nationalist, a struggling businessman, an impoverished worker, an anti-Communist, an anti-Semite—all could find compelling reasons to support Hitler. The orbit of fears encompassed by National Socialist ideology was greater than that of any other party, and it was always far easier to determine what the Nazis were against than what they were for.[2] A world depression and the collapse of the Weimar Republic magnified these fears and brought Hitler to power. In 1928 Hitler's party garnered a mere 2.6 percent of the German vote; in 1932, when almost six million Germans were unemployed, the National Socialists received 37.4 percent of the vote—most of it at the expense of middle-class parties.[3]

In power, Hitler was free to pursue the single coherent theme in his grab-bag ideology of fears and dreams: the destruction of the Jews. In power the full force of the Third Reich's propaganda machine could be focused on the phantom activities of "international finance Jewry" (Hitler's phrase), which plotted the destruction of Germany. In time, writes Hilberg, "The theory of world Jewish rule and of the incessant Jewish plot against the German people penetrated into all offices."[4] With the coming of war, and as the military situation deteriorated, the dimensions of the Jewish conspiracy grew. Jews were spies, saboteurs, the architects of the allied bombing campaign, the liaison between partisans and the Red Army, among the ancestors of allied leaders, and the originators of both communism and capitalism. All misfortune stemmed from the international Jewish conspiracy.

The degree to which the Nazi moral landscape was concocted of a mythical biology has to be appreciated before the Holocaust can be, in small part, explained. Hitler literally regarded Jews as a biological fifth column; in his mind and therefore in the organizational ethic of the SS, Jews represented the ultimate internal conspiracy that destroyed a society at its most fundamental level. The existence of an imaginary "inner enemy" gave credence to Hitler's Aryan utopias and provided the SS with its primary and most murderous goal.[5]

Hitler's statements advocating the destruction of the Jews bracket his public life. As early as 1919 he wrote that the final goal of anti-Semitism must be the complete elimination of the Jew; and in the final paragraph of his political testament, signed the day before his death, he charges the German people "to the scrupulous observance of the laws of race and to the merciless opposition to the universal poisoner of all peoples, International Jewry."[6] His intervening calls to vengeance fill volumes. In Hitler's mental world, the existence of Judaism in the form that he imagined it—as an antihuman biological entity—explained everything: all the sins of the world and all of the obstacles in his path sprang ultimately from this single unified source of evil.[7]

In keeping with many, if not most, literate Europeans, Hitler was influenced by the popular social Darwinists of the era, but to characterize his racial visions as pseudoscience is to miss their essential nature. They were instead a deeply mythological configuration of German Volkisch Romanticism, anti-Semitism, and racism. Perhaps more than any nation state of this century, the Third Reich, Hitler's creation, can be said to have been morphogenetic. Form follows fantasy.[8]

That Hitler, born in nineteenth-century Austria, was an anti-Semite is unsurprising. His transformation into a *racial* anti-Semite seems to have taken place in the context of his Vienna frustrations. Young Hitler was, by all accounts, a compulsive but eclectic reader; the only topic to which he seems to have systematically applied himself was anti-Semitism. A listing of the racist literature readily available to Hitler in the virulently anti-Semitic Vienna of the period would be long and repetitive. One such publication may be usefully mentioned: the journal *Ostara*. This raw and lurid racial tract was the creation of Lanz von Liebenfels, who was also the founder of the "New Temple," a secret society that was the precursor of a "New Order." According to Schleunes, particulars of Nazi ideology crop up first in the pages of *Ostara*, and in a postwar interview, Liebenfels recalls Hitler, in person, requesting back issues.[9]

Liebenfels et al. aside, much of the root mythology of National Socialism derives from Wagner. There can be no doubt that Hitler was spellbound by Wagner the musical dramatist and Rauschning quotes Hitler as declaring that "whoever wishes to comprehend National Socialism must first know Richard Wagner."[10] It is far from extreme to suggest that Hitler viewed the world in terms of a vast Wagnerian drama and that Nazi ideology was ultimately the political formulation of a Manichaean illusion of stupendous struggles of good against evil.[11] National Socialist ideology was a peculiar sort of mythology, basically a kind of Wagnerian biology.

Hitler's granitic hatreds were born of absolute conviction. There is no evidence that Hitler ever seriously considered the possibility that Jews represent a religious community and not a "race." To Hitler, world Jewry represented an organic evil, and the terminology used by him to describe Jews is relentlessly biological. Jews are "maggots, poisoners, rats, vipers, defilers of race, the ferment that causes peoples decay" and "bacilli." Indeed, in a reflective moment, Hitler once compared himself to Robert Koch, the German bacteriologist.

SCAPEGOAT

Hitler's pronouncements on Jews fall basically into two categories. There are his diatribes against their phantom machinations accompanied by specific threats of retaliation, and, less often, there are frank admissions of their political usefulness to him. In the absence of the Jew "We should have then to invent him. It is essential to have a tangible enemy not merely an abstract one."[12] In an interview with Josef Hell in 1922, he elaborates:

... In no case has revolution succeeded without the presence of a lightning rod that could conduct and channel the odium of the general masses. ... I came to the conclusion that a campaign against the Jew would be as popular as it would be successful. There are few Germans who have not been vexed with the behavior of Jews or else have not suffered losses through them in some way or other. ... Once the hatred and the battle against the Jews have been really stirred up, their resistance will necessarily crumble in the shortest possible time. They are totally defenseless, and no one will stand up to protect them."[13]

It is quite clear, then, that Hitler regarded the Jew in his ancient role as scapegoat as a means to power. It is also true that economic chaos, a crushing and popularly inexplicable military defeat, and nationalism were also potent concerns, but to isolate these several factors from anti-Semitism is misleading.[14] "Jewish intrigues," after all, provided the entire explanation for economic chaos and defeat. No aspect of National Socialist ideology was separable from anti-Semitism; racial anti-Semitism was the core of Hitler's ideology and the one thing that rendered it coherent. The Jew was not just subhuman; the Jew was anti-human and thereby rendered all misfortune explicable. By extension, if the Jew was eliminated, all would be well.

Anti-Semitism served Hitler well in the realm of practical politics. When Hitler's prophecies of widespread domestic reform did not materialize in any significant way, the separation of the Jew from German social and economic life was pointed to as a concrete achievement—utopia would surely follow.[15] It was especially useful for maintaining party unity.[16] Outside the party faithful, Hitler could always draw upon the centuries-old wellspring of religious anti-Semitism to attack his enemies, and he seldom, if ever, felt the need to tone down his anti-Semitic rhetoric except in response to international considerations (notably during the 1936 Olympics). It is easily overlooked that the series of legal restrictions imposed on Jews provided Hitler with considerable political and economic patronage. The first of a flood of restrictive racial decrees—effective 7 April 1933, two months after Hitler took power—retired all officials of "non-Aryan" descent (anyone with a Jewish parent or grandparent). Subsequent decrees restricted or denied employment in the legal and medical professions, public schools and universities, publishing, and the armed forces. The effect was to isolate the German Jewish community and strip it of position and property. Non-Jewish Germans benefitted directly from this process, or thought they soon would, and it is reasonable to assume that in many individual cases their allegiance to the regime increased in proportion. It must be accepted that this dynamic profoundly influenced the descending moral and intellectual path taken by German medicine. The swift removal of many thousands of Jewish physicians from the practice of medicine, in combination with the growth of a vast state apparatus of racial hygiene, proved a windfall to the "Aryan" medical community, and ultimately a near majority of German doctors joined the National Socialist Physicians League, which was an administrative and ideological organ of the party.[17]

THE RACIAL WAR

Hitler fought two wars: a war of conquest to the east to gain living space for Germanic peoples, and a war of destruction against the Jews. These two wars were distinct in his mind and were waged more or less independently.[18] Both sprang from Hitler's racial world view. If the Jews were the despoilers of humanity—a sort of biological fifth column—then Aryans represented the true potential of the species. To Hitler, it followed that Aryans within and without Germany must be provided with living space and protected from the inroads of further miscegenation. The conquest of Russia would ensure living space and the Holocaust would eliminate the Jew who "goes his way, the way of sneaking in among nations and boring from within."[19]

The destined Aryan utopia envisioned by Hitler extended from the Atlantic to the Urals, its blond, blue-eyed "nucleus" to be defended in the East by Germanic outposts that dominated servile subhuman (untermenschen) populations. And "the Jew, that destroyer, we shall drive out."[20] In dreamy nocturnal monologues taken down on orders from Martin Borman during the war years, Hitler often expanded on his eastern visions.

The real frontier is the one that separates the Germanic world from the Slav world. It's our duty to place it where we want it to be.... It's inconceivable that a higher people should painfully exist on a soil too narrow for it, whilst amorphous masses, which contribute nothing to civilization, occupy infinite tracts of soil that is one of the richest in the world. . . . We must create conditions for our people that favor its multiplication and we must at the same time build a dike against the Russian flood.

The German colonists ought to live in handsome, spacious farms. The German services will be lodged in marvelous buildings, the governors in palaces. . . . Around the city to a depth of thirty to forty kilometers, we shall have a belt of handsome villages connected by the best roads.[21]

Hitler acted upon such fantasies, and they should not be dismissed as merely the ramblings of a chronic insomniac. Chapter 14 of the second volume of *Mein Kampf* could not have been more specific. It is a foreign policy statement that only the combined intervention of England, Russia, and the United States prevented from being fully implemented.

1. The foreign policy of the folkish state must safeguard the existence on this planet of the race embodied in the state.
2. And so we National Socialists consciously draw a line beneath the foreign policy tendency of our pre-War period. We take up where we broke off six hundred years ago. We stop the endless German movement to the south and west, and turn our gaze toward the land in the east. At long last we break off the colonial and commercial policy of the pre-War period and shift to the soil policy of the future.

   If we speak of soil in Europe today, we can primarily have in mind only Russia and her vassal border states.
3. Since for this we require strength, and since France, the mortal enemy of our nation, inexorably strangles us and robs us of our strength, we must take upon ourselves every sacrifice whose consequences are calculated to contribute to the annihilation of French efforts toward hegemony in Europe.[22]

In other words, once Germany is rearmed and France neutralized, Germany shall strike east and conquer Russia. It nearly worked out that way. But imbedded within this call to arms and conquest is also a call for destruction.

The danger to which Russia succumbed is always present for Germany. Only a bourgeois simpleton is capable of imagining that Bolshevism has been exorcised. With his superficial thinking he has no idea that this is an instinctive process; that is, the striving of the Jewish people for world domination, a process which is just as natural as the urge of the Anglo-Saxon to seize domination of the earth. And just as the Anglo-Saxon pursues this course in his own way and carries on the fight with his own weapons, likewise the Jew. He goes his way, the way of sneaking in among nations and boring from within, and he fights with his weapons, with lies and slander, poison and corruption, intensifying the struggle to the point of bloodily exterminating his hated foes. In Russian Bolshevism we must see the attempt undertaken by the Jews in the twentieth century to achieve world domination.

But the impotence of nations, their own death from old age, arises from the abandonment of their blood purity. And this is a thing that the Jew preserves better than any other people on earth. And so he advances on his fatal road until another force comes forth to oppose him, and in a mighty struggle hurls the heaven-stormer back to Lucifer.[23]

THE SS

Just as Hitler fought two wars, strategic and racial, so too he fostered the development of two parallel governments. Hitler's race war, the war against the Jews, was fought by the SS—the *Schutzstaffel* (Guard Detachments). The development, organization, and career of this predatory bureaucracy are central to the discussion of the Holocaust.

National Socialism has much of its tangled root system in the Freikorps movement of postwar Germany. Hitler's Storm Troopers (SA), from which the SS emerged, were organized along the lines of a Freikorps unit, even to the point of continuing the leaden titles of rank (*Obergruppenfuehrers, Obersturmbannfuehrers,* and the like) used by the Freikorps—a legacy continued by the SS. The brown shirt, the swastika, and the Hitler salute were first employed by Freikorps units.[24]

The principal function of the SA membership is amply described by their initial designation within the budding Nazi party: "Strong Arm Squads." Hitler adopted the term Storm Troopers (*Sturm-Abteilung,* hence SA) to advertise the nationalistic and militaristic ideals of his party. Four years of warfare had left Germany with a virtually inexhaustible reservoir of economically and emotionally displaced veterans who often gravitated into one or the other of Germany's many paramilitary units. One of the reasons for the sustained growth of the SA is simply the demise over time of comparable organizations to join. SA membership was characterized by, among other things, a predisposition to violence. In a country in which party politics was at times only cosmetically different from civil war, a protective organization of brawlers was to Hitler's advantage; but by its very nature the SA was ill disciplined and hard to control.

The SS emerged by fits and starts from the "brown masses" of the SA as a disciplined Praetorian Guard. Its hallmark came to be corpse-like obedience to Hitler. SS functions rapidly expanded beyond ceremonial guarding and intelligence gathering to duties as a paramilitary police force to control the SA when its predations upon the Jewish community became too extreme or, more accurately, too public. The SS could be relied upon; the SA could not.

Koehl argues that the SS represents a perversion of middle-class values.[25] The SS motto, taken quite literally at all levels of the SS, was: "My honor is my loyalty." Ruthlessly and idealistically pursuing the realization of Hitler's fantasies, this most criminal of all organizations always had the stamp of prudery upon it. From the beginning, SS men unquestioningly murdered ("special tasks") in obedience to orders issued in the quest for a higher ideal. Therein lay the morality. Disorder and lack of discipline were officially out of bounds to these men, but the orderly slaughter of millions represented an opportunity for self-sacrifice. Nothing makes this clearer than Himmler's infamous Poznan speech. The occasion was a meeting of ranking SS leaders in 1943.

One principle must be absolute for the SS man: We must be honest, decent, loyal and comradely to members of our own blood and to no one else. What happens to the Russians, what happens to the Czechs, is a matter of utter indifference to me. Such good blood of our own kind as there may be among the nations we shall acquire for ourselves, if necessary by taking away the children and bringing them up among us. Whether the other peoples live in comfort or perish of hunger interests me only in so far as we need them as slaves for our culture; apart from that it does not interest me. Whether or not 10,000 Russian women collapse from exhaustion while digging a tank ditch interests me only in so far as the tank ditch is completed for Germany. We shall never be rough or heartless where it is not necessary; that is clear. We Germans, who are the only people in the world who have a decent attitude to animals, will also adopt a decent attitude to these human animals, but it is a crime against our own blood to worry about them and to bring them ideals.

I shall speak to you here with all frankness of a very serious subject. We shall now discuss it absolutely openly among ourselves, nevertheless we shall never speak of it in public. I mean the evacuation of the Jew, the extermination of the Jewish people. It is one of those things which is easy to say. "The Jewish people is to be exterminated," says every party member. "That's clear, it's part of our programme, elimination of the Jews, extermination, right, we'll do it." And then they all come along, the eighty million good Germans, and each one has his decent Jew. Of course the others are swine, but this one is a first-class Jew. Of all those who talk like this, not one has watched, not one has stood up to it. Most of you know what is means to see a hundred corpses lying together, five hundred or a thousand. To have gone through this and yet—apart from a few exceptions, examples of human weakness—to have remained decent, this has made us hard. This is a glorious page in our history that has never been written and never shall be written.[26]

Much of the shape of the SS, its manifold departments and quasi-religious ceremonials, was the work of Heinrich Himmler, *Reichsfuehrer SS*. Himmler, the consummate toady, has been described by Albert Speer as "half schoolmaster, half crank." Apart from the fact that Himmler did not personally steal, he typifies the leaders of Nationalist Socialist Germany. Fest writes:

The basic pathological characteristic of the Nationalist Socialist movement so often and erroneously sought out in clinically obvious psychopaths like Julius Streicher, showed itself rather in the curious amalgam of crankiness and "normality," of insanity and sober administrative ability.[27]

A skilled and relentless bureaucrat, Himmler's personal ambitions were reflected by the cancerous growth of the SS state within Germany. Himmler took over the leadership of the SS in 1929, just before the depression swelled the party ranks. SS elitism proved a magnet for the ambitious; professionals, technocrats, failed academics, and petty nobility abounded in the SS. Sometimes these men were aggressive; more typically they were merely able. Himmler drew from a deep pool of bureaucratic tendencies: SS administrators were "chosen average men." Himmler totally embraced the notion of the SS as

a racial aristocracy, literally a community of blood (blutgemein-
schaft). To this end a functionary within the SS Race and
Resettlement Main Office (*Rasse- und Siedlungs Hauptamt*—
RuSHA) drew up a complex set of standards that, although
ostensibly medical and anthropological, was essentially a vari-
ant of livestock judging, an approach that Himmler, formerly
a poultry farmer, knew well.[28]   SS applicants submitted photo-
graphs of themselves, which Himmler personally scrutinized
for undesirable characteristics. Naturally, genealogical considerations were paramount, and it was necessary to demonstrate
the absence of a single Jewish ancestor as far back as 1800
to be admitted to the ranks and as far back as 1750 to be officers.
After 1931 an SS man could marry only "if the necessary condition of race and healthy stock were fulfilled."[29]

To set this elite apart, the trappings of rank and status were
emphasized. The black uniform, boots, death's-head insignia,
and a multiplicity of badges and symbols of rank were designed
to be imposing. No detail, however minor, seems to have been
overlooked. SS typewriters, for example, were equipped with
special runic keys. Deserving SS men of all ranks could be
awarded the death's head signet ring, and officers could receive
the coveted ceremonial dagger. Important SS leaders were provided with coats of arms designed by the Ancestral Heritage
Office of the SS. Always the historical romantic, Himmler re-
vived or simply concocted a whole series of supposedly ancient
Germanic ceremonies, which even Hitler thought to be a little
silly. The imposition of this lodge brother mentality upon the
SS officer corps quickly produced an emphasis on arcane ritual comparable to what might be expected had the Ku Klux
Klan, in a previous incarnation, joined forces with the Teutonic
knights. Himmler's preoccupation with ritual is perhaps best
epitomized by the refurbishing of Wewelsburg castle in Westpha-
lia into a sort of SS Valhalla (total cost thirteen million reich
marks), which was used by Himmler for high-level meetings
and to initiate future SS "Knights of Blood and Soil." It was
in the great hall of Wewelsburg Castle, directly over a burial
crypt designed to hold the ashes of SS *Obergruppenfuehrers,*
that Himmler, in March of 1941, spoke to a group of SS colonels
and generals of the planned elimination of millions of Jews
and Slavs.[30]

Although Himmler was an admirer of the Society of Jesus,
the SS more closely resembled the Spanish Inquisition. The
SS emphasized racial purity. It was allowed to manage its own

finances and to solicit sponsoring members. Additionally, it
maintained its own court system, which policed its membership
and which in principle and in practice superseded the German
court system. A defendant could be exonerated in civil court
only to be arrested anew by an agency of the SS, a practice
defined as "correction of justice."[31] It maintained its own system
of prisons. But unlike the Spanish Inquisition, the SS had no
system of internal restraint.

THE ORGANIZATION OF THE SS

In its manner of growth the SS was both cancerous and entrepreneurial: cancerous in the sense that existing political and
administrative structures were interpenetrated and ultimately
taken over by the SS, and entrepreneurial in that vast new agencies and institutions were formed within the SS (the Waffen
SS, for example). Add to this the fact that the ranking leadership
of the SS was linked together by a system of feudal loyalties,
and the result is an organization of Byzantine complexity, so
much so that it is arguably impossible to draw up a table of
organization that adequately conveys the internal structure of
the SS State.[32]

The fact that the SS functioned at all, much less with its
infamous efficiency, is difficult to explain, but German rever-
ence for efficiency and a willingness to follow orders offer a
partial explanation. Raul Hilberg has commented on the singular
fact that a minor functionary of the Reich Security main office
(RSHA), office 1V-B, one Adolf Eichmann, and a small team
of perhaps a dozen "emigration specialists" could arrange for
the transportation of over one million people to the death camps.
Hilberg concludes:

> The German administration was not deterred by the pressures of
> other assignments; it never resorted to pretenses, like the Italians,
> it never took token measures, like the Hungarians, it never procrasti-
> nated like the Bulgarians. The German bureaucrat worked efficiently,
> and with a sense of urgency. Unlike other collaborators, the Germans
> never did the minimum. They always did the maximum.[33]

Just the same, it must be emphasized that the Third Reich
was a totalitarian state and the SS, its institution of social control. Alternatives to obedience did not beckon. But it is a mistake

to conclude that refusal to carry out a crime, particularly among high-ranking officers, would automatically result in execution or incarceration. The normal outcome seems to have been punitive reassignments. By and large the principal sanction against disobedience and the *violation of an oath* seems to have been internal and psychological, with the result that regardless of personal feelings, enthusiasm in all endeavors, and not dull reluctant obedience, was the most characteristic behavior within the SS.

THE GROWTH OF RSHA

One of the main pillars of the SS state was its security apparatus. In 1931 Himmler hired a cashiered naval officer, Reinhard Heydrich, to head the infant SS security department (Sicherheitsdienst SD). Heydrich, a ruthless and effective organizer, rapidly formed a network of operatives and informers that kept tabs on rival organizations. Heydrich's long-term ambition was to expand the SD to the point that the official German security systems were rendered superfluous.[34] However, the manner of Hitler's consolidation of power was such that this course of action became unnecessary. Instead, the SS took over the existing German police structure.

One of Hitler's predictable goals was to bring all German police, and most especially the political police, under party control. In the context of much intraparty squabbling, the first stage of this process was accomplished when Himmler gained firm control over two skilled and efficient police organizations: the *Kriminal Polizei* (KRIPO) and the secret police, the *Geheime Staatspolizei (Gestapo)*. Together these organizations formed the SS Security Police (*Sicherheitspolizei*—SIPO), which was placed under the authority of Heydrich. Thus it developed that the SS contained two essentially parallel security structures— the SIPO and the SD. Similarly, the regular uniformed German police (*Ordnungspolizei*—ORPO) also became an appendage of the SS, so that in effect the entire German police establishment was centralized and put under the control of the Reichsfuehrer.

Centralization of party control was formalized in June of 1936 when the party post of Reichsfuehrer was joined with the new government office of chief of German police. Reichsfuehrer SS and Chief of German Police Himmler shortly thereafter announced the appointment of Heydrich as the chief of Security

Police (SIPO) and Kurt Daluege as chief of the Uniformed Police (ORPO). And finally, as a result of another major reorganization of the SS in September 1939, Heydrich was lofted to the status of *Obergruppenfuehrer* and placed in charge of the Reich Security Main Office (RSHA). As the core of this department, the SD and the SIPO provided much of the administration and manpower for the Holocaust machinery.[35]

HIMMLER'S INTENDANTS

Superior SS and Police Leaders *(Hoehere SS und Polizei Fuehrer—HSSPF)* had authority that spanned all branches of the armed SS and the SS police. In 1941 all HSSPF were given the rank of general in the SS and in the police. These plenipotentiaries often acted as Himmler's troubleshooters and led combined operations. Koehl argues that this administrative gambit greatly facilitated the accomplishment of the Holocaust.

> Thus, a powerful institution had come of age, and the way was prepared to coordinate and protect the most daring and reprehensible actions in the east from intervention and sabotage by other parts of the German state and society. Though their hands were to run all the threads, both of information and control, of Himmler's web dealing with the most delicate and political matters, including relations with the party—especially the gauleiters—the army, the state bureaucracy, and leading figures of Germany's business and professional world.[36]

WAFFEN SS, WVHA, RKFDV

During the Second World War, the various departments of the SS were shaped by the tasks assigned to them and by the relentless ambition of the Obergruppenfuehrers commanding them. The military arm of the SS, the Waffen SS, grew to half a million men and earned a reputation for combat effectiveness and ruthless brutality.[37] At least part of this reputation is correct since many Waffen SS leaders had former careers in the *Totenkopfverbande* (Death's-Head Formations—concentration camp guards), which early on were administratively under Waffen SS headquarters.

The SS main office for economy and administration (WVHA) under Obergruppenfuehrer Oswald Pohl became an empire in itself responsible for the administration and supply of the Waffen SS, all SS and police building projects, all SS business endeavors, and the administration of the labor camps and death camps.[38] The WVHA ultimately controlled and operated with slave labor hundreds of factories that made everything from china nicknacks to V2 rockets. Under Pohl the concentration camps existed to support SS industry; however, the fact that the WVHA ran the concentration camps is only partly explained by the need for slave labor. The SS regarded the destruction of European Jewry to be an extractive industry. To be sure, the extortion of Jewish money and property was an activity that all segments of the Third Reich participated in, but only the WVHA was organized to systematically steal the clothing, eyeglasses, hair, and teeth of millions of people. Hilberg describes this process.

How was it possible to be so thorough? The answer lies in the assemblyline, a method which was foolproof. Inmate work parties picked up the luggage left in the freight cars of the transports and on the platform. Other inmate Kommandos collected clothes and valuables in the dressing rooms. Women's hair was cut off in the barber shops near the gas chambers. Gold teeth were extracted from the mouths of the corpses, and the human fat escaping from the burning bodies was poured back into the flames to speed the cremations. Thus, the two organic processes of the death camp, confiscation and killings, were fused and synchronized into a single procedure which guaranteed the absolute success of both operations.[39]

The Reich Commission for the Strengthening of Germandom (RKFDV) was the colonial arm of the SS charged with the job of Aryanizing the conquered territories in the east, which involved the displacement of existing populations of Slavs and Jews and the resettlement of ethnic Germans. Local populations were screened and categorized and their fates determined. "Racially useful" children obtained by a variety of strategies, including kidnapping, were sent to Germany for adoption into SS families. In this activity the SS Well of Life Society (Lebensborn), the SS welfare organization, was instrumental in providing the services of its adoption agency. SS Lebensborn officers vigorously protected "their" pool of blond children from the inroads of other non-SS agencies, and Himmler evidently toyed with the idea of using some of these children to form a sort of SS Janissary.[40] The war ended before selected boys could grow into this fate.

The demand for suitable racial stock to meet the manpower requirements of the casualty-prone Waffen SS was partly met by the RKFDV, but in time the Waffen SS siphoned off so many ethnic Germans that it actually interfered with the resettlement program.[41] A similar interdepartmental dependency is more grimly manifested in the RKFDV role in the Holocaust. The RKFDV dramatically rearranged the ethnic map in those territories in which it was allowed free play and in the process helped to concentrate the Jews of Eastern Europe. Also the RKFDV, with its enormous population of ethnic Germans to house and clothe, provided an enormous market for the products of death and labor camps. A WVHA report of February 1943, for example, makes note of 211 freight cars of confiscated clothing sent to resettlement camps.[42]

THE ARYAN PARADISE

It was the express mission of no less than three separate departments of the SS to bring about the Aryan paradise through the selection of suitable racial stock; each fiercely defended its piece of the action. Before the war, the Liaison Office for Ethnic Germans (*Volksdeutsche Mittelstelle*—VOMI) maintained contact with German enclaves in the East and surreptitiously subsidized them. VOMI teams often went into newly conquered territory to establish contact with German communities. Always overshadowed by the RKFDV, VOMI personnel were often in charge of the nuts and bolts of the massive resettlement program, maintaining hundreds of resettlement camps, arranging for transportation, etcetera.[43]

The agricultural romantics and racial typologists of the Race and Settlement Office (RuSHA) worked closely with the RKFDV and were the principal appraisers of human stock. The resettlement camps were, among other things, racial categorization centers. New arrivals would have their paperwork inspected for documentary evidence of Germanic background and be given a medical examination that was also an appraisal of race. The "racial estimate" of each individual (am/I—"racially very valuable," to IV3C—"racial reject") was noted on his or her medical examination card. When prospective settlers questioned the necessity of receiving a racial estimate, they were pointedly advised that this was a life and death matter.[44]

While the RKFDV, VOMI, and RuSHA manfully sought to husband the "racially useful" populations of Eastern Europe in order to bring about Hitler's biological utopia, other SS departments—notably the RSHA, the WVHA and the *Totenkopf* formations—worked towards the same end by the equally direct method of murdering those of "unsuitable" racial stock. The perpetration of the Holocaust is then all of one piece with the various SS departments working hand-in-glove to bring about a Jew-free Europe.

Defining a Jew

As Hitler tells us, a "visible enemy is needed. . . ." The task of manufacturing a visible enemy—of defining a Jew—fell largely to the Ministry of the Interior. The initial decree of 7 April 1933 simply excluded all "non-Aryans" from official positions. For a variety of reasons, including especially the terrible (to Hitler) and no doubt intractable problem of miscegenation, this and other pioneering restrictions were deemed insufficient, and on the occasion of the Nuremberg Rally of 13 September 1935, Hitler ordered a comprehensive "Law for the Protection of German Blood and Honor." Hammered out in great urgency with the Nuremberg Rally as a backdrop, the Nuremberg laws defined the "Jew" (and not a non-Aryan) and also non-Jews of "mixed Jewish blood."[45]

Protecting German blood and honor turned out to be a very complicated business. Defined as Jews were: anyone with three or four Jewish grandparents; anyone with two Jewish grandparents who was a practicing Jew as of 15 September 1935; anyone with two Jewish grandparents who was married to a Jew as of 15 September 1935; or anyone who was the child of a marriage contracted with a three-quarter Jew or a full Jew after 15 September 1935 or was a child born of a similar extra-marital arrangement after 31 July 1936. Marriage between Jews (as above) and citizens of "German or related blood" and any sexual intercourse between these two categories of people became a crime.

Not a Jew but a person of "mixed Jewish blood," a *Mischling*, was someone with two Jewish grandparents who was not a practicing Jew as of 15 September 1935 or not married, as of that date, to a Jew. A subsequent elaboration defined Mischlinge of the first degree (as immediately above) and Mischlinge of the second degree, those people with only one Jewish grandparent. One's grandparents were presumed to be Jewish if they practiced Judaism; therefore, in most cases, only parental fractions entered into the determination of racial status. Fractions of grandparents were, however, important to SS officer candidates.

In the end result, Germany, by law, consisted of three kinds of humans; Germans (Aryans), and two kinds of non-Aryans— Jews and Mischlinge. Mischlinge were subject to certain legal discriminations, but all subsequent racial decrees leading to the Holocaust applied only to Jews.[46] Needless to say, the Nuremberg decrees produced a series of complex court cases that the judiciary of the Third Reich solemnly adjudicated. The degree to which these legal categories penetrated German culture is difficult to appreciate, but it may be noted that almost instantaneously a whole new profession of "family researchers" materialized whose services were essential to office holders, aspirants, the offspring of unmarried mothers, and those who wished to join the SS.[47]

It is important to emphasize that the Nuremberg laws, which were intended to protect German blood and honor, were entirely geared to religious criteria. In fact, no other means were available to the German leadership to render the Jewish "race" visible. The ersatz nature of the racial villain is obvious, but this made no difference whatsoever: a scapegoat had been defined with legal precision and was then put to work.

Well over four hundred anti-Semitic decrees and directives came into effect between 1933 and 1943, all of which had the clear purpose of defining Jews as pariahs. The intent of some of these decrees was entirely symbolic; Jews were, for example, forbidden to raise the German flag. But most of these laws were punitive—designed to isolate or to facilitate exploitation.[48] Nothing was overlooked: Jews were forbidden to enter German dining cars, recreational areas, and even German forests; a variety of curfews were imposed; and access to basic commodities such as milk, meat, and cereal was restricted. Through time the character of these laws became increasingly strident and more ominous. No indignity was too trifling or cruel to escape the attention of the Nazi authorities. Jews could not visit Aryan hairdressers, use public telephones, buy books in a store, or use automatic ticket machines. In 1942 the Third Reich managed to hit upon an innovation that even a millennium of inspired anti-Semitism had failed to produce. The pets of Jews, now tainted with Jewish blood, had to be turned into dog pounds for extermination—to share the fate of their owners.[49]

1938 seems to have been a watershed; after that year decrees and directives expropriating Jewish property and limiting their movements tumbled rapidly onto the German scene. A decree requiring the registration of Jewish property was published in April of that year. In July all Jews were required to carry identification cards, and in October the passports of Jews were identified with the "J-stamp." In addition to the J-stamp, these documents displayed a further uniformity in that all German Jews now had a state-provided middle name—either Sarah or Israel. The mandatory Jewish star, a medieval practice, was first introduced in occupied Poland (1939) and then later (1941) implemented within Germany.[50] The Nuremberg laws, in particular, were made more stringent by numerous supplementary decrees until, finally, all Jews became outlaws, subject to death if identified.

CRYSTAL NIGHT

Jews were at the same time subjected to an ongoing and only technically illegal pogrom at the hands of the stormtroopers (SA), who viewed strong-arm tactics as a rewarding and patriotic duty. Bullying, beatings, destruction of property, and "wild concentration camps" were largely the product of the SA. The degree to which the Nazi authorities directed these activities is amply indicated by the period of relative tranquility imposed during the 1936 Olympic Games. Depending on the political climate, SA "mischief" was encouraged, ignored, or discouraged.

The culmination of such attacks came in the early morning hours of 10 November 1938 in the form of an organized nationwide pogrom. The catalytic event, at least officially, was the assassination of a German embassy secretary in Paris by a German-born Polish Jew, Herschel Grynspan. Upon learning that his parents had been deported to Poland by the security police, Grynspan, then living in Paris, proceeded to shoot the nearest available German official.

The reaction in Berlin was a "spontaneous demonstration" by the German public. A series of directives engineering this "demonstration" went out to both the SA and to the SS (the SS—that is, all police—were instructed not to interfere). Goebbels seems to have been the principal instigator of this pogrom, but Hitler evidently gave him the nod. In any event, Hitler and Goebbels spent much of the evening of the 9th in conversation during which Hitler is reported to have said, "The SA should be allowed to have its final fling."[51] Assembled by party leaders, stormtroopers throughout Germany responded with the alacrity of long-bored Cossacks, and in the ensuing destruction dozens of people (all Jews) lost their lives and close to two hundred synagogues and thousands of Jewish shops were destroyed or pillaged. By morning German towns and cities were in a sea of broken glass—hence, "Crystal Night."[52]

Crystal Night also provided an opportunity for the SS to incarcerate twenty thousand Jews, a figure that was geared to the available capacity of Germany's burgeoning concentration camps. Most of those arrested were wealthy—this distinction had also been specified—and were shortly released upon promise that they would emigrate. Emigration, of course, involved almost total expropriation of property, but the alternative was the camp.

For the sake of appearance and perhaps in the interest of discipline, a few of the SA murderers were brought to trial, but in all cases the sentences were ridiculously light. Instances of "race defilement" (rape) were, however, treated harshly.[53] Looting, unsurprisingly, was universal and was denounced by the authorities only because the loot remained in private hands.

Crystal Night represents a sharp turning point. Party factions had been at odds over how to best exploit politically and economically the now well-defined scapegoat. The SS initially pursued a policy of calculated and orderly exploitation, leading to the massive emigration of Jews. The scapegoat, in short, was first to be sheared and then ejected, bearing the racial sins of Germany. "Aryanization," the transfer of Jewish property to German control, was the official policy, and the fundamental folly of the SA pogrom lay in the fact that it destroyed property that in very little time could have been expropriated. The full dimension of Goebbels's blunder became apparent when it was discovered that the bulk of Jewish business establishments destroyed were insured by non-Jewish insurance companies. This unwelcome development became the subject of acrimonious debate at a meeting between Goering and other high officials on 12 November 1938.[54]

Actually, the way out of this impasse was relatively easy. Using a logic that was lost on insurance officials, who had hoped to escape payment altogether, Goering announced that the damaged party was the Third Reich and that the insurance payments would go to the government. It was also decided that German Jews would pay an "atonement" of one billion marks. Apart from being a standard medieval gambit, this action also had certain internal logic since Hitler had always regarded German Jews as a hostage against the phantom machinations of international Jewry.[55]

The long-term consequences of the Crystal Night were far more severe. The fuehrer had ordered, said Goering at the outset of the meeting of the 12th, "that the Jewish question be settled and once and for all coordinated or solved in one way or the other."[56] The total isolation of the Jews from German society in large measure hails from this meeting. Virtually all of the strategies suggested to deal with the Jewish "problem" and the several recommended palliatives for bruised Nazi honor were thereafter put into effect. The stenographic record shows that these discussions were wide ranging and included the following: the crowded beaches, parks, forests, trains, and schools and the fact that Jews were still to be found in them; the possibility of marking all Jews with badges (Goering would have preferred uniforms); various refinements to the Aryanization process; the potential for rapid forced emigration; and the advantages and disadvantages of ghettos.[57]

As Hilberg clearly demonstrates, most Nazi anti-Semitic legislation has ancient precedent.[58] The summary accomplishment of this web of laws, directives, and decrees was to compress the laws and regulations accumulated during one thousand years of religious anti-Semitism into the span of a mere eight years. After 1940, however, precedent was largely abandoned and the Nationalist Socialist policy took a direct path to the Holocaust.

THE CRUSADE FOR RACIAL PURITY

A major debate exists among the Holocaust historians between "intentionalists," those who argue that Hitler planned the Holocaust from the beginning of his political career, and the "functionalists," those who argue that the Holocaust resulted from a series of ad hoc solutions to the problems of occupation.[59] The principal point of agreement within these two academic camps is that the search for a document ordering the destruction of the Jews of Europe signed by A. Hitler will almost certainly

fail. By the beginning of the war, the principle of leader absolutism, the "Fuehrer principle," had so penetrated the German
state that policy emanated fundamentally from ministerial and
departmental perception of the fuehrer's will. In practice this
perception was gained from written decrees, often secret, from
verbal orders, or, even less formally, from an expressed wish.[60]
A written order from Hitler was therefore unnecessary and very
likely never issued.

But the trail is not cold.[61] There are many references by Hitler's
Lieutenants (Goering, Goebbels, Himmler, Heydrich, Bormann,
et al.) to *fuehrer orders* to systematically liquidate the Jews of
Europe. Again and again the documentation reveals specific
references to extermination orders "from the highest level."
In a communication dated 2 October 1942 from Himmler to
Oswald Pohl regarding the concentration of Jews into WVHA
labor camps, Himmler closes in typical fashion: "However, one
day the Jews there, in conformity with the Fuehrer's wish, are
also to disappear."[62]

In addition, there is from Himmler a signed report to Hitler
(report number 51, 29 December 1942), prepared on a large-type
"fuehrer typewriter," detailing with customary precision the accomplishments of the RFSS in Russia for the months of August
to November. Under the heading "Jews Executed" is the number
363,211. A notation by Hitler's adjutant indicates that this report
crossed Hitler's desk on 31 December 1942.[63]

In addition, a number of high-level conferences were called
to coordinate the Final Solution. These are well documented.
The first Wannsee conference (20 January 1942) dealt specifically
with this issue and was attended by representatives from the
ministries of the Interior, Justice, the Foreign Office, Reich
Chancellary, RuSHA, and RSHA, among others. The meeting
was chaired by Heydrich, who did most of the talking. Adolf
Eichmann organized the meeting and kept the minutes, which,
although highly sanitized, make chilling reading: in view of
the "possibilities in the east," there had been a change of policy
from "emigration" to "evacuation." Europe was "to be combed
from west to east" for Jews, who would be transported "group
by group into transit ghettos, to be transported from there farther
to the East." "Even now," said Heydrich, "practical experience
is being gathered that is of major significance in view of the
coming Final Solution of the Jewish Question."[64] At his trial,
Eichmann was questioned about the reality behind the antiseptic
Wannsee minutes. He answered: "The discussion covered kill-

ing, elimination and annihilation."[65] It is difficult to believe that Hitler did not at least indirectly instigate this conference, and even harder to suppose that he could have long remained ignorant of its true agenda.

Furthermore, it is simply idle to believe that any process so fundamentally at odds with the Third Reich's war effort, and ultimately its survival, could have been maintained without Hitler's express approval. The events leading to the Holocaust were useful to national socialism not only ideologically but also politically in that the extortion of Jewish property provided a common pool of victims from which all segments of the Third Reich could benefit. At the same time, however, there can be no doubt that the Holocaust was inimical to the military goal of the Reich. It can be argued that the use of slave labor benefitted the war effort, and it can be argued that the resettlement program paid some dividends in the form of cannon fodder for the Waffen SS. But the Holocaust industry, apart from a great deal of used clothing, furniture, and human hair produced only death.[66]

Protests against the diversion of badly needed transport and resources to the needs of the Holocaust were common. Carefully reasoned arguments against the German occupation policy (by Canaris among others) are documented, and early in the war Goering is on record as stating flatly, "It is more important to win the war than to implement racial policy."[67] All of these calls to reason were futile. Direct and vigorous appeals to morality on the part of the German authorities do not exist in the extant documentation. Probably they never existed.

In a word, the Holocaust has all the earmarks of an organizational crusade: nothing else satisfactorily explains the overweening priority accorded this endeavor. A statement issued by the Ministry of Eastern Occupied Territories is perfectly direct on this issue: "Economic questions should not be considered in the solution of the Jewish question."[68] So too were military considerations regarded. Between 1 November and 4 December 1941, as the German Army pushed near Moscow, fifty trainloads of Jews traveled east; and even during the battle for Stalingrad the deportation trains were subject to only a brief embargo, which Himmler easily overrode. On several occasions when compelling military emergency brought drastic restrictions to all civilian transport, trainloads of Jews were dispatched as "armed forces trains."[69] Throughout the war the situation on the eastern front did not change; dangling at the end of hundreds of miles of railway, the *Wehrmacht* routinely found its supply lines clogged with cargoes of men and women and children.

Even the impending fall of the Third Reich did not diminish the effort to kill all the Jews of Europe. The Jews of Hungary were not killed until the summer of 1944; the SS had only been waiting until the Jews from other regions had been exterminated before they fell upon the Hungarians. By the time the government of Hungary came solidly under German control, Italy had turned on its German ally, the Russians had advanced to the borders of Rumania and Hungary, and a massive cross-channel invasion was momentarily expected in the West. None of this mattered, for it was at this same time that the Holocaust machine had reached full potential. Within the space of three months, a team of veteran RSHA "deportation specialists" had sealed the Jews of Hungary within ghettos, stripped them of property, and shipped 470,000 of their number to the camps; of those who survived the journey, only about one-fourth were judged to be suitable for labor. All others were immediately killed. The most intense destruction took place between 15 May and 8 June 1944; during this span of twenty-four days, ninety-two trains, according to SS records, transported 289,357 Hungarian Jews to Auschwitz. The vast majority were gassed in a continuous slaughter that, to the dismay of the camp commander, outstripped the capacity of his crematoriums.[70] Most of those who remained alive subsequently died of disease or were simply worked to death. Such was the standard fate; the Hungarian experience differed from that of other nationalities only in that the stages of the Holocaust—identification, extortion, concentration, death—were dramatically telescoped in time.

Always the Holocaust is surrounded by an aura of compelling urgency. Transport log jams must be untangled, personnel problems corrected, corruption [sic] controlled, the killing done faster, and the disposal of bodies made more efficient. In the end all of these problems were handled and the Holocaust became a fact.[71]

THE BUREAUCRATIZATION OF VIOLENCE

The fundamental approach of the SS to any problem was always the same: the calculated and orderly application of violence. Nothing illustrates this better than the Holocaust, which was from beginning to end perceived by Himmler to be a particularly thorny administrative task. It was in the organizational tradition of the SS to put a bureaucratic and technological gloss on any activity. The destruction of the Jews was no different. By 1938, the tireless academicians of the RuSHA had compiled a "Jewish List," a history of Jewish surnames in Germany, which ran to 175 pages. New departmental sections were established, notably within the SD, and new areas of expertise were encouraged. The SS Jewish expert, Adolf Eichmann, who had formerly toiled in another SD section compiling a list of German freemasons, is a prime example of one who capitalized on this new bureaucratic niche, which in time would become the infamous Section IV B of the RSHA. Esoteric specialties such as "emigration specialist" and "deportation specialist" appeared. The most efficient men in these positions were consummate bureaucrats since the essence of their job was administrative liaison. The scheduling of death trains was a "science" according to Eichmann.[72] All of these specialties within the SS drew heavily upon organizational and administrative ability. The Holocaust, in sum, became a reality because the SS was able to routinize the transport, concentration, and murder of millions of people.

THE CAMP SYSTEM

The transport was basically a matter of interdepartmental and interministry cooperation. It was here that the emigration specialists were so invaluable. The process of concentration drew upon the ancient European system of ghettos and upon newly evolved organizational skill—the concentration camp.

Emergency powers that were granted Hitler after the Reichstag fire contained a sweeping provision allowing "protective custody" arrests of anyone deemed a threat to the regime. The protective custody provision spurred a growth industry in the form of SA "wild" concentration camps, which stormtroopers used to settle private vendettas, intimidate political opponents, and extort money. Since all of these activities could be readily combined, it is difficult to determine what the primary motivation was, but by the end of 1933 there were more than fifty such improvised jails scattered throughout Germany holding an uncertain number of people (probably around ten thousand) for Communist party activities, suspicion of treason, threats to public safety, and subversive remarks.[73]

Himmler needed no encouragement to establish SS camps that initially differed from the SA variety only in that extortion was obviously not their central purpose. In March of 1933 Himmler ordered that a camp be established in an old powder factory near Dachau. It was to become the model and the primary training ground for the SS concentration camp system. The Death's-Head Formations were first formed at Dachau, and many of the top SS camp administrators were trained at Dachau, including Rudolf Hoess, the commandant of Auschwitz.

The commander of Dachau, Theodor Eicke, a long-time SA member who had jumped to the SS in 1930, was a man of fanatical loyalties with a capacity for leadership and organization. He soon distinguished himself in Himmler's eyes by introducing a system of harsh and unfailing discipline into the operating procedures of Dachau. His regulations for the "Maintenance of Discipline and Order" are a model of calculated brutality and consist of an inflexible system of punishments ranging from denial of mail, to periods of solitary confinement, to a variety of standardized beatings. Beatings at Dachau, as at all other camps, were savage, but under Eicke they were delivered publicly and by rotation. The intent of Eicke's policy was to utterly depersonalize camp discipline. In this Eicke was enormously successful; the effect on the inmates, and on the guards, was utter dehumanization. Accordingly, efficiency increased.

Other qualities endeared Eicke to Himmler. Eicke's hatred for all inmates, and most especially Jews, was profound. Prisoners, in his eyes, were the enemy with which his guards were constantly at war.[74] Hoess recalled that Eicke constantly drummed home the same themes.

> Any pity whatsoever for 'enemies of the state' was unworthy of an SS man. There was no place in the ranks of the SS for men with soft hearts. . . . He could only use hard, determined men who ruthlessly obeyed every order. It was not for nothing that the emblem was the Death's Head and that they carried a loaded gun. They were the only soldiers who even in peace time faced the enemy day and night, the enemy behind the wire. . . .[75]

Eicke came to view his Death's-Head Formations as the elite

of the SS. Whatever Himmler may have thought of this notion, it is clear that he saw in Eicke his model jailer, and in 1934 Eicke was made inspector of concentration camps with full authority to introduce his system of control into other camps. Dachau became a training center. Cadres of Death's-Head NCOs and officers, thoroughly indoctrinated with Eicke's merciless brand of national socialism and trained in the Dachau system, were sent to other camps. By 1935 the camp system had been consolidated into seven large camps, all under Death's-Head control and operating according to a common routinized system of numbing inhumanity.[76]

From the very beginning, manufacture and repair of equipment for SS paramilitary organizations was a concentration camp function. This too was done on Eicke's initiative, but Himmler was quick to see the potential of slave labor, and in 1938 the concentration camp system was wedded to the National Socialist building program. Major brickworks were established near existing camps (Sachsenhausen and Buchenwald), and new camps were established near rock quarries (Flossenburg and Mauthausen).[77] Henceforth, industrial considerations were always a major factor within the camp system, which by 1942 was largely under WVHA control.

By September 1939, the population of the concentration camps exceeded twenty thousand. The outbreak of war, as would be expected, fostered an increase in the camp population, and by late 1941 the population of the camps reached one hundred thousand. By then the camps had become very deadly places, and the figure of one hundred thousand in no way tallies the number of people who went into the camps. Overwork, brutality, malnourishment, and disease, by design, took a fearful toll. Jews, Gypsies (defined as people "who move about in a gypsy-like manner"), and other ethnic and social "undesirables" increasingly made up the camp population.[78] In the years to follow, Eicke's procedures of indoctrination and calculated brutality achieved their full potential: the Dachau system allowed a small number of marginal people to control, intimidate, and murder millions. As such it was a model of bureaucratic efficiency.

The period of 1942 to 1945 was the period of maximum growth during which the camp system was totally devoted to the twin goals of liquidation and slave labor, which was manifested in the selection process on the "ramp" at Birkenau, the largest of the Auschwitz complex of camps. Immediately upon arrival, those who could work—able bodied boys, men, and women without children—were sent to labor camps; all others were killed within a matter of hours. At other, more specialized camps, all would be killed upon arrival excepting a small work force to labor in the crematoriums. These detachments, the *Sonderkommando*, were themselves killed after a period of months since camp administrators correctly saw in them a potential for rebellion.

Gearing up for the final stage of the Holocaust—the industrialization of murder—took very little time because the necessary technology was already in place. It had already been developed in the context of another National Socialist hygienic endeavor.

EUTHANASIA

There is a clear administrative path from sterilization to euthanasia to industrial murder. Much of the ground work for the Holocaust was established by the willing nazification of German medicine. Roughly half of all German doctors became party members, far more than any other profession, and fully 7 percent were members of the SS. Many German physicians took completely to heart Rudolf Hess's dictum that "National Socialism is nothing more than applied biology" and embraced the image, artfully presented in such SS publications as *The Face of the German Doctor Over Four Centuries*, of the German physician as guardian of the volk.[79] Those doctors drawn into the euthanasia program looked upon themselves as healers of the Aryan race, and euthanasia was to them literally a kind of surgery.

As stated in *Mein Kampf*, National Socialist policy required laws to protect against the transmission of hereditary disease, and with the Nazi realization of power there soon came dire warnings from high officials that Germany was in danger of *Volkstod* (death of the race). In July of 1933 the Law for the Prevention of Offspring with Hereditary Diseases was enacted.[80] This statute provided that "anyone who is suffering from a hereditary disease can be sterilized by a surgical operation," and it also established "hereditary health courts" consisting of two physicians and a district judge. Appeal was possible but almost always futile.[81] An obsessive concern for racial hygiene can also be found in the law (passed in July of 1934), which created a centralized system of state health offices housing the Departments of Gene and Race Care. Among the many duties of these departments (such as marriage approvals and the selection of proper candidates for sterilization) was the maintenance of an exhaustive index of the hereditary value of German citizens.[82]

The National Socialist definition of hereditary disease was very broad and included schizophrenia, manic depressive disease, severe bodily deformation, various types of blindness and deafness, epilepsy, and hereditary [sic] alcoholism.[83] Evidently somewhere between 200,000 and 350,000 people were sterilized on the basis of these and other criteria. Having, from the standpoint of German national pride, an undesirable father seems to have been one criterion. In 1937 Hitler ordered that all children fathered by French and Belgian occupation troops in the Rhineland be rounded up and sterilized. This was accomplished without detectable resistance from the German medical establishment.[84]

Public advocates for euthanasia were not lacking in the Third Reich, but Hitler was at this time not among them. He is reported to have told the Reich Medical Leader Gerhard Wagner that the question of euthanasia would have to wait until wartime.[85] As would be expected in matters of this nature, Hitler kept to his word; however, developments preliminary to the full installation of the euthanasia program precede the war. Sometime in early 1939, Hitler's personal chancellory entertained an appeal from the father of a deformed child for a mercy killing. When this request was brought to the fuehrer's attention, he readily agreed and entrusted the matter to Dr. Karl Brandt, the reich commissioner of health and sanitation, and to the director of his personal chancellory, Philip Bouhler. Hitler also authorized that in the event of similar request, euthanasia be performed as a matter of routine, and shortly after the invasion of Poland a broad statement of authorization in Hitler's handwriting went to Bouhler and Brandt to establish a comprehensive program of euthanasia.[86]

Administratively, there were two euthanasia programs within Germany. Both programs originated in the Fuehrer Chancellory and broadly overlapped in personnel. Initially focusing on infants and very young children, all of Germany's institutionalized population soon became subject to the scrutiny of Germany's racial guardians.

Killing infants and children proved to be relatively simple. Questionnaires requesting detailed health information were sent by the Reich Health Ministry to all childcare institutions in Germany. Officially this search was conducted by the "Reich

Committee for the Scientific Registration of Serious Hereditary and Congenital Disease," and receiving physicians quite naturally assumed that the information requested was for registration purposes only. The completed questionnaires were then examined by three physicians to determine, on the basis of very broad standards, whether or not the children in question should be killed. As a rule, the children were killed within childcare institutions dominated by like-minded doctors by means of a variety of drugs. Such hospitals and care centers were designated by the Fuehrer Chancellory as "children's speciality institutions.[87]

The far more ambitious T4 Program (for *Tiergarten Strasse 4*, the Berlin address of the Fuehrer Chancellory) was aimed at adults and operated under a comprehensive administrative cover, the Reich Work Group for Sanitoriums and Nursing Homes (*Reichsarbeitsgemeinschaft Heil—und Pflegeanstalten;* or RAG). Questionnaires designed to identify Germany's "useless eaters" were sent to all care centers in Germany; upon return of the questionnaire, panels of "experts" (typically psychiatrists) passed judgment on patients. A red plus on the questionnaire within a box bearing the familiar bureaucratic warning "do not mark in this space" brought death.[88]

From its inception, the T4 Program was characterized by a sense of urgency. Understaffed in the wake of the invasion of Poland, hospitals and nursing homes were showered with questionnaires that had to be completed in short order. One physician recalls filling out fifteen hundred forms in the space of two weeks.[89] The evaluation of these forms by T4 "experts" was equally hurried and superficial; the inclination was strongly towards a "positive judgment" (death).

"Physicians commissions," consisting in practice largely of medical students and typists, would often descend on institutions that had been tardy in filling out questionnaires. When this happened, as it often did, institutional physicians had little control over the information entered on a questionnaire, which then tended to exaggerate a patient's infirmities. At the Neuendettelsauer nursing home in Bavaria the clerical handiwork of one dedicated commission slated more than one thousand patients for "treatment" in the span of one week.[90]

The T4 Program preyed on a much larger patient population than the children's euthanasia program and often drew from the resources of the SS. Separate and specialized euthanasia centers for adults were deemed a necessity. On 12 October 1939,

Himmler expropriated Grafeneck, a care center for handicapped children in Wurttemburg operated by the Samaritan Brothers. Under the direct supervision of the Criminal Police Commissioner of Wurttemburg, Christian Wirth, the children entrusted to the care of this institution were killed by injection or by means of drugs introduced into their food.[91] Grafeneck, soon empty, was the first of six euthanasia centers ultimately scattered throughout Germany—in Grafeneck, Brandenburg, Bensburg, Hartheim, Sonnenstein, and Eichberg.[92] One suspects that in all cases these killing centers, converted from isolated and walled mental hospitals, nursing homes, and prisons, murdered the original inhabitants in the general cause of the T4 Program. Apart from a desire for racial purity, T4 was also motivated by the need to create space within Germany's hardpressed medical facilities for military casualties. Hence, the emphasis on "useless eaters."

Secretly transporting and killing many thousands of disabled and severely retarded people was a formidable undertaking but one that was readily handled under the guise of the Charitable Transport Company for the Transport of the Sick (German acronym Gekrat), which brought the patients to the killing centers, and The Charitable Foundation for Institutional Care—known as "the Foundation" (Stiftung), which staffed the killing centers. These fronts, although not SS organizations, were heavily staffed with SS personnel, both medical and nonmedical. Gekrat, for example, hailed from the SS transport fleet.[93]

As the adults slated for execution came flooding in from the institutions of Germany, the process of murder by injection proved to be too costly and far too slow. This bottleneck, however, was short-lived. Euthanasia physicians, upon expert advice from the Reich Criminal Police Office, devised a primitive gas chamber that after some experimentation demonstrated a capability of killing up to thirty people at a time. Pure carbon monoxide, obtained from German chemical companies in bottled form, was the gas of choice.

Improvements followed. Arriving patients were understandably fearful about being crammed into a small windowless room. Wirth, or possibly Bouhler, who closely monitored every aspect of the euthanasia program, then hit upon an easy and effective deception; shower heads and benches were installed in the chamber, thereby creating a familiar institutional setting. All six euthanasia centers soon had such arrangements, which increased productivity to the point that crematoriums became a necessity. An uncertain but very large number of people were killed in this manner between late 1939 and the Fall of 1941 (variously estimated at between 60,000 and 275,000).[94]

All institutionalized German Jews were killed, at first within Germany and in segregated groups (T4 policy stipulated that Aryans and Jews not be murdered together). By the fall of 1940, German Jews falling within the purview of the T4 Program were shipped to Poland to die in the death camps.[95] It was in the euthanasia centers that the practice of robbing Jewish corpses of their gold teeth was first introduced.[96]

The secrecy of the T4 Program relied on the use of a formal Aesopian language (as did the Holocaust) and on a variety of bureaucratic departments that existed only to foster the illusion of civilization. Secretly murdering a patient required, at a minimum, three prevaricating letters. The first letter notified the family of the patient's transfer "because of war-related measures"; the second indicated that the patient had arrived safely and sternly advised against visits; and the third letter, sent by the "Condolence Letter Department," informed the family of the death of their relative.[97] Often, to further ensure secrecy, the patient was transferred to the killing center by way of an intermediate institution; that is, the euthanasia program "laundered" patients.[98]

Death certificates required a major bureaucratic conjuring act. Since all patients were murdered, it was necessary to come up with a satisfactory reason for death. It would not do, as happened once, to list the cause of death as appendicitis when the patient did not have an appendix.[99] Timing was also a preoccupation; an accurate date of death would have soon revealed that all patients who went for "treatment" died shortly after arrival. A Special registry office within each killing center produced bogus death certificates (signed by a physician but not dated) listing, on the basis of elaborate "time cards" and "death files," a plausible date and cause of death. Cremation was explained as a precaution against epidemics, and families were provided with a standard funeral urn that contained equally standard ashes (bodies were not cremated individually).[100]

Inevitably this remarkable bureaucratic subterfuge began to break down. Families were informed that their loved ones had died more than once—of different causes and in different places. Too many healthy patients died suddenly. A family that had lost one child received multiple urns. Otherwise healthy epileptics would report for sterilization only to disappear. Once thriving institutional care centers all of a sudden stood empty or contained only convalescing soldiers. But the major problem was that the T4 Program took place largely within Germany and murdered people that Germans defined as Germans. The endless one-way traffic into the euthanasia centers, coupled with the smoke of crematoriums, provided solid evidence of what was going on. Denunciations from the pulpit and inquiries by relatives made it clear to Hitler that the T4 Program was widely known and unpopular. In the fall of 1941 the T4 Program was officially shut down, but by this time the biggest part of Germany's "useless eaters," a social category that was beginning to include the institutionalized elderly, had been killed.

In fact, the public dismantling of the T4 Program was yet another bureaucratic dodge. The visible and offending euthanasia centers were closed, and, naturally, the several bureaucratic fronts that screened them dematerialized. But there was no change in policy.

Within Germany the silent murder of children and infants continued essentially unabated. Indeed, this practice, now unofficial but no less firm, was expanded to include children up to the age of 16, engulfing in some instances institutionalized adolescents who had eluded the administrative coils of the T4 Program.[101] The children's euthanasia program was maintained throughout the war and (such was the zeal of some German physicians) for some time after.[102]

Nazi medical authorities also tapped the initiative of ideologically committed doctors to foster a "wild euthanasia" program, which eliminated adults by the same inconspicuous methods used in the children's program, by means of drugs or starvation and usually within the institutions that ostensibly cared for them. This agenda seems to have been obtained by merely continuing to officially refer to mental patients as "useless eaters" (or similar euphemisms) and by maintaining an obvious policy of not punishing medical murder.[103] The fiction that the euthanasia program applied only to hereditary disease was soon abandoned; wild euthanasia preyed more or less randomly on the medically burdensome, including, for example, tubercular slave laborers.

In the occupied east and within the labor camps there was much for T4 personnel to do. By the spring of 1940 the useless eaters of the occupied territories were being eliminated by an itinerant euthanasia kommando under *Hauptsturmfuehrer* Herbert Lang. Specializing in gas vans, which in the tradition of the T4 Program used bottled carbon monoxide, the Lang Kommando fanned out from its base in Poznan to murder mental patients and, increasingly, Jews who could not work. Lang and his team drove to the hospital or transit camp and then, at intervals of two or three hours, drove away with cargoes of designated patients.[104] The driver released the gas from inside the cab. Simple and efficient, the gas vans were constrained only by a limited supply of bottled gas.

Himmler was quick to grasp the potential of a T4 program for his empire of concentration camps. With Bouhler's concurrence, this was put in place by early 1941 (if not earlier) and was officially designated Operation 14f13 (camp code for type of death; 14f1 indicated natural death, 14f2 suicide, and so on; 14f13 denoted "special treatment"). Operation 14f13 greatly enhanced the efficiency of the labor camps (the death camps, of course, did not need its services) by quickly ridding them of the sick, infirm, and psychologically troublesome. In time 14f13 operatives advanced to killing whole categories of people, but throughout they kept up the pretense of executing people, usually by injection, on the basis of a much abbreviated medical form.[105]

The most sinister manifestation of the T4 hydra lies in the death camps. It was no accident that the first generation of death camps—Auschwitz represents the second—closely followed the official demise of the T4 Program since these installations were, absent the paperwork, vastly expanded and more efficiently murderous euthanasia centers. The first death camps were designed, staffed, and commanded by T4 personnel who continued to think of themselves in terms of the Foundation. The connection could not be more direct; the first and most primitive death camp was established in November of 1941 when the Lang Kommando was ordered into a sedentary existence at the small village of Chelmno in occupied Poland. The murder of the Jews of the Lodze Ghetto began on 8 December 1941, shortly after Lang, who had been ordered to Berlin for consultation, returned to Chelmno with three redesigned gas vans. At first only vaguely defined useless eaters were gassed—then all.[106]

THE INVASION OF POLAND

At the declaration of the war, a motley assortment of SS paramilitary units made up of personnel drawn from the SD, Security Police, and Death's-Head regiments recently released from concentration camp duty, followed the Wehrmacht into Poland. Acting on the basis of a sweeping directive to "clean-up once and for all . . . Jews, intelligentsia, clergy, nobility, . . ." these units proceeded to concentrate the Jews of Poland into ghettos and to destroy the Polish leadership. Independent of Wehrmacht control, the actual execution of this directive by SS units was, to Himmler's chagrin, reminiscent of the wildest excesses of the Crystal Night pogrom. Drunkenness, looting, rape, and murder were the essential characteristics of SS activities during the months that followed the invasion. The wholesale murder of Jews was routinely tolerated. When, for example, an SS man and a member of the army's Secret Field Police shot fifty Jews out of hand, the incident was chalked up to "youthful initiative." An estimated 250,000 Jews had died by December of 1939.[107]

SS behavior in Poland brought protests from the army. As always, these protests were couched in terms of violations to the honor of German soldiers, and, as always, they came to nothing. Himmler raised the specter of an SS commissar breathing down the neck of every German field general, and that was enough to silence further criticism.[108]

After the invasion of Poland, roughly two million Jews fell under Nazi control. The concentration of these people into ghettos proved an enormous undertaking beyond anything in the experience of the SS at that time. It was Himmler's goal to have all Jews resettled into the region known as the General Government, comprising much of occupied Poland, and closed within ghettos by the summer of 1940. Virtually the entire rail network of occupied Poland was allocated after 15 November for the purpose of shipping Jews to the ghettos of central Poland. In December these shipments began to include Jews and Gypsies from within the reich.[109]

Disorganization reigned. The basic process at this time seems to have been to load as many Jews as possible onto trains and ship them east, often without any clear destination. These conditions are a reflection of the urgency behind the "resettlement" program. Another contributing factor was Himmler's absolute conviction that an unlimited number of Jews could be put into any ghetto. However crowded conditions became within the ghettos of the General Government, Jewish resettlers continued to arrive at an undiminished pace. The effect of such a policy is easily predicted but hard to appreciate. To take a single instance: in November 1940 a little more than one square mile of Warsaw was fenced in—the Warsaw Ghetto—and within this area resided four hundred thousand people. Disease in combination with a policy of systematic starvation brought the monthly death toll to five thousand.[110] Conditions in other Polish ghettos were no different.

EINSATZGRUPPEN

It is clear that the decision to go ahead with the Final Solution had been made before the invasion of Russia, most probably in the early spring of 1941.[111] A policy of outdoor massacre was embraced, but Himmler was concerned that this organizational commitment would degenerate into an enlargement of the debaucheries that characterized the Polish campaign. Closely scrutinized by Heydrich, a brigade of murderers was formed and trained for the invasion. By May, three thousand men from the SD, Security Police, Order Police, and the Waffen SS (specifically, from the Death's-Head units that had been formed by Eicke) were organized into four battalion-sized special action groups (Einsatzgruppen). Drilled and indoctrinated anew by RuSHA racial instructors, a commitment to the necessity for savagery toward the racial enemy developed among them. The leadership, drawn exclusively from the SD or the Security Police, represented a cross section of the SS middle-level management and included a physician, a theologian, an opera singer, a number of Ph.Ds and many lawyers.[112]

These newly booted bureaucrats were given special training at the Frontier Police School at Pretsch, near Wittenberg. One week before the invasion of Russia, Heydrich had the entire unit pass in review and then assembled them for a speech. Heydrich spoke of the necessity of taking on difficult tasks in the service of the state and of the need for "unparalleled hardness." Later that day, in the privacy of the castle at Pretsch, Heydrich provided the leadership of the Einsatzgruppen with the specifics of their mission. If we are to believe the testimony of Otto Ohlendorf, the commander of Einsatzgruppe D, many of these formerly chairbound SD and Security Police professionals balked at their assignment; but, all obeyed—it was, they were told, a fuehrer order.[113]

At the highest level it was determined that the Einsatzgruppen would be supplied by the army but would otherwise be under RSHA control, an arrangement that was no doubt a legacy of the Wehrmacht's modest attempts at interference in Poland. A further stipulation was that the Einsatzgruppen would have complete freedom of movement, including access to the front-line areas. It was correctly assumed that this would greatly facilitate the process of mass murder.[114]

Each Einsatzgruppe (A, B, C, and D) was assigned to a specific army group and moved into Russia at the heels of the Wehrmacht. The Jews of Russia—some four million within the regions occupied by Germany—were largely concentrated into urban areas and lived within the context of a highly anti-Semitic population that was in many case, if not in most cases, willing to assist in the task of assembling and murdering Jews. Thus, it does not surprise us that the Einsatzgruppen were enormously successful. Altogether roughly 1,400,000 Russian Jews were murdered.

The actual number of people directly involved in liquidation of Russian Jewry was of course much greater than the three thousand in the Einsatzgruppen. Units of Ukranians and Baltic Germans were often incorporated within the Einsatzgruppen, and Himmler's ever-present HSSPFs were always eager to assist with the loan of a spare unit of Order Police. In simple pattern it can be said that two waves of murderers swept over occupied Russia. Behind the Einsatzgruppen, locally organized kommandos of SD, Gestapo, and Order Police fanned out to eliminate those Jews who had escaped the first wave of destruction.[115]

The actual process of killing was brutally simple: Jews were assembled, often on the pretense of resettlement, had their clothing and valuables collected, were herded into groups before an antitank ditch or ravine, and shot. With minor variations and in numbers up to thirty-five thousand (Babi Yar), this process was repeated hundreds of times in occupied Russia.

Himmler found that the massacre method held certain inherent shortcomings. In the first place, secrecy was impossible to maintain. The occupied population, ordinary soldiers (who wrote home and took pictures), and, increasingly, Jews were learning the truth of resettlement. Feeble but highly placed complaints about damage to the honor of the Wehrmacht once again added to Himmler's burdens. Where possible, Jews fled the invaders or went into hiding. And, in the light of the universally savage nature of the German occupation, non-Jews came to suspect that they might be included in future cycles of mass murder. There were also major personnel problems. Among the Einsatzgruppen leadership, nightmares and intestinal complaints (something that also plagued Himmler) were common. In a few instances, hospitalization was required. At the enlisted level, the Einsatzgruppen often degenerated into collections of inebriates.

Himmler on only one occasion witnessed a massacre. On his own initiative he asked the commander of Einsatzgruppe B, Arthur Nebe, to shoot a hundred Jews so that he might observe the liquidation process. Afterwards, he was visibly shaken but recovered sufficiently to deliver a speech on obedience to a higher law and to duty. "Look in the eyes of the men in this Kommando," Himmler was then told. "These men are finished for the rest of their lives."[116] Later in the day, Nebe and Himmler toured an insane asylum, after which Himmler ordered that Nebe kill the inmates. Toward their parting, Himmler suggested that Nebe turn his mind to "more humane" methods of killing, but the only innovation that Nebe could think of on short notice involved the use of explosives.[117]

The difficulties experienced by the Einsatzgruppen were sufficient to bring in the services of the RSHA technical units (IID), which contrived gas vans that used exhaust gases (and not bottled CO) to kill women and children. Ostensibly more "scientific," and hence in Himmler's eyes more humane, these devices were enormously unpopular with the Einsatzgruppen rank and file since it was they who had to do the unloading.

THE COMMISSAR ORDER

As the pockets of Russian Jewry dwindled and as organizational problems mounted, the Einsatzgruppen began to emphasize other activities. Throughout the course of the Russian campaign, the enemy was not the Russian or the Jew but the "Jewish-Bolshevik," the "Jewish-Commissar," or the "Jewish-Partisan." The Commissar Order issued by the Wehrmacht on 6 June 1941, directing that all captured political commissars be "as a matter of principle" shot immediately, is a concrete reflection of this attitude. Compliance with this unpopular order, which was in fact a fuehrer order, varied from commander to commander, but a common practice was to avoid direct complicity by handing over suspects to the Einsatzgruppen.[118] A further and related duty of the Einsatzgruppen was to screen the oceans of Russian prisoners of war for Jewish soldiers. Once identified, of course, such people were shot.

The Commissar Order provides yet another example of the

uncanny ability of Nationalist Socialist thinkers to turn social categories into biological categories. The SS, for example, sponsored several attempts to identify "racial blood." These efforts, naturally, failed. In the Commissar Order another approach beckoned to SS Hauptsturmfuehrer Hirt, a professor of anatomy at the University of Strasbourg and a dedicated member of Ahnenerbe, an SS anthropological institute formed to study the heritage of the "Nordic Indo-Germanic Race." Hirt wrote to Himmler that anthropometric studies of Jewish skulls were sadly lacking but that a supply of "Jewish-Bolshevist-Commissar" skulls would fill this void. A precise man, Hirt suggested that captives so identified should not be killed until after they had been measured and photographed and that the undamaged head should be placed in a hermetically sealed can before it was sent to Ahnenerbe.

Himmler was enthusiastic, and to an undetermined degree Hirt's program became a reality. It is known that Himmler ordered that 150 suitable people be culled from among the inmates of Auschwitz and that an Ahnenerbe official was sent to Auschwitz to make the selection. The bodies of some of these men and women were ultimately discovered by the American Army when it captured Strasbourg.[119]

THE ROOTS OF THE HOLOCAUST INDUSTRY

The demise of the T4 Program in August of 1941 proved to be timely. It was at this time that Himmler's attention was directed towards the problems associated with the policy of outdoor massacre by which the Jews of Russia were being exterminated. The organizational commitment had already been made to exterminate all the Jews of Europe, but it was only now that Himmler was beginning to grapple with the immensity of this task; it was therefore with some urgency that Himmler sought guidance from the technologically pioneering mass murderers of the General Foundation for the Affairs of Insane Asylums.

Beginning in the fall of 1941 a large contingent of men drawn from Hitler's Chancellory and from the euthanasia centers reported to HSSPF Odilo Globocnik, who had been entrusted with the command of Operation Reinhard: killing the Jews of Poland. Among those reporting to Globocnik at the inception of Operation Reinhard were Christian Wirth, who was at that time accompanied by an entire "euthanasia kommando," Bouhler's consulting chemist, Dr. Kallmeyer, and Viktor Brack, Bouhler's chief liaison officer in the T4 Program. Wirth set up the gas chambers of Operation Reinhard and then became commandant of Belzec. He later became Operation Reinhard's extermination camp inspector. The commandants of all three extermination camps under operational control of Globocnik were drawn from the euthanasia centers.[120] In sum, among those who staffed and directed the euthanasia program can be found the cadre of the extermination camps; indeed, Wirth and his colleagues, many of whom remained on the payroll of Hitler's Chancellory, continued to refer to themselves as a "foundation" long after they arrived in Poland.[121]

Events would prove Himmler's administrative instincts murderously astute. With only minor modifications, the procedures and equipment prototypically developed by the General Foundation were amenable to virtually unlimited expansion. The Grafeneck gas chamber, as noted, held thirty people; the gas chambers at Auschwitz held in excess of six thousand.[122] Perhaps hundreds died each day during peak periods of murder in the euthanasia program: for many days running in June of 1944, ten thousand Hungarian Jews a day were gassed at Auschwitz.

THE DEATH CAMPS

In the final accomplishment of the Holocaust, three organizational initiatives are apparent: the Einsatzgruppen in Russia, the death camps of Himmler's HSSPFs, and the combined work camps and death camps of the WVHA. There were six major killing installations: Chelmno, established by HSSPF Koppe, located near the Lodze Ghetto just outside the territory of the General Government; Treblinka, Sobibor, and Belzec, erected in the course of Operation Reinhard and located within the territory of the General Government; and the killing installations within the WVHA camps at Lublin (Majdanek), located within the territory of the General Government, and at Auschwitz, located in Upper Silesia. Once the decision had been made to finally destroy all of European Jewry, the technology of mass destruction rapidly evolved to the point of industrial mass production. Auschwitz could kill people as fast as they could be shipped in by rail.

The first operational killing center was Chelmno. At the request of the local *Gauleiter*, Himmler gave his permission to kill one hundred thousand Jews. It was at this juncture, in late 1941, that the RSHA gas vans came into play. Again, simplicity beckoned. Apart from the associated graveyards, Chelmno was basically a loading dock and a storehouse. The entire complex was enclosed within an area of less than 2 hectares.[123]

Beginning in December 1941, under the authority of HSSPF Koppe, Jews from the Lodze Ghetto were transported in groups of a hundred or so to an old chateau in the Chelmno (Kulmhof) woods some forty miles away. There the Lang Kommando, re-equipped with RSHA gas vans, simply told the new arrivals to undress, herded them through a corridor marked "to the bath," and loaded them into the vans. Instead of taking them to the showers, the gas vans drove them to their place of burial. Usually, but not always, they were dead upon arrival. In this manner a thousand people a day could be killed.[124]

The Operation Reinhard camps erected by HSSPF Globocnik were in all ways more efficient. In full production by the summer of 1942, Belzec, Sobibor, and Treblinka were centralized complexes designed to process and kill whole trainloads of people. All three installations had stationary gas chambers (never less than three) that, in keeping with their euthanasia heritage, were disguised as showers. Indeed, as Hilberg emphasizes, the layout of all of the Operation Reinhard camps centered on the fiction that they were just transit camps.[125] Treblinka, the largest (encompassing roughly 20 hectares) and most efficient of these camps, was also in its arrangement the most deceptive. A fake hospital and a fake train station greeted new arrivals, but, quite often, so did mounds of unburied dead.[126]

Construction on Belzec, the prototype for Operation Reinhard, began as early as November of 1941, and the camp was in operation by March of the following year. Initially, bottled CO seems to have been used at Belzec, but this practice was quickly abandoned; thereafter, diesel exhaust from a captured soviet tank engine was piped into the gas chambers. At Treblinka and Sobibor diesel exhaust was employed from the beginning.

In the normal routine, new arrivals would have their valuables collected at the railhead, told over a loudspeaker that they would be sent to the shower building, have their clothes collected (women would also have their hair shorn), and then they would be herded a distance of a hundred yards or so to the gas chambers. Afterwards, their remaining valuables (gold teeth) would be collected and their bodies disposed of either by mass burial or by burning in open pits.

By Hilberg's tabulation, Chelmno killed 150,000 people, Sobibor, 200,000, Belzec, 550,000, and Treblinka, the resettlement destination of the residents of the Warsaw Ghetto, 750,000. Very few escaped these camps. At Chelmno, Treblinka, and Sobibor the Jewish Sonderkommando rebelled, and there were altogether a few dozen survivors. There were two survivors of Belzec.[127]

In the Fall of 1943 the Wirth Kommando, which had constructed Treblinka, Sobibor, and Belzec, was ordered to destroy them and remove all traces that they had ever existed. The really hard work had already been accomplished by the SS exhumation unit. This was Kommando 1005, a group of Jewish slaves, commanded by Standartenfuehrer Paul Blobel, a former member of the Einsatzgruppen and a man who had in some manner offended Heydrich.[128] After disinterring many of the numberless hecatombs that now contained one fourth of Russian Jewry and burning the contents on great pyres constructed of rails and timbers, Blobel and his kommando turned their attention to the vast graves of Chelmno and Operation Reinhard. In these places both burning and a "bone crusher" were employed. The ground was then plowed and seeded.[129] Chelmno was closed in March of 1943 and then reopened in February of 1944 for fitful killings that ended in January of 1945. Burning the bodies produced by Chelmno removed all but documentary evidence since there was little to Chelmno but graveyards.

Majdanek, second in size only to Auschwitz, was the major labor camp complex within the General Government. The main camp, located in the suburbs of Lublin, covered an estimated 275 hectares. With the advent of Operation Reinhard, Majdanek became a killing center. Three gas chambers, two equipped to use carbon monoxide or hydrogen cyanide gas interchangeably and the third using hydrogen cyanide only, then began to destroy the Jewish inmate population. Estimates for the number of people murdered at Majdanek vary enormously. Hilberg provides a figure of fifty thousand.[130] Other estimates suggest that more than three hundred thousand were murdered at Majdanek.

Majdanek has a tangled administrative history because it became a bone of contention between Globocnik and the WVHA. In the end, Himmler lost patience with the corruption found in Globocnik's "Lublinland Reserve." Many Jewish labor camps in the Lublin area were in the hands of an SS company, OSTI, headed by Globocnik and his SS cronies. When Globocnik's profiteering caught up with him in the Fall of 1943, OSTI was transferred to Oswald Pohl and the WVHA. On 3 November

1943, five of these work camps were closed, and the seventeen thousand Jews in excess of current needs were immediately sent to Majdanek. Numerous reports, consistent on particulars, reveal that upon arrival all seventeen thousand were machine-gunned into great pits. Their bodies were then burned, casting a pall of ash and smoke over the city of Lublin.[131]

AUSCHWITZ

Auschwitz was ideally located near a juncture of rail lines in a relatively isolated region of Upper Silesia. In the summer of 1941, camp Commander Rudolf Hoess was, by his own recollection, called to Berlin and told by Himmler of the Final Solution and also told to prepare for a dramatic expansion of the facilities at Auschwitz. Eighteen square miles around the existing facility were ultimately acquired by the Land Office for the strengthening of Germandom on which on which the main camp Auschwitz I and Birkenau (Auschwitz II) were constructed. Monowitz (Auschwitz III), some miles away, was the industrial camp of the I. G. Farben Company, which produced synthetic rubber.[132]

Everywhere the sure hand of experience is evident in the design of Auschwitz. It was not, as were the camps of HSSPFs, a makeshift operation. Auschwitz was a modern factory. The vast installation of Auschwitz II in the Birkenau Woods was the death camp. This function was carried out in four "combination units"—combined crematoriums and gas chambers. Two of these units were located near the "ramp," the rail platform where the selections were made, and the remaining two were located some five hundred yards to the north next to "Canada," the block of warehouses that held plundered goods. The two larger units centered on underground gas chambers equipped with elevators to lift the corpses to the crematoriums. These chambers were very large, roughly 7 by 30 meters, and could hold up to two thousand people.[133] The gas chambers in the other combination units were above ground and were somewhat smaller. All of these combination units had large connected rooms for undressing. The gas chambers, as elsewhere, were designed to look like showers.

At Auschwitz, Zyklon B (cyanide) gas was used. Experimentation on Russian POWs had demonstrated to Hoess the efficiency of this gas, which was a commercial product used for fumigation—something that no doubt enhanced its appeal to SS decision makers. However that may be, great effort was made to ensure a regular supply. Since, oddly enough, Zyklon B was something that the SS industries did not manufacture, orders for Zyklon B were placed by the chief disinfectant officer of the Waffen SS on behalf of the Auschwitz "Extermination and Fumigation Division." Zyklon B disintegrated over time, and at Auschwitz a supply had to be on hand at all times; shipments of "materials for the Jewish Resettlement" (Zyklon B) therefore arrived about every six weeks.[134]

By the summer of 1944 the WVHA empire of concentration camps had grown enormously. A map sent by Pohl to Himmler shows 20 major camps and 165 satellite camps. A report dated 15 August 1944 lists the total number of concentration camp inmates at 524,296. Auschwitz was a big part of this. In addition to Auschwitz I, the parent camp, and Birkenau, there were 39 satellite installations of which Monowitz was by far the largest. Birkenau covered 440 acres and at its peak may have housed as many as 100,000 people in appalling conditions. From its completion in the spring of 1943 and throughout all of 1944, it never seems to have held less than 30,000.[135]

Auschwitz, then, was the River Rouge of concentration camps. It did everything on an assembly-line basis. Six hundred thousand people were gassed at Birkenau between May and October of 1944, and the overall death toll is greatly in excess of one million. On a *routine* day, trains bearing four thousand people (not all of them alive) would arrive at the Birkenau rail platform, and of these people roughly a thousand would be culled for brief survival. The remainder would be killed. By nightfall, their bodies would have been cremated and their clothes stored away in the vast warehouses of "Canada," waiting to be shipped to Germany.

The selection process performed by SS physicians (men such as Mengele) "on the ramp" was keyed to current needs for exploitable labor: able-bodied men, boys, and women without children as a rule were not immediately gassed. But for Jews, the labor camps and industrial camps (such as Monowitz) were really an extension of the confiscation process. The established practice with the Jews was to extract the maximum amount of labor in the shortest possible time. As a matter of policy, Jews were worked to death. At Monowitz, for example, the factory police worked closely with the SS guards who carried out their duties with characteristic brutality. At least one group of inmates was told point blank that they would "perish in concrete."[136] This, as it turns out, was literally true since it was company practice to throw the dead and dying into ditches dug for electrical cables, which would then be sealed with concrete. Roughly thirty-five thousand inmates worked at the Monowitz complex at one time or another; of these, perhaps ten thousand survived.[137] No one, in or out of the SS, has ever supposed that such labor practices were economically efficient. But that was never the issue. This murderous policy was the means of reconciling the WVHA concern for industrial output with the higher organizational goal of exterminating European Jewry.

In July of 1944 Majdanek fell into the hands of the Russians, yet Auschwitz, less than two hundred miles away, continued to operate at full capacity until October. It was Himmler's intention that none of the inmates escape SS control. In November, the last of the crematoriums was ordered demolished, and in a routine organizational ritual, the Sonderkommando were taken into the Birkenau Woods and shot. In January more than sixty thousand inmates still within the Auschwitz complex were marched to the Reich camps—a distance of roughly four hundred miles. A small but unknown percentage of people completed the journey.[138]

1945

Conditions within the Reich camps during 1945 were, if anything, worse than in the death camps. Sanitation and health care were virtually nonexistent. Typhus was endemic. At Mauthausen, for example, thirty thousand people died from starvation, disease, and murder in 1945. Mauthausen remained under German control until the very last days of the war; the killing, as was typical, did not stop until the camp was overrun.[139]

At Bergen-Belsen a small British advance force was greeted at the camp entrance by the SS commander Josef Kramer and staff. Kramer, who had once commanded Birkenau, then announced, "They are calm at present." The reason for "calm" became apparent to the British when sporadic firing indicated that other camp personnel, those not involved in this welcoming ceremony, were still busily murdering prisoners at the other end of the camp. An inspection of the camp revealed forty thousand inmates, most of whom were in advanced stages of starvation, and ten thousand unburied dead. Thirteen thousand more died shortly after liberation.[140]

Nothing better indicates the disarray of the camp system in the final days of the war than the vast numbers of corpses that greeted the Allies as each camp, in turn, gave up its horrors. Under normal circumstances such untidiness, from the SS perspective, was never permitted. The SS carefully balanced the production of corpses with the institutional capacity for burial and cremation ("body flow"). Logistically, the living almost always proved more cooperative than the dead, for even a day's delay in disposing of the corpses at a place like Treblinka or Auschwitz could produce hopeless tangles within the complicated system of assemblage and transport that allowed the Holocaust machine to work at peak capacity. It is known that an excess of corpses once forced Treblinka to an absolute standstill.[141] During the slaughter of Hungarian Jews (an operation as tightly scheduled as an amphibious landing), when the capacity of the Auschwitz crematoriums proved hopelessly insufficient, a huge program of open-air burning was instituted to alleviate the bottleneck. Long experience during Operation Reinhard had demonstrated that a sufficiently hot fire and the correct mix of corpses–the correct percentage of men, women, and children—produced enough body fat for efficient cremation. It was only necessary to set the Sonderkommando to ladling it back onto the pyre.[142]

DISCUSSION

In his last testament Hitler makes reference to his single enduring accomplishment. The Jews, he tells us, "atoned" for their "guilt" by "humane means." Like Hitler, the SS often spoke and thought in Aesopian language. This too was an organizational decision. Just as the enormous logistical burden of murdering six million people was ultimately subject to administrative and technological solution, so too was the psychological burden of mass murder. As much as possible the bestial activities associated with the Holocaust were kept at arms length, both psychologically and physically, and the higher a person was within the SS hierarchy, the more the Holocaust became a matter of organizational dreams and paperwork. Himmler, we know, dealt firsthand with death on only one occasion. He did not choose to repeat the experience and, thereafter, lived as before in a world of futuristic dreams, ersatz ritual, herbal medicines, and sanitized bureaucratic reports.

It was organizational policy that SS administrators follow the emotional career of their leader: they were blooded. New HSSPFs were routinely acclimatized to the SS world of "hard tasks" by temporary assignments to the Waffen SS—especially Theodor Eicke's savage battalions—and mid-level technocrats, such as Otto Ohlendorf, were often plucked from some quiet administrative den to briefly command a mobile killing operation.[143] Among SS personnel, at least, participation in the obdurate reality of racial policy tended to invigorate their commitment to the crusade. Ranking SS technocrats accepted the organization's odious rationalizations and gulled themselves into a sense of self-worth with the virtues of remaining "decent" among fields of corpses and the ethics of "hard tasks"; the morality, as Himmler put it, of being "superhumanly inhuman." As the Nuremberg testimony makes clear, duty and bonds of oath often allowed all sense of guilt to be abandoned to the next higher organizational level. All the same, SS policy distanced its men as much as possible from the suffering, murders, and corpses with "scientific methods" (i.e., gas chambers and crematoriums) and the use of ethnic auxiliaries and conscript Jews motivated by fear of death.

Even the elaborate secrecy that surrounded the Holocaust was as much a psychological ploy as it was a strategic deception. No undertaking as large as the Final Solution could long remain a secret. But it remained enough of a secret that people outside the SS could choose not to know, and both victim and administrative accomplice often made that choice.

In its ultimate refinement the Holocaust industry manipulated human emotions as efficiently as it scheduled trains. Except children, few among the four and five thousand victims arriving daily at Auschwitz in 1944 could have been totally ignorant of their fate; but, by design, frightened, bewildered, filthy, and dehydrated, many could hope that the showers were really showers. Lightly guarded and lulled, perhaps, by the music of Mozart, they walked the short distance from the ramp to the combination units, undressed, carefully folded their clothes as per instructions, and entered the chambers. Quickly filled, the gas chamber would be sealed, and before many had discovered that the "showers" did not work, an SS medical corpsman wearing a gas mask would pour the prescribed amount of cyanide crystals down the chamber's ventilation shaft.[144] In minutes all would be dead and the Sonderkommando, clinging to a few extra weeks of life, would take over. The SS looked upon the hopes and fears of its victims in much the same way that it regarded their body fat—as a hitherto untapped commodity.

The SS attracted and created corrupt and horribly sadistic people by the tens of thousands, but that presence within the organization does not explain the Holocaust. The Final Solution was accomplished in spite of such people; they were, after all, inefficient. Administrative talent and dutiful, methodical, personnel were the key to assembling, murdering, and burning the bodies of more than five million people, and neither the inhumanity nor the irrationality of this organizational goal provided much hindrance to its accomplishment. Himmler, banal, loyal, and efficient, was the archetypical SS man. He embraced the beliefs expected of him and did what he was told with enthusiasm. This was overwhelmingly true of the entire administrative apparatus of the Third Reich.

The Holocaust looms before us as a ghastly exaggeration of a fundamental process of this century—the rationalization of mythical reality. How were the Jews of Europe killed? "From the start," writes Raul Hilberg in the preface to The Destruction of the European Jews,

> I have wanted to know how the Jews of Europe were destroyed, I wanted to explore the sheer mechanism of destruction, and as I delved into the problem, I saw that I was studying an administrative process carried out by bureaucrats in a network of offices spanning a continent.[145]

Kren and Rappaport observe that "far from being irrational, the Holocaust can only be epitomized in terms of excessive rationality, an example of logical thought slipping the bonds of human feeling."[146] It was "the bonds of human feeling" that the SS was designed to guard itself against; it was just this "weakness" that was the central topic of Himmler's infamous Poznan speech. "And then they come along, the eighty million good Germans, and each one has his decent Jew. . . ." This Himmler feared: any consistent exercise of feelings, even in small ways, would have crippled the Holocaust.

CORRESPONDENCES

I argue here that the Holocaust and especially the events leading up to it conform in *most* respects, but not all, to the explanatory scheme presented above.

1.0; 1.1; 1.2 - The image of World Jewry as a biological evil was,
in Hitler's words, "The granite basis of my conduct." Hitler acted
on a biological imperative, however delusional, that allowed no com-
promise. Jews, in his world view, would infallibly destroy all that
he cherished. An obsessive fear of Jews, as Hitler imagined them,
was at the core of his personality; he would have sooner taken his
life than abandon his war against the Jews—as he did. In his political
testament of 29 April 1945, he expresses his fear of becoming a "spectacle organized by Jews for the amusement of their hysterical masses."

2.0; 2.1; 2.2 - The vast SS organization, if anything, rivaled the
NKVD in its immunity to accountability. It had its own army and
its own industrial base. It answered only to Hitler and was, therefore,
able to pursue its policy of destruction without interference. Economic
and military considerations, as we know, counted for nothing.

3.0 - The history of the Third Reich and its principal organ of
social control bears out the prediction of this summary proposition.

4.0 - The steady grown of the SS "state" and the parallel erosion
of the reich judiciary is a matter of record. German fear of the Communist left (a "Jewish conspiracy") as much as Hitler's political clout
brought about his appointment as chancellor. The growth of Hitler's
one-party state proceeded from the instant of his appointment; the
possibly fortuitous Reichstag fire was used by Hitler to render the
Communist menace more palpable and dramatically accelerated the
pace of his "legal revolution." Thus began the established pattern.
Throughout the history of the regime, the perceived menace to Germany, from within and without, nourished the principle of fuehrer
absolutism.

4.1 - The link between the steady and unremitting radicalization
of racial policy and the power of the SS is direct and without exception.
The destruction of the Jews was preceded by a steady and progressive
degradation of German society: law was replaced by an emphasis on
administrative fiat, which was, in turn, replaced by a reliance on
verbal orders and directives.[147]

5.0; 5.1; 5.2 - The view that the Nazi state was absolutely monolithic
is no longer accepted. In fact, the Nazi state was shot through with
redundant and often competing institutions. Competition, however,
invariably took the form of currying the fuehrer's favor. In the final
analysis, the Holocaust took place because Hitler demanded it, but
one cannot fail to be impressed by the degree to which all segments

of German society participated in the destruction of the Jews. German institutional resistance to the Holocaust simply did not exist: the Foreign Office, the military, German industry, civil service, and the railways all dutifully and efficiently participated. Far beyond that, once cleansed of Jews, independent minds and the morally courageous (overlapping categories to be sure), German medicine, and indeed the whole of German academia entered into a productive coalition with party ideologues. With an exuberance born of self-interest, German physicians and academics justified Hitler's murderous image of reality and in many, many instances actively enabled the colossal crimes perpetrated in defense of that cold, twisted myth.[148]

6.0 - Given the outcome of the Second World War, this cannot be assessed.

* * *

The Holocaust does *not* conform in all respects to the pattern revealed during the Red Scare and the Great Purge. The comparison holds for the events leading up to the Holocaust but not for all aspects of the Holocaust itself, which took place during wartime and in occupied territory. The Jewish scapegoat was politically and ideologically useful to the Nazi regime. In the absence of the antihuman Jew, Hitler's entire scheme of sham biology would have been rendered incoherent, weakening the coalition of fears upon which Hitler had founded his party. The legal definition, isolation, and exploitation of the German Jew, far from rendering the Jew invisible, made the Jew an obvious and recognizable pariah in German eyes—"a visible enemy."

The policy of mass murder comes about immediately upon the invasion of Russia and the attempted translation of Hitler's eastern visions into reality. Yet the savage German occupation policy in the east, of which the Holocaust was the central horror, did incalculable harm to the German war effort. "We started," said General Heinze Guderian, "to mistreat them too soon."[149]

Hilberg demonstrates that the cost of the Holocaust was by any objective assessment very great and fundamentally inimical to the war effort.[150] Even in the strict accounting of Jewish goods extorted against the cost of maintaining the Holocaust industry, the destruction of European Jewry was a burden; but when the loss of Jewish labor and the diversion of transport and scarce manpower are factored in, the cost to the German war effort must be regarded as immense. It cannot be supposed that these considerations escaped the Nazi leadership. The point is that *the cost of the Holocaust never had any impact on policy.* The SS waged its war against the Jews to the very end of Hitler's regime, and it must be accepted that there was no process internal to the Third Reich except, *perhaps*, the death of Hitler, that could have shut down the death factories. Accordingly, the expectation that the rate of deviance production will be reduced when the mass production of deviance begins to menace the interests of dominant groups is *not* born out. The Holocaust, therefore, hints at the full potential of industrial bureaucracy to mass produce deviance and victims. Only a hint: had the war taken the course anticipated by Hitler, few who survived the German occupation in the east believe that the hungry SS factories would have been shut down once they had consumed all of European Jewry.

11
Moral Landscapes and the Persistence of Enchantments

To learn that a totalitarian state may, if it chooses, easily destroy its supposed internal enemies—basically what is asserted in proposition 3.0—is no great revelation to a citizen of the twentieth century. At the same time, however, the fact that consistent social conditions preceded these destructions and, further, that the conspiracy being destroyed is largely or entirely imaginary is not self-evident. Most Western observers of Stalin's show trials thought there must have been, somewhere, a genuine conspiracy afoot. And, regardless of the nature of the social control system, the overriding impact of external demand (proposition 4.0) is far from accepted wisdom. To tens of thousands of Americans of Japanese descent this dynamic, nevertheless, meant confinement within concentration camps.

In the months following Pearl Harbor, virtually everyone of Japanese descent residing within the continental United States (roughly 112,00 people of whom 70,000 were U.S. citizens) were labeled as "potentially disloyal," stripped of their property, and incarcerated for years in "relocation camps." Lieutenant General John DeWitt, commander of the Fourth Army on the West Coast, reacted to reports of clandestine radios, signal lights, phantom aircraft, and "mysterious" traffic jams by calling for the removal of enemy aliens and *all* people of Japanese ancestry from the coast.

The call for removal became a general hue and cry in an atmosphere so charged with war hysteria that even the absence of sabotage was taken as evidence for an elaborate Japanese fifth column. In testimony before a congressional committee headed by John Tolan of California on national defense migration, the attorney general of California and candidate for governor, Earl Warren, spoke of the ominous lack of sabotage: ". . .

254

We are just being lulled into a false sense of security. . . . Our day of reckoning is bound to come in that regard."[1] However illogical, such allegations were soberly accepted by the Tolan Committee—but only when directed at Japanese-Americans and Japanese nationals. After reflecting on the fact that Joe DiMaggio's parents were also enemy aliens, committee members, to a man, showed a commendable willingness to trust in the loyalty of German and Italian nationals.[2] In fact, the policy of removal had already been approved in Washington and was being put into place as the committee sat. Racism, hysteria, and the very material interests of well-organized white farmers[3] had by then translated into intense congressional pressure for the removal of everyone of Japanese ancestry from the West Coast. The president signed Executive Order 9066 on 19 February 1942, providing General DeWitt with blanket authority, and the Japanese exclusion orders soon followed. The enforcement statute, Public Law 503, passed both houses of congress as rapidly as the declaration of war against the Empire of Japan and with, if that is possible, even less debate. The lone vocal critic, Senator Taft of Ohio, noted ruefully that "this is probably the sloppiest criminal law I have ever read or seen anywhere. . . . I have no doubt that in peacetime no man could be convicted under it. . . ."[4]

Evidence that there was any military necessity for the relocation of Japanese nationals, much less Japanese-Americans, was entirely absent. *All* of the reports of spying, signaling, and attempted sabotage chased down by the FBI proved groundless. On the issue of any potential collective disloyalty, the record was equally clear. Both the FBI and naval intelligence had kept the Japanese community under surveillance for several years prior to the war and on that basis had found no reason to suspect its loyalty as a group. J. Edgar Hoover strongly disapproved of any "round-up procedure" and advocated dealing with disloyal citizens and aliens on an individual basis.[5] Similarly, a report to the chief of naval operations in January of 1942 concluded that "the Japanese Problem has been magnified out of its true proportion . . . [and] . . . should be handled on the basis of the individual, regardless of citizenship, and *not* on a racial basis."[6] The State Department initiated yet another investigation, which resulted in the Munson Report. Again and again, this report documents the loyalty of the Japanese community, stating, for example, that the empire would rather depend on "imported agents" since the Japanese are "afraid of and do not trust the Nisei."[7] The Munson Report, submitted in November

1941, circulated to the Departments of State and War and to the Navy, as well as to the president.[8] The conclusion is unavoidable that the political leaders of the United States simply ignored the findings of its intelligence services. The FBI, naval intelligence, and the investigative apparatus of the State Department *all* recommended dealing with the potential for treasonous behavior among Japanese-Americans on an individual basis, that is, in the same manner as with other national groups.

The chimerical Japanese fifth column was kept alive by the desire of powerful people to believe in its existence. This desire was also strongly evident among liberal groups, which by and large supported relocation as a military necessity. Although internally torn, the ACLU was reticent on the matter of relocation and generally kept the issue at arm's length throughout the war.[9]

There was at the same time not the slightest consideration given to incarceration of American citizens of German or Italian descent, and even the merest hints that German and Italian nationals might be relocated provoked immediate and impassioned denials by the administration.[10] The underlying motivation for the relocation of Japanese-Americans was racism, which for official consumption was coded as "loyalty to the Emperor" and "national characteristics." General DeWitt's celebrated statement, "A Jap is a Jap," provoked dismay only because it accurately reflected a fundamental dynamic in the relocation process.

In stormy sessions, the Supreme Court grappled with the legality of the exclusion order and relocation on several occasions. The majority decision upholding relocation on the grounds of military necessity in the case of *Korematsu vs. the United States* provides a clear statement of the overweening impact of external demand. In this decision, which was soon to haunt the American Tribunal at Nuremberg, Justice Hugo Black could not totally ignore the racial issue: "Legal restrictions which curtail the rights of a single racial group are immediately suspect . . . [but] . . . pressing public necessity may sometimes justify the existence of such restrictions." In grander terms, Black summed up the thinking of the majority: "When . . . our shores are threatened by hostile forces, the power to protect must be commensurate with the threatened danger."[11]

America's wartime treatment of Japanese-Americans has a clear and illuminating geography. Hawaiian shores, surely as endangered as those of California, encompassed 150,000 people of Japanese descent. But better assimilated and comprising the bulk of the Islands' skilled labor force, they were never, despite strong mainland pressure, subjected to relocation. Urged at one point to send 15,000 to 20,000 of the "most dangerous" to the mainland relocation camps, the Hawaiian department rejoined that it did not "want to arbitrarily select 15,000 Japanese" and that it found the existing situation "highly satisfactory." And when Secretary of the Navy Knox, the most phobic man in Roosevelt's Cabinet, continued to harp for removal, he was rounded on by Chief of Staff Marshall and Chief of Naval Operations King in a bluntly worded memo to the president. Logistical burdens would have made significant inroads into military shipping and neither Marshall nor King were willing to contemplate that prospect.[12] Only some 2,000 individuals of Japanese ancestry were incarcerated in the Hawaiian Islands.

The government's policy toward Japanese-Americans during the Second World War reflects the interplay of accountability and demand in the production of deviance. Where external demand was high and unalloyed by accountability, constitutional safeguards counted for nothing. But in Hawaii, where powerful military and economic considerations were in place, the very considerable push for relocation of all Americans of Japanese descent to the mainland or the Island of Molokai (the leper colony!) was overridden. On the mainland the perception of the military situation was guided by the interest of powerful groups. The belief in an imminent Japanese invasion of the mainland (never possible) and in the existence of an elaborate network of saboteurs, which had no corroboration, was a self-serving myth—the "myth of military necessity"—founded upon a sort of spectral evidence constructed of rumor and fear.[13]

DEMONOLOGY IN THE INDUSTRIAL AGE

It is true, as Erikson suggests, that deviance manifests itself in the form that is most feared, but it is equally true that it is feared in a form that is most useful to powerful interests. In early modern Europe the primary focus of attention was religious misbehavior and most especially an obsessive concern over the activities of Satan's agents. During the twentieth century those who dominate society are most preoccupied by the activities of ideological deviants. But in this technological age one is continually struck by the supposedly demonic nature of the ideologically deviant. People so defined are alleged to derive their wickedness from some dark, fantastical province of mind and politics, and they are invariably given credit for feats that are beyond ordinary human capabilities. A case can be made that such people literally become demonic in the mental world of the powerful (this was surely so for Hitler). It is simply a matter of record that during periods when deviance is being mass produced by the modern state, virtually all social disorder and collective failure is credited to them. "The Bolshevik mind," writes Ulam, "was unable to distinguish between theoretical and factual reality, between the world of ideologically inspired dreams or suspicions and the world of hard fact."[14]

The amount of treasure and ingenuity that has been lavished on the public display of selected varieties of deviants is striking. In any complex society certain people are culled out from the pool of potential deviants and presented to the public as the embodiment of evil. There is no reason to doubt that the intent of ritualized events such as the burning of a witch, the mandatory Jewish star, an auto-da-fé, a show trial, or the hearings of the House Committee on Un-American Activities was anything less than theater. Undoubtedly, too, the desired effect of such spectacles was (and is) the presentment of a moral boundary and, thereby, the imposition of the moral landscape of dominant groups upon the remainder of society. Very much connected with this strategy is a preoccupation with "naming names." The centerpiece of the show trial in Stalinist Russia was the confession, and the standard questions asked of everyone by the NKVD were: "Who recruited you?" and "Whom have you recruited?"[15] Similarly, informing, confessing, and, in general, the public abasement of "fellow travelers" and sympathizers were the primary reasons for the numerous investigations of the House Committee on Un-American Activities.[16] The underlying purpose was to render the purported evil a reality.

The witch, as with modern day ideological apostates, was defined with legal precision but also in such a way that a very broad category of people could be so labeled. As we know, during a panic-trial anyone could be defined as a witch. A visible "Enemy of God" was needed and was typically supplied by the trial and burning of selected women. But an invisible enemy was equally necessary to keep the conspiracy alive since a conspiracy that is obvious and therefore easily rooted out serves no lasting purpose. During early modern times the official construction of reality amply provided for an invisible conspiracy. Witches were thought to be only a small part of the devil's constituency—the part that could be brought to trial. Demons and an entire host of other preternatural creatures, largely detectable through their mischief and by definition beyond the reach of the social control system, also worked in close alliance with the devil's human agents.

The process of manufacturing a bogus conspiracy is much the same in this century. During the McCarthy Era the visible enemy was subject to narrow definition—a "card-carrying communist." Such people were few.[17] "Fellow travelers," on the other hand, were essentially unlimited and embodied the enormous, hidden potential of the Communist conspiracy. The pattern is recurring: "Wreckers" and "enemies of the people" could be made visible through public trial but by definition could be found anywhere biding their time, waiting to strike. Kulaks were not only defined with precision but were subject to official quantification; "subkulaks," on the other hand, were unlimited and pursued to the success of the Second Five-Year Plan. Jews were subject to a precise legal definition, but the genes and blood (identical concepts in the mind of Hitler and his racial police) of Jews had an independent, hidden existence manifested only in Aryan misfortunes. By an undetermined metabolic pathway, the presence of "Jewish" blood, even in small amounts, supposedly inspired all carriers to complex financial and political conspiracies.[18] Nor was this all. In addition to "antihuman," that is, Jewish, "blood," there was also the equally self-serving problem of "subhuman" (untermenschen) blood and genes within the vast population of Slavs and Poles who fell under German control. Thus were the slaughters of non-Jews on the eastern front justified. It is impossible to avoid the conclusion that the Third Reich's thirst for racial villains was inexhaustible.[19] In short, the modern day racial and ideological villain, just as with the devil's servants, is both visible and invisible, defined with precision but also existing in nebulous, insidious forms and in vast numbers.

The suppression of diabolical witchcraft—the "Great Conspiracy" of early modern Europe—was integral to the process that brought about the modern state. What the witch cult did for the role of prince in the sixteenth and seventeenth century, the conspiracy of ideological apostates does today for the industrial state. Political deviants, mythically configured and possessed of diabolical attributes, provide modern regimes with an ideological charter in the same manner that the contrived reality of Satan's kingdom gave credence to the king's claim of divine legitimacy. It would seem that the modern "rational" world is far from disenchanted. The realm, in Weber's words, of "souls, demons, and deities" persists but is now subject to chillingly purposeful, bureaucratic control.[20] Demons in this century are standardized and, upon demand, producible en *masse*.

Notes

CHAPTER 1: MASS PRODUCTION OF DEVIANCE

1. Murray Edelman, *Politics as Symbolic Action* (Chicago: Markham, 1971), 1.

2. Notable and exceedingly scholarly exceptions can be found in: Elliot Currie, "Crimes without Criminals: Witchcraft and Its Control in Renaissance Europe," *Law and Society Review* 3, no. 1 (1968): 7–32; Walter D. Connor, "The Manufacture of Deviance: The Case of the Soviet Purge 1936–1938," *American Sociological Review* 37 (1972): 403–13; Kia Erikson, *Wayward Puritans* (New York: Wiley, 1966); Christina Larner, *Enemies of God* (Baltimore: Johns Hopkins University Press, 1981).

3. Raul Hilberg, *The Destruction of the European Jews*, 2d ed. (New York: Holmes and Meier, 1985), 9.

4. Norman Cohn, *Europe's Inner Demons* (New York: Basic Books, 1975), 255.

5. See in particular: Gustave Henningsen, *The Witches' Advocate* (Reno: University of Nevada Press, 1980); Julio Caro Baroja, *Inquisición, Brujeriá y Criptojudáismo* (Barcelona: Ediciones Ariel, 1972).

6. Keith Thomas, *Religion and the Decline of Magic* (New York: Charles Scribner's Sons, 1971), 520–21.

7. Austin Turk, "The Sociological Relevance of History: A Footnote to Research on Legal Control in South Africa," in Michael Armer and Allen D. Grimshaw (eds.), *Law and Deviance*, (Beverly Hills, Calif.: Sage, 1973), 288.

8. Turk, "The Sociological Relevance of History," 290.

9. Ernest Nagel, *The Structure of Science* (New York: Harcourt, Brace and World, 1961), 452–53.

10. Nagel, *The Structure of Science*, 54.

11. Austin Turk, *Criminality and the Legal Order* (Chicago: Rand McNally, 1969).

12. Turk, *Criminality*, 9.

13. Erikson, *Wayward Puritans*, 11.

14. Erikson, *Wayward Puritans*, 14.

15. Pat Lauderdale, "Deviance and Moral Boundaries," *American Sociological Review* 41 (1976): 660–76.

16. Erikson, *Wayward Puritans*, 59; William Chambliss, "Toward a Political Economy of Crime," *Theory and Society* 2 (1975): 156.

17. See, for example, Albert K. Cohen, *The Elasticity of Evil: Changes in the Social Definition of Deviance* (Oxford: Basil Blackwood, 1974).

18. George B. Vold, *Theoretical Criminology* (New York: Oxford University Press, 1958), 203–19.

19. Max Black, *Models and Metaphors* (Ithaca: Cornell University Press, 1962), 236–40.

20. Currie, "Crimes without Criminals," 11.

21. Ibid., 17.

22. The debt to Currie's analysis is obvious. Mine differs primarily in that I have set apart *external demand*. See Currie, "Crimes without Criminals," 16, 20.

23. Paul Reynolds, *A Primer in Theory Construction* (Indianapolis, Ind.: Bobbs-Merrill, 1971), 91.

24. This closely follows the discussion by Schattschneider on the displacement of political conflict. E. E. Schattschneider, *The Semi-Sovereign People* (Hinsdale, Ill.: Dryden, 1975), 60–74.

25. Carl G. Hempel, "The Functions of General Laws in History, *Journal of Philosophy* 39 (1942): 35.

CHAPTER 2: THE PRODUCTION OF DEVIANCE

1. Monica Wilson, "Witch Beliefs and Social Structure," *American Journal of Sociology* 56 (1951): 307–13.

2. Scarlett Epstein, "A Sociological Analysis of Witch Belief in a Mysore Village," *Eastern Anthropologist* 12 (1958): 234–51.

3. Epstein, "A Sociological Analysis," 250.

4. S. F. Nadel, *Nupe Religion* (New York: Schocken, 1970), 174.

5. Nadel, *Nupe Religion*, 169.

6. Lucy Mair, *Witchcraft* (New York: McGraw-Hill, 1969), 169.

7. Edward Harper, "Fear and the Status of Women," *Southwestern Journal of Anthropology* 25 (1969): 80–91.

8. Ibid., 81.

9. Ibid., 85.

10. Ibid., 84.

11. E. E. Evans-Pritchard, *Witchcraft Oracles and Magic among the Azande* (Oxford: Clarendon Press, 1937), 99.

12. Henry A. Selby, *Zapotec Deviance* (Austin: University of Texas Press, 1974), 92–98.

13. Bernard Lovell, *Emerging Cosmology* (New York: Columbia University Press, 1981), 35–36.

14. See, for example, Jeanne Favret-Saada, *Deadly Words* (New York: Cambridge University Press, 1980); Gustave Henningsen, "Informe sobre tres años de investigaciones etnológicas en España," *Revista de Anthropologia* 1 (1971): 61–90; Hans Sebald, *Witchcraft: The Heritage of a Heresy* (New York: Elsevier, 1978).

15. Jeffrey Russell, *A History of Witchcraft, Sorcerers, Heretics, and Pagans* (New York: Thames and Hudson, 1980), 7.

16. Cohn, *Europe's Inner Demons*, 126–46; Richard Kieckhefer, *European Witch Trials: Their Foundation in Popular and Learned Culture 1300–1500* (Los Angeles: University of California Press, 1976), 11–26.

17. H. C. Erik Midelfort, *Witch Hunting in Southwestern Germany: 1562–1684* (Stanford, Calif.: Stanford University Press, 1972), 11–19; Cohn, *Europe's Inner Demons*, 147; Kieckhefer, *European Witch Trials*, 103–94; Jeffrey Russell, *Witchcraft in the Middle Ages* (Ithaca: Cornell University Press, 1972), 227–64.

18. Russell, *A History of Witchcraft*, 113; Mair, *Witchcraft*, 222.

19. E. William Monter, *Witchcraft in France and Switzerland* (Ithaca: Cornell University Press, 1976), 18.

20. Russell, *Witchcraft in the Middle Ages*, 230.

21. Monter, *Witchcraft in France and Switzerland*, 24.

22. H. R. Trevor-Roper, *The European Witch-Craze of the Sixteenth and Seventeenth Centuries* (New York: Harper and Row, 1969), 104; Russell, *Witchcraft in the Middle Ages*, 231.

23. Monter, *Witchcraft in France and Switzerland*, 21; Cohn, *Europe's Inner Demons*, 230, 238; Russell, *Witchcraft in the Middle Ages*, 220, 221. It may be noted that Jakob Sprenger, one of the authors of the *Malleus Maleficarum*, was born at Basel and there entered the Dominican order; Russell, *Witchcraft in the Middle Ages*, 230.

24. Rossell Hope Robbins, "Introduction," to *Catalogue of the Witchcraft Collection in Cornell University Library* (Millwood, NY: KTO Press, 1977), xxii; Trevor-Roper, *The European Witch-Craze*, 104.

25. Robbins, "Introduction," xxiv.

26. Trevor-Roper, *The European Witch-Craze*, 104–5.

27. Cohn, *Europe's Inner Demons*.

28. Mair, *Witchcraft*, 237–41.

29. Kieckhefer, *European Witch Trials*, 11–26.

30. Ibid., 104.

31. Russell, *Witchcraft in the Middle Ages*, 229.

32. Quoted in Rossell Hope Robbins, *The Encyclopedia of Witchcraft and Demonology* (New York: Bonanza Books, 1981), 265.

33. Monter, *Witchcraft in France and Switzerland*, 25.

34. Midelfort, *Witch Hunting*, 21.

35. Ibid., 60.

36. Monter, *Witchcraft in France and Switzerland*, 35; Robbins, "Introduction," xxviii–xxxvi.

37. Geoffrey Parker, *Europe in Crisis, 1598–1648* (Ithaca: Cornell University Press, 1980), 298.

38. The Salem episode is unusual only in its timing (1692).

39. Russell, *A History of Witchcraft*, 11.

40. Quoted in Midelfort, *Witch Hunting*, 23.

41. Christina Larner, "Crimen Exceptum? The Crime of Witchcraft in Europe," in V. A. C. Gatrell, Bruce Lenman, and Geoffrey Parker, eds., *Crime and the Law* (London: Europa Publications, 1980), 50; Larner, *Enemies of God*, 17.

42. Midelfort, *Witch Hunting*, 9.

43. Ibid., 201–30.

44. Ibid., 122.

45. Ibid., 85.

46. Quoted in Midelfort, *Witch Hunting*, 28.

47. Ibid., 27–28.

48. Quoted in H. C. Erik Midelfort, "Witch Hunting and the Domino Theory," in James Obelkevich, ed., *Religion and the People, 800–1700* (Chapel Hill: University of North Carolina Press, 1979), 279.

49. H. C. Erik Midelfort, "Heartland of the Witchcraze: Central and Northern Europe," *History Today* 31 (1981): 27–31.

50. Monter, *Witchcraft in France and Switzerland*, 191.

51. Russell, A History of Witchcraft, 86.

52. Henry Kamen, The Iron Century 1550–1660 (New York: Praeger, 1971), 245.

53. Midelfort, "Heartland of the Witchcraze," 28, 29; Trevor-Roper, The European Witch-Craze, 150.

54. Henningsen, The Witches' Advocate, Table 15; Monter, Witchcraft in France and Switzerland; Trevor-Roper, The European Witch-Craze; Larner, Enemies of God.

55. Henningsen, The Witches' Advocate, 23–25; Trevor-Roper, The European Witch-Craze, 112.

56. Nicholas Remy, Demonolatry, trans. A. E. Ashwin (1595; reprint, New York: Barnes and Noble, 1970), 74.

57. Christina Larner, "James VI and I and Witchcraft," in A. G. R. Smith, ed., The Reign of James VI and I (New York: Saint Martin's, 1973), 79.

58. Larner, Enemies of God, 63.

59. Monter, Witchcraft in France and Switzerland, 47–48, 102.

60. Russell, A History of Witchcraft, 122; Midelfort, "Witch Hunting and the Domino Theory," 285; Trevor-Roper, The European Witch-Craze, 163–64.

61. Midelfort, Witch Hunting, 88–90.

62. Ibid., 90–94.

63. Ibid., 98–112, 212–15.

64. Ibid.96–98.

65. As quoted in Robbins, "Introduction," xix.

66. George Lincoln Burr, "The Literature of Witchcraft," Papers of the American Historical Association 4 (1890): 48.

Chapter 3: The Origins of the European Witchcraze

1. See in particular: Hans Sebald, "Franconian Witchcraft: A Discussion of Functionalism," Deviant Behavior 2 (1981): 349–69; Alan Macfarlane, Witchcraft in Tudor and Stuart England (London: Routledge and Kegan Paul, 1970).

2. Favret-Saada, Deadly Words, 6.

3. Nadel, Nupe Religion, 201.

4. Mair, Witchcraft, 215.

5. Macfarlane, Witchcraft in Tudor and Stuart England, 169–84.

6. As quoted in Macfarlane, Witchcraft in Tudor and Stuart England, 188.

7. Nadel, Nupe Religion, 205–6.

8. Thomas Rogers Forbes, The Midwife and the Witch (New Haven: Yale University Press, 1966), 113.

9. Larner, Enemies of God, 3, 100–102.

10. Monter, Witchcraft in France and Switzerland, 23; Midelfort, "Heartland of the Witchcraze," 28.

11. Midelfort, Witch Hunting, 183–86.

12. Michael W. Flinn, The European Demographic System 1500–1820 (Baltimore: The Johns Hopkins University Press, 1981), 19–20; see also Table 7.

13. E. William Monter, "Historical Demography and Religious History in Sixteenth Century Geneva," Journal of Interdisciplinary History 9 (1979): 418; Flinn, The European Demographic System, 207.

14. Monter, "Historical Demography," Table 7.

15. Ibid., 421.

16. Ibid., 424.

17. Flinn, The European Demographic System, 28.

18. Midelfort, Witch Hunting, 185.

19. Quoted in Larner, "James VI," 86.

20. Keith Thomas, Religion and the Decline of Magic, 520–21.

21. Quoted in Thomas, Religion, 520.

22. Lynn White, Jr., "The Spared Wolves." Saturday Review of Literature, 37 (1954): 23–35; Max Marwick, "Witchcraft as a Social Strain Gauge," in Max Marwick, ed., Witchcraft and Sorcery (Baltimore: Penguin Books), 1970.

23. Robert K. Merton, "Social Structure and Anomie," American Sociological Review 3 (1938): 672–82.

24. Albert Cohen, Deviance and Control (Englewood Cliffs, N.J.: Prentice Hall, 1966), 76.

25. Quoted in Parker, Europe in Crisis, 16.

26. Parker, Europe in Crisis, 21.

27. Ester Bosenrup, Population and Technological Change (Chicago: University of Chicago Press, 1981), 99; Kamen, The Iron Century, 3–46.

28. Hugh Trevor-Roper, "The General Crisis of the 17th Century," Past and Present 16 (1959): 31–66.

29. Kamen, The Iron Century, Figures 9 and 13; Immanuel Wallerstein, The Modern World System (New York: Academic Press, 1974), 1: 77–84; for a discussion of sixteenth-century population growth, see Flinn, The European Demographic System, 76–79.

30. Parker, Europe in Crisis, 29.

31. V. G. Kiernan, State and Society in Europe 1550–1650 (New York: St. Martin's Press, 1980), 209.

32. Parker, Europe in Crisis, 299.

33. Kamen, The Iron Century, 250.

34. Norman Cohn, The Pursuit of the Millenium (New York: Oxford University Press, 1970).

35. Kieckhefer, European Witch Trials, 19.

36. Larner, Enemies of God, 41.

37. Ibid., 2.

38. Ibid., 23.

39. C. L'Estrange Ewen, Witch Hunting and Witch Trials (London: Kegan Paul, Trench, Trubner, 1929), 112; Larner, Enemies of God, 65.

40. J. S. Cockburn, "The Nature and Incidence of Crime in England: A Preliminary Survey," in J. S. Cockburn, ed., Crime in England 1500–1800 (Princeton: Princeton University Press, 1977), 54; Thomas, Religion, 451.

41. Arnold Pritchard, Catholic Loyalism in Elizabethan England (Chapel Hill: University of North Carolina Press, 1979), 5.

42. Quoted in Macfarlane, Witchcraft in Tudor and Stuart England, 104.

43. Thomas, Religion, 449.

44. Ibid., 452.

45. Henningsen, The Witches' Advocate, 38–40.

46. Henry Kamen, The Spanish Inquisition (New York: The New American Library, 1971), 173.

47. Kamen, The Spanish Inquisition, 174.

48. Henningsen, The Witches' Advocate, 39.

49. Ibid., 51–67.

50. Ibid., 118.

51. Quoted in Henningsen, *The Witches' Advocate*, 184.

52. For *saco bendito* (sacred sack). Usually a yellow robe with a black St. Andrew's Cross. Those condemned to death wore sambenitos displaying devils and the flames of hell. Reconciled heretics were sentenced to wear a sambenito as punishment; afterwards it hung in the miscreant's parish church for generations.

53. Caro Baroja, *Inquisición*, 198.

54. Quoted in Henningsen, *The Witches' Advocate*, 195.

55. Henningsen, *The Witches' Advocate*, 209–16.

56. Quoted in Henningsen, *The Witches' Advocate*, 301.

57. Quoted in Henningsen, *The Witches' Advocate*, 304.

58. Henningsen, *The Witches' Advocate*, 388.

59. E. William Monter, "French and Italian Witchcraft" *History Today* 30 (1980): 31–35.

60. Quoted in Caro Baroja, *Inquisición*, 256, emphasis added, trans. E. Gonzalas.

61. Henningsen, *The Witches' Advocate*, 37.

62, Quoted in Henningsen, *The Witches' Advocate*, 350.

63. Ibid., 378, emphasis added.

64. Ibid., 382.

65. Ibid. 383.

CHAPTER 4: THE POLITICAL GEOGRAPHY OF WITCHCRAFT

1. Cf. Thomas, *Religion*, 460.

2. Larner, *Enemies of God*, 22.

3. R. M. Jackson, *The Machinery of Justice in England* (New York: Cambridge University Press, 1977), 18.

4. Frederick Pollack and Frederick William Maitland, *The History of English Law* (Cambridge: Cambridge University Press, 1923) 2:601.

5. Quoted in Cohn, *Europe's Inner Demons*, 161.

6. Cohn, *Europe's Inner Demons*, 162.

7. Ibid., 163.

8. John H. Langbien, *Torture and the Law of Proof* (Chicago: University of Chicago Press, 1977), 6–8; Russell, *Witchcraft in the Middle Ages*, 153; both authors note that officially the use of torture replaced the ordeal but that in the pragmatic view of contemporaries it amounted to the same thing. God, it was assumed, would protect the innocent.

9. Midelfort, *Witch Hunting*, 19; Larner, *Enemies of God*, 49.

10. Langbien, *Torture*, 55.

11. Russell, *Witchcraft in the Middle Ages*, 158.

12. Midelfort, *Witch Hunting*, 69.

13. Russell, *Witchcraft in the Middle Ages*, 42.

14. Quoted in Russell, *A History of Witchcraft*, 82.

15. Quoted in Langbien, *Torture*, 5.

16. Monter, *Witchcraft in France and Switzerland*, 196.

17. Ibid., 196.

18. Jackson, *The Machinery of Justice,* 18.
19. Reinhard Bendix, *Kings or People* (Berkeley: University of California Press, 1978), 277.
20. Midelfort, *Witch Hunting,* Table 1.
21. Midelfort, "Heartland of the Witchcraze," 28.
22. H. C. Lea, *Materials Toward a History of Witchcraft* (Philadelphia: University of Pennsylvania Press, 1939).
23. Currie, "Crimes Without Criminals," 21.
24. Midelfort, *Witch Hunting,* 178.
25. Quoted in Robbins, "Introduction," liii–liv.
26. Larner, *Enemies of God,* 115.
27. Ibid.
28. Midelfort, *Witch Hunting,* 164–69.
29. *Ibid., 195.*
30. *Larner, Enemies of God, 197.*
31. Thomas, *Religion,* 457.
32. Kamen, *The Spanish Inquisition,* 153–55.
33. Alfred Soman, "Criminal Jurisprudence in Ancien-Regime France: The Parlement of Paris in the 16th and 17th Centuries," in *Crime and Criminal Justice in Europe and Canada,* ed. A. Knafla (Waterloo, Ont.: Wilfrid Laurier University Press, 1981), 59.
34. Henningsen, *The Witches' Advocate,* 17.
35. H. C. Lea, *A History of the Inquisition of the Middle Ages* (New York: The Harper Press, 1955), 191.
36. Edith Simon, *The Piebald Standard* (London: Cassell, 1959); Barbara Tuchman, *A Distant Mirror* (New York: Knopf, 1978), 42–44; Cohn, *Europe's Inner Demons,* 77–99.
37. Russell, *A History of Witchcraft,* 90.
38. Stuart Clark, King James' Daemonologie: Witchcraft and Kingship," in Sydney Anglo, ed., *The Damned Art* (London: Routledge and Kegan Paul, 1977), 164; Larner, "James VI," 81.
39. George Lyman Kittredge, *Witchcraft in Old and New England* (Cambridge: Harvard University Press, 1929), 370–71.
40. C. L'Estrange Ewen, *Witchcraft and Demonism* (London: Heath Cranton Limited, 1933), 261; Wallace Notestein, *A History of Witchcraft in England, 1558–1718* (1911; reprint, New York: Russell and Russell, 1965), 164.
41. Ewen, *Witchcraft and Demonism,* 259; Notestein, *A History of Witchcraft in England,* 193.
42. Russell, *A History of Witchcraft,* 100; Ewen, *Witchcraft and Demonism,* 255–313.
43. Notestein, *A History of Witchcraft in England,* 67.
44. Thomas, *Religion,* 458.
45. Notestein, *A History of Witchcraft in England,* 201; Russell, *A History of Witchcraft,* 97.
46. Ewen, *Witchcraft and Demonism,* 259.
47. Richard Ollard, *This War without an Enemy* (New York: Atheneum, 1976), 92.
48. Thomas, *Religion,* 500.
49. Ibid., 448; Ewen, *Witchcraft and Demonism,* 260.
50. Ewen, *Witchcraft and Demonism,* 259–60.

51. Thomas, *Religion*, 458.
52. Quoted in Ewen, *Witchcraft and Demonism*, 260.
53. Ewen, *Witchcraft and Demonism*, 281.
54. Notestein, *A History of Witchcraft in England*, 180–81.
55. Quoted in Ewen, *Witchcraft and Demonism*, 260.
56. Notestein, *A History of Witchcraft in England*, 192–93.
57. Adrian Morey, *The Catholic Subjects of Elizabeth I* (Totowa, N.J.: Rowman and Littlefield, 1978); Carol Z. Wiener, "A Study of Elizabethan and Early Jacobean Anti-Catholicism" *Past and Present* 51 (1971): 27–62; Thomas, *Religion*, 458.
58. Quoted in Ronald Homes, *Witchcraft in British History* (London: Frederick Muller Ltd., 1974), 138.
59. Notestein, *A History of Witchcraft in England*, 199.
60. Ewen, *Witchcraft and Demonism*, 260.
61. Notestein, *A History of Witchcraft in England*, 179, 198.
62. Ibid., 164–204.
63. Ibid., 198.
64. Macfarlane, *Witchcraft in Tudor and Stuart England*, 142.
65. Notestein, *A History of Witchcraft in England*, 182.

CHAPTER 5: THE SALEM PANIC TRIAL

1. Erikson, *Wayward Puritans*, 155.
2. John Demos, "Underlying Themes in the Witchcraft of Seventeenth-Century New England," *American Historical Review* 75 (1970): 1314.
3. Marian Starkey, *The Devil in Massachusetts* (New York: Knopf, 1949), 7.
4. Charles W. Upham, *Salem Witchcraft* (1867; reprint, New York: Frederick Unger, 1959), 10.
5. Upham, *Salem Witchcraft*, 10.
6. Starkey, *The Devil*, 13–14.
7. Perry Miller, *The New England Mind: From Colony to Province* (Cambridge: Harvard University Press, 1953), 27–39.
8. Robert Calef, *More Wonders of the Invisible World*, in George L. Burr, ed., *Narratives of the Witchcraft Cases, 1648–1706* (New York: Charles Scribner's Sons, 1914), 342.
9. Chadwick Hanson, *Witchcraft at Salem* (New York: Signet, 1970), 22–23.
10. Calef, *More Wonders*, 341–42.
11. Quoted in Starkey, *The Devil*, 42.
12. Quoted in Paul Boyer and Stephen Nissenbaum, *Salem Possessed* (Cambridge: Harvard University Press, 1974), 3.
13. Calef, *More Wonders*, 342.
14. Deodat Lawson, "A Brief and True Narrative of Some Remarkable Passages Relating to Sundry Persons Afflicted by Witchcraft, at Salem Village . . . 1692," in Burr, *Narratives*, 154.
15. Boyer and Nissenbaum, *Salem Possessed*, 146.

16. Starkey, *The Devil*, 66.

17. Quoted in Boyer and Nissenbaum, *Salem Possessed*, 173.

18. Calef, *More Wonders*, 346.

19. Upham, *Salem Witchcraft*, 113–14, emphasis added.

20. Boyer and Nissenbaum, *Salem Possessed*, 31.

21. Starkey, *The Devil*, 21.

22. Erikson, *Wayward Puritans*, 149.

23. Stephan Foster, *Their Solitary Way* (New Haven: Yale University Press, 1971), 67.

24. Erikson, *Wayward Puritans*, 48, 72–73.

25. James G. Moseley, *A Cultural History of Religion in America* (Westport, Conn.: Greenwood Press, 1981), 12.

26. Starkey, *The Devil*, 52.

27. Paul Boyer and Stephan Nissenbaum, *Salem Village Witchcraft: A Documentary Record of Local Conflict in Colonial New England* (Belmont, Calif.: Wadsworth Press), 405–15; Boyer and Nissenbaum, *Salem Possessed*, 89–90.

28. Boyer and Nissenbaum, *Salem Possessed*, 63.

29. It may also be noted that one of these men, George Burroughs, was hanged as a witch.

30. Boyer and Nissenbaum, *Salem Possessed*, 51.

31. M. Wynn Thomas, "Some metamorphoses of Salem Witchcraft," in Anglo, *The Damned Art*, 212; Miller, *The New England Mind*, 180.

32. Boyer and Nissenbaum, *Salem Possessed*, Map 1.

33. Calef, *More Wonders*, 370.

34. Boyer and Nissenbaum, *Salem Possessed*, 80–109, 115.

35. Upham, *Salem Witchcraft*, 390.

36. Evans-Pritchard, *Witchcraft Oracles*, 99.

37. Boyer and Nissenbaum, *Salem Possessed*, 182–83.

38. Moseley, *A Cultural History*, 8.

39. Quoted in Erikson, *Wayward Puritans*, 151; Starkey, *The Devil*, 172.

40. Quoted in Burr, *Narratives*, 170.

41. Calef, *More Wonders*, 376.

42. Burr, *Narratives*, 375, note 2.

43. Quoted in Calef, *More Wonders*, 374–75.

44. Burr, *Narratives*, 291–93; Upham, *Salem Witchcraft*, 447–55.

45. Boyer and Nissenbaum, *Salem Possessed*, 32.

46. Burr, *Narratives*, 377, note 1, supra.

47. Upham, *Salem Witchcraft*, 345; "I do admire [I am Surprised]," writes Brattle in his open letter, "that some particular persons . . . should be much complained of by the afflicted persons and yet that the Justices should never issue out their warrants to apprehend them. . . ." Quoted in Burr, *Narratives*, 178.

48. Quoted in Burr, *Narratives*, 179.

49. John Higginson, "Epistle to the Reader," in Burr, *Narratives*, 400.

50. Calef, *More Wonders*, 369.

51. Quoted in Starkey, *The Devil*, 155.

52. Thomas J. Holmes, *Increase Mather: A Bibliography of his Works* (Cambridge: Harvard University Press, 1931), 124.

53. Starkey, *The Devil*, 227.

54. Upham, *Salem Witchcraft*, 459.
55. M. Halsey Thomas, ed., *The Diary of Samuel Sewall* (New York: Farrar, Straus, and Giroux, 1973), 299.
56. Starkey, *The devil*, 235.
57. Calef, *More Wonders*, 382.
58. M. Wynn Thomas, "Some Metamorphoses," 213.
59. Moseley, *A Cultural History*, 12.
60. James Truslow Adams, *The Founding of New England* (Boston: Atlantic Monthly Press, 1921), 450; Henry A. Shipton, "A Plea for Puritanism" *American Historical Review* 40 (1935): 461.
61. As per the discussion in Randall Collins, *Conflict Sociology* (New York: Academic Press, 1975), 364–80.
62. Robert L. Heilbroner, *Marxism: For and Against* (New York: W. W. Norton, 1980), 62.
63. Erikson, *Wayward Puritans*, 10–11.
64. Upham, *Salem Witchcraft*, 8.
65. M. Halsey Thomas, *Diary*, 86.
66. Larzer Ziff, *Puritanism in America* (New York: The Viking Press, 1973), 244–46.
67. Homer Cary Hockett, *Political and Social Growth in the United States* (New York: Macmillan Press, 1933), 1:125.
68. Terence Morris, *Deviance and Control: The Secular Heresy* (London: Hutchinson and Company), 40.
69. Miller, *The New England Mind*, 200.
70. Erikson, *Wayward Puritans*, 19–23.
71. Larner, "Crimen Exceptum?" 57.
72. Boyer and Nissenbaum, *Salem Possessed*, 29.
73. Midelfort, "Witch Hunting and the Domino Theory," Table 3.
74. William Phips, "Letter to Earl of Nottingham, Whitehall, London," dated 21 February 1693, in Burr, *Narratives*, 199.
75. Thomas J. Holmes, *Cotton Mather: A Bibliography of His Works* (Cambridge: Harvard University Press, 1940), 1257–58.
76. Quoted in M. Wynn Thomas, "Some Metamorphoses," 213.
77. Miller, *The New England Mind*, 203.
78. Quoted in Miller, *The New England Mind*, 206.
79. Miller, *The New England Mind*, 201.
80. Ibid., 207.
81. John Hale, *A Modest Inquiry into the Nature of Witchcraft*, in Burr, *Narratives*, 404.
82. Hale, *A Modest Inquiry*, 421.
83. Quoted in M. Halsey Thomas, *Diary*, 367.
84. Miller, *The New England Mind*, 209.
85. Ibid., 195.
86. Thomas Hutchinson, *The History of the Province of Massachusetts Bay* (1764; reprint, Cambridge: Harvard University Press, 1936) 2:37.
87. *The History*, 45.

CHAPTER 6: IDEOLOGY AND THE EUROPEAN WITCHCRAZE

1. Parker, *Europe in Crisis*, 228–29.

2. Jean Delumeau, *Catholicism Between Luther and Voltaire: A New View of the Counter-Reformation* (Philadelphia, Pa.: Westminster Press, 1977), 175–230.

3. William Beik, "Popular Culture and Elite Repression in Early Modern Europe," *Journal of Interdisciplinary History* 1 (1980): 97–103.

4. John Bossy, "The Counter-Reformation and the People of Catholic Europe" *Past and Present* 47 (1970): 57.

5. Bossy, "The Counter-Reformation," 66.

6. Dietrich Gerhard, *Old Europe: A Study of Continuity, 1000–1800* (New York: Academic Press, 1981), 104–7; V. G. Kiernan, *State and Society in Europe, 1550–1650*, 1980), 29; Larner, "Crimen Exceptum?" 74.

7. Larner, *Enemies of God*, 199.

8. William Haller, *Foxe's Book of Martyrs and the Elect Nation* (London: Jonathon Cope, 1963), 13; Morey, *The Catholic Subjects of Elizabeth I*, 64; Morris, *Deviance and Control*, 21.

9. Nachman Ben-Yehuda, *Deviance and Moral Boundaries* (Chicago: University of Chicago Press, 1985), 36–38, 70.

10. Larner, *Enemies of God*, 195.

11. Quoted in Larner, "James VI," 77.

12. Quoted in Clark, "King James' Daemonologie," 158.

13. Larner, "James VI," 85.

14. Clark, "King James' Daemonologie," 166.

15. Larner, "James VI," 84.

16. Larner, *Enemies of God*, 70.

17. Quoted in Clark, "King James' Daemonologie," 161.

18. Quoted in Larner, *Enemies of God*, 70.

19. Larner, *Enemies of God*, 71.

20. Ibid., 71.

21. Ibid., 83.

22. Ibid., 74.

23. Ibid., 74.

24. Ibid., 76.

25. Trevor-Roper, *The European Witch-Craze*, 164.

26. Antero Heikkinen, *Paholaisen Liitolaiset*, English Summary pp. 374–94 (Helsinki, 1969), 387.

27. Heikkinen, Summary, 375.

28. Ibid., 375.

29. Ibid., 386.

30. Trevor-Roper, *The European Witch-Craze*, 176.

31. Alfred Soman, "The Parlement of Paris and the Great Witch Hunt (1565–1640)" *Sixteenth Century Journal* 9 (1978): 34–35.

32. Midelfort, "Witch Hunting and the Domino Theory," 280.

33. Midelfort, *Witch Hunting*, 191.

34. Midelfort, "Witch Hunting and the Domino Theory," 281.

35. Roger Brown, *Social Psychology* (New York: Free Press, 1965), 549.

36. Leon Festinger, *A Theory of Cognitive Dissonance* (Stanford, Calif.: Stanford University Press, 1957), 1.

37. Elliot Aronsen, "Persuasion via Self-Justification: Large Commitments for Small Rewards," in L. Festinger, ed., *Retrospectives on Social Psychology* (New York: Oxford University Press, 1980), 18.

38. F. Verbruggen, *Looking for Leon Festinger in the 18th Century* (Ghent:

University of Ghent, 1974); Alfred Lindsmith et al., *Social Psychology* (Hindsdale, Ill.: The Dryden Press, 1975), 106.

39. Festinger, *A Theory*, 11.

40. Midelfort, "Witch Hunting and the Domino Theory," 281.

41. Robbins, "Introduction," xix, quotes a letter written by the Chancellor of the Prince-Bishop of Wurzburg in 1629, which so claims.

42. Midelfort, *Witch Hunting*, 192.

43. Ibid., 137; Midelfort, "Witch Hunting and the Domino Theory," 281–82.

44. Midelfort, *Witch Hunting*, Table 2.

45. Quoted in Midelfort, *Witch Hunting*, 104.

46. Quoted in Robbins, "Introduction," xix.

47. Midelfort, *Witch Hunting*, 125–26.

48. Ibid., 127–31.

49. Midelfort, "Witch Hunting and the Domino Theory," 285.

50. Soman, "The Parlement of Paris," 31.

51. Ibid., 38.

52. As quoted in Notestein, *A History of Witchcraft in England*, 173, emphasis added.

53. Midelfort, "Witch Hunting and the Domino Theory," 285.

54. Larner, *Enemies of God*, 91.

55. Ibid.

56. Midelfort, *Witch Hunting*, 162, emphasis added.

57. Brian Easlea, *Witch Hunting, Magic and the New Philosophy* (Atlantic Highlands, N.J.: Humanities Press, 1980), 1.

58. Easlea, *Witch Hunting*, 201.

59. Ibid., 201–7; Russel, *A History of Witchcraft*, 100.

60. Richard A. Horsley, "Further Reflections on Witchcraft and European Folk Religion," *History of Religion* 19 (1979): 90–94.

61. Edward Peters, *The Magician, the Witch and the Law* (Philadelphia: University of Pennsylvania Press, 1978), 176.

62. Quoted in Larner, *Enemies of God*, 83, spelling modernized.

63. Gordon Donaldson, *Scotland: The Shaping of a Nation* (London: David and Charles, 1974), 81.

64. Robbins, *The Encyclopedia of Witchcraft*, 35–37.

CHAPTER 7: THE RED SCARE

1. Burl Noggle, *Into the Twenties* (Urbana: University of Illinois, 1974), 84–93.

2. As quoted in Ellis W. Hawley, *The Great War and the Search for a Modern Order* (New York: St. Martin's Press, 1979), 22.

3. David Burner, "1919: Prelude to Normalcy," in John Greaman, Robert H. Bremmer, and David Brody, eds., *Change and Continuity in 20th-Century America* (Columbus: Ohio State University Press, 1968), 17.

4. Stanley Coben, *A. Mitchell Palmer: Politician* (New York: Columbia University Press, 1963), 199; and see Joan M. Jensen, *The Price of Vigilance* (Chicago: Rand McNally, 1968) for an extended discussion of the American Protective League. On the matter of "slacker raids," Jensen (p. 194) notes that federal authorities announced early on that the government would pay up

to fifty dollars for the "necessary and reasonable expense" of apprehending a deserter, thereby placing a bounty on unidentified males.

5. Noggle, *Into the Twenties*, 98–99.

6. Hawley, *The Great War*, 29.

7. Quoted in Robert K. Murray, *Red Scare: A Study in National Hysteria* (Minneapolis: University of Minnesota Press, 1955), 14.

8. Hawley, *The Great War*, 3–6.

9. Burner, "1919," 11.

10. Stanley Coben, "A Study in Nativism: The American Red Scare of 1919–1920" *Political Science Quarterly* 79 (1964): 59; Burner, "1919," 27; Murray, *Red Scare*, 7.

11. Hawley, *The Great War*, 50.

12. Coben, "A Study in Nativism," 60.

13. Murray B. Levin, *Political Hysteria in America* (New York: Basic Books, 1971), 96.

14. Noggle, *Into the Twenties*, 90.

15. William E. Leuchtenburg, *The Perils of Prosperity, 1914–1932* (Chicago: University of Chicago Press, 1958), 68; Noggle, *Into the Twenties*, 91.

16. Richard Gid Powers, *Secrecy and Power: The Life of J. Edgar Hoover* (New York: The Free Press, 1987), 59. Powers counts this an "uncomfortably close parallel" to the mission of the German right-wing paramilitary units (Freikorps) that fought the "war after the war" and brutally crushed all attempted communist coups.

17. Cedric Belefrage, *The American Inquisition* (New York: Bobbs-Merril Press, 1973), 12.

18. Murray, *Red Scare*, 61–63; Leuchtenburg, *The Perils of Prosperity*, 71.

19. Murray, *Red Scare*, 194–95.

20. Ibid., 64.

21. Ibid., 70.

22. Ibid., 73–75.

23. Powers, *Secrecy and Power*, 63.

24. Murray, *Red Scare*, 193.

25. Ibid., 194.

26. Ibid., 99.

27. *New York Times*, 21 February 1919.

28. Burner, "1919," 21.

29. David Brody, *Labor in Crisis* (Philadelphia: Lippincott, 1965), 144.

30. Murray, *Red Scare*, 129.

31. Interchurch World Movement, *Report on the Steel Strike of 1919* (New York: Harcourt, Brace and Howe, 1920), 11–13.

32. William A. Gengarelly, "Resistance Spokesmen: Opponents of the Red Scare 1919–1921" (Ph.D. diss., Boston University, 1972), 72; Leuchtenburg, *The Perils of Prosperity*, 79; Interchurch World Movement, *Report*, 240–42; Brody, *Labor in Crisis*, 157–58.

33. National Popular Government League, *Report Upon the Illegal Practices of the United States Department of Justice* (Washington, D.C., May 1920) Exhibit 8. This exhibit states, in part, that:

> 1. Under-cover informants employed by private detective agencies which in turn are employed by the steel and coal companies, supply to those detective agencies,

and through them to the companies and to the Department of Justice, information concerning members of labor organizations.

2. Arrests are frequently made upon the unsupported statements of these undercover private informants; these arrests are made by local police without warrant and reported to the Department of Justice, which sends its investigator to go through the men arrested and ascertain if there are any extreme radicals among them; and then sets the machinery of the Department of Labor in motion for their deportation. In other words, the steel and coal companies use the local and Federal governments to harass and get rid of "troublesome" workers.

34. Interchurch World Movement, *Report*, 221–27.

35. Quoted in Levin, *Political Hysteria*, 191.

36. Interchurch World Movement, *Report*, 34.

37. Ibid., 227.

38. Ibid., 31.

39. Leuchtenburg, *The Perils of Prosperity*, 77; Brody, *Labor in Crisis*, 128–29.

40. Quoted in Murray, *Red Scare*, 17, emphasis added.

41. Coben, "A Study in Nativism," 62; Burner, "1919," 16; Murray, *Red Scare*, 206.

42. Quoted in Coben, "A Study in Nativism," 62.

43. William Preston, Aliens and Dissenters (Cambridge: Harvard University Press, 1963), 220.

44. Louis F. Post, *The Deportation Delirium of Nineteen-Twenty* (Chicago: Charles H. Kerr and Company, 1923), 52.

45. Post, *The Deportation Delirium*, 52.

46. Constantine Panunzio, *The Deportation Cases of 1919–1920* (1921; reprint, New York: Da Capo Press, 1970), 83.

47. Murray, *Red Scare*, 197.

48. Levin, *Political Hysteria*, 55,

49. Powers, *Secrecy and Power*, 73.

50. Quoted in Powers, *Secrecy and Power*, 73.

51. Levin, *Political Hysteria*, 58.

52. Preston, *Aliens and Dissenters*, 218.

53. Post, *The Deportation Delirium*, 67.

54. Panunzio, *Deportation Cases*, 44; Post, *The Deportation Delirium*, 67, 80.

55. Quoted in Coben, *A. Mitchell Palmer*, 225.

56. Panunzio, *Deportation Cases*, provides the full text of this change, p. 37.

57. Dominic Candeloro, "Louis F. Post and the Red Scare of the 1920s" *Prologue* 11 (1979): 41–55; Coben, "A Study in Nativism," 73.

58. Candeloro, "Louis F. Post," 51.

59. Syndicalism advocated the use of direct methods by labor—general strikes and so on—to overthrow the government and place worker's cooperatives in control. Criminal syndicalism encouraged the use of violence to bring about the same end. In actual practice, the syndicalist laws were used to render any effective anticapitalist activity illegal.

60. Murray, *Red Scare*, 212; Post, *The Deportation Delirium*, 101.

61. Post, *The Deportation Delirium*, 101.

62. Coben, "A Study in Nativism," 73; Leuchtenburg, *The Perils of Prosperity*, 78; Panunzio, *Deportation Cases*, 8–84.

63. Frederick L. Allen, *Only Yesterday* (1931; reprint, New York: Harper and Row, 1964), 48.

64. Post, *The Deportation Delirium*, 92.

65. Panunzio, *Deportation Cases*, 35.

66. Post, *The Deportation Delirium*, 94–95.

67. Hawley, *The Great War*, 52.

68. Preston, *Aliens and Dissenters*, 222.

69. Murray, *Red Scare*, 247.

70. Thomas Vadney, "The Politics of Repression, A Case Study of the Red Scare in New York." *New York History* 49 (1968): 50–73. Quoted in Levin, *Political Hysteria*, 74.

71. Candeloro, "Louis F. Post," 44; Gengarelly, "Resistance Spokesmen," 179.

72. Murray, *Red Scare*, 247.

73. National Popular Government League, *Report*, Exhibit 16.

74. Candeloro, "Louis F. Post," 48–49.

75. Murray, *Red Scare*, 252–53.

76. Quoted in Candeloro, "Louis F. Post," 50.

77. Gengarelly, "Resistance Spokesmen," 202–3; Candeloro, "Louis F. Post," 50.

78. Levin, *Political Hysteria*, 80–81.

79. Gengarelly, "Resistance Spokesmen," 229.

80. Post, *The Deportation Delirium*, 167.

81. Murray, *Red Scare*, 251.

82. Quoted in Post, *The Deportation Delirium*, 192.

83. Murray, *Red Scare*, 251.

84. Candeloro, "Louis F. Post," 45.

85. Murray, *Red Scare*, 257–59.

86. Ibid., 265.

87. David M. Oshinski, *A Conspiracy So Immense: The World of Joe McCarthy* (New York: The Free Press, 1983), 89.

88. Powers, *Secrecy and Power*, 103.

89. Ibid., 105.

90. Post, *The Deportation Delirium*, 80.

91. Oshinsky, *A Conspiracy*, 87; Coben, *A. Mitchell Palmer*, 254–55.

92. Gengarelly, "Resistance Spokesmen," 90.

93. Powers, *Secrecy and Power*, 93–121.

94. Quoted in Powers, *Secrecy and Power*, 71.

95. Richard M. Freeland, *The Truman Doctrine and the Origins of McCarthyism* (New York: Knopf, 1972); Alan D. Harper, *The Politics of Loyalty* (Westport, Conn.: Greenwood Press, 1969); Peter Irons, "America's Cold War Crusade: Domestic Politics & Foreign Policy, 1942–1948" (Ph.D. diss., Boston University, 1972).

Chapter 8: The McCarthy Era

1. Richard H. Rovere, *Senator Joe McCarthy* (New York: Harcourt, Brace and Co., 1959), 17–18; Leuchtenburg, *The Perils of Prosperity*, 36.

2. Freeland, *The Truman Doctrine*, 36: Edwin R. Bayley, *Joe McCarthy and the Press* (Madison: University of Wisconsin Press, 1981), 5–6.

3. David Caute, *The Great Fear* (New York: Simon and Schuster, 1978), 38.

4. William R. Tanner and Robert Griffith, "Legislative Politics and 'McCarthyism': The Internal Security Act of 1950," in Robert Griffith and Athan Theoharis, eds., *The Specter* (New York: Franklin Watts Inc., 1974), 179.

5. Robert Justin Goldstein, *Political Repression in Modern America* (New York: Schenkman, 1978), 324.

6. Richard M. Fried, *Men Against McCarthy* (New York: Columbia University Press, 1976), 13.

7. Robert Griffith, "American Politics and the Origins of McCarthyism," in Griffith and Theoharis, eds., *The Specter*, 8.

8. Quoted in Griffith, "American Politics," 8.

9. Freeland, *The Truman Doctrine*, 225.

10. Ibid., 119–22; Griffith, "American Politics," 13.

11. Edward Schneier, "White Collar Vigilantism: The Politics of Anti-Communism in the United States," in H. Jon Rosenbaum and Peter C. Sederberg, eds., *Vigilante Politics* (Philadelphia: University of Pennsylvania Press, 1976), 127; Irons, "America's Cold War Crusade: Domestic Politics and Foreign Policy, 1942–1948." (Ph.D. diss., Boston University, 1972), 93; Caute, *The Great Fear*, 30; Freeland, *The Truman Doctrine*, 97.

12. Quoted in Freeland, *The Truman Doctrine*, 101.

13. Alan D. Harper, *The Politics of Loyalty* (Westport, Conn.: Greenwood Press, 1969), 25; Athan Theoharis, "The Escalation of the Loyalty Program," in Jack Stuart, ed., *Realities of the Truman Presidency* (New York: Simon and Schuster, 1975), 88; Freeland, *The Truman Doctrine*, 127.

14. Goldstein, *Political Repression*, 300.

15. Hoover's perception of the Communist menace was often partly shaped by organizational goals. Thomas C. Reeves, *The Life and Times of Joe McCarthy* (New York: Stein and Day, 1982), 222, notes that in February of 1950, in the midst of an effort to fund seven hundred new agents, Hoover advised an influential group of senators that there were at least 540,000 communists and fellow travelers in the United States.

16. Freeland, *The Truman Doctrine*, 233, 238.

17. Donald F. Crosby, *God, Church and Flag: Senator Joseph R. McCarthy and the Catholic Church 1950–1957* (Chapel Hill: University of North Carolina Press, 1978); David M. Oshinsky, *Senator Joseph McCarthy and the American Labor Movement* (Columbia: University of Missouri Press, 1976); Griffith, "American Politics," 1–17.

18. Peter Irons, "The Cold War Crusade of the United States Chamber of Commerce" in Griffith and Theoharis, eds., *The Specter*, 76–77.

19. Oshinsky, *Senator Joseph McCarthy*, 61–62.

20. Irons, "America's Cold War Crusade," 118.

21. Irons, "America's Cold War Crusade," 137.

22. Caute, *The Great Fear*, 349.

23. Irons, "America's Cold War Crusade," 101.

24. Caute, *The Great Fear*, 350; Irons, "The Cold War Crusade," 79–82.

25. Irons, "America's Cold War Crusade," 96, 100.

26. Richard M. Fried, *Men Against McCarthy*, 102; Ronald J. Caridi, *The Korean War and American Politics: The Republican Party as a Case Study* (Philadelphia: University of Pennsylvania Press, 1968), 86–90; Peter Good-

child, *J. Robert Oppenheimer: Shatterer of Worlds* (Boston: Houghton Mifflin, 1981), 203–4.

27. Freeland, *The Truman Doctrine*, 348.

28. Paul Michael Rogin, *The Intellectuals and McCarthy: The Radical Specter* (Cambridge: MIT Press, 1967), 224, 251–52; Earl Latham, *The Communist Controversy in Washington* (Cambridge: Harvard University Press, 1966), 417.

29. Quoted in Reeves, *The Life and Times of Joe McCarthy*, 225.

30. Reeves, *The Life and Times of Joe McCarthy*, 227.

31. Quoted in Oshinsky, *A Conspiracy*, 111.

32. Latham, *The Communist Controversy*, 423.

33. Quoted in Freeland, *The Truman Doctrine*, 347.

34. Rovere, *Senator Joe McCarthy*, 222; Bayley, *Joe McCarthy and the Press*, 203.

35. Charles J. V. Murphy, "McCarthy and the Businessman" *Fortune* 49 (1954): 58; Oshinsky, *Senator Joseph McCarthy*, 125–26; Goldstein, *Political Repression*, 399–401.

36. Bayley, *Joe McCarthy and the Press*, 193.

37. Oshinsky, *A Conspiracy*, 174.

38. Rovere, *Senator Joe McCarthy*, 239.

39. Except, of course, as it affected the organized labor movement.

40. Oshinsky, *A Conspiracy*, 140. The Milwaukee *Journal*, 2 May 1950, reports that on May Day 1950, American Legionnaires disguised as Russian soldiers and evidently bent on enlightening their fellow citizens occupied the small town of Mosinee, Wisconsin. The Mayor was dragged from his house and all clergy incarcerated in a "stockade" just off "Red Square." Firearms were confiscated (an adventurous thing to do in a rural American community), and all businesses were nationalized in the sense that restaurants were forced to serve only potato soup, dark bread, and black coffee. Not until nightfall was the town "liberated" to the sounds of patriotic music and the burning of communist literature. The Mayor, who had not been informed of this charade, suffered a heart attack the following day. Oshinsky (p. 139) accounts this "the most bizarre display of anti-Red fervor," but it seems likely that close inspection of the popular culture of this era would unearth similar such episodes. At least some Catholic parishioners in Detroit were informed that their first duty in the event of a Communist take-over was to rush to their church and consume the Host (J. M. Johimsthal, personal communication).

41. Don E. Carleton, *Red Scare!* (Austin: Texas Monthly Press, 1985), 151.

42. Caute, *The Great Fear*, 22.

43. Ibid., 80, 445.

44. Victor Navasky, *Naming Names* (New York: The Viking Press, 1980), 314–29.

45. Powers, *Power and Secrecy*, 299.

46. Schneier, "White Collar Vigilantism," 111.

47. Walter Goodman, *The Committee* (London: History Book Club Ltd., 1969), 299.

48. Navasky, *Naming Names*, 85.

49. Caute, *The Great Fear*, 502.

50. Ibid., 527.

51. Navasky, *Naming Names* 95.

52. Adam Yarmolinsky, "How a Lawyer Conducts a Security Case," *The Reporter* 10 (1954): 18–22.

53. Les K. Adler, "The Politics of Culture: Hollywood and the Cold War," in Griffith and Theoharis, eds., *The Specter*, 251.

54. Quoted in Rovere, *Senator Joe McCarthy*, 270; see also Fried, *Men Against McCarthy*, 314; Bayley, *Joe McCarthy and the Press*, 210; Goldstein, *Political Repression*, 400–402.

55. Athan Theoharis, *Seeds of Repression* (Chicago: Quadrangle Books, 1971), 190.

CHAPTER 9: THE GREAT PURGE

1. Stephan F. Cohen, *Bukharin and the Bolshevik Revolution* (New York: Knopf, 1973), 131.

2. Quoted in Christopher Hibbert, *The Days of the French Revolution* (New York: Morrow, 1981), 225.

3. Merle Fainsod, *Smolensk Under Soviet Rule* (Cambridge: Harvard University Press, 1958), 6.

4. Peter H. Juviler, *Revolutionary Law and Order* (New York: The Free Press, 1976), 20.

5. Fainsod, *Smolensk*, 6.

6. E. H. Carr, *The Bolshevik Revolution* (New York: Macmillan Company, 1952), 149.

7. Jerry F. Hough and Merle Fainsod, *How the Soviet Union is Governed* (Cambridge: Harvard University Press, 1979), 88.

8. Quoted in George Legget, *The Cheka: Lenin's Political Police* (Oxford: Clarendon Press, 1981), 16.

9. Quoted in Legget, *The Cheka*, 15.

10. Legget, *The Cheka*, 102, 114.

11. Alexander Yanov, *The Origins of Autocracy* (Berkeley: University of California Press, 1981), 67–73; Legget, *The Cheka*, 202. From the Russian *oprich*—apart, beside. Oprichnina denotes a separate state within the Moscovite state. It was the creation of Ivan the Terrible. Nicholas Raisonovsky, *A History of Russia*, 4th ed. (New York: Oxford University Press, 1984), 150.

12. Simon Wolin and Robert M. Slusser, "The Evolution of the Soviet Secret Police," in Simon Wolin and Robert H. Slusser, eds., *The Soviet Secret Police* (New York: Praeger, 1957), 9.

13. Legget, *The Cheka*, 352.

14. Quoted in Wolin and Slusser, "The Evolution of the Soviet Secret Police," 10.

15. Hough and Fainsod, *How the Soviet Union is Governed*, 171.

16. Wolin and Slusser, "The Evolution of the Soviet Secret Police," 13.

17. Robert Conquest, *The Great Terror: Stalin's Purge of the Thirties* (New York: Macmillan, 1968), 547.

18. Quoted in Hough and Fainsod, *How the Soviet Union is Governed*, 88.

19. Quoted in Adam B. Ulam, *The Bolsheviks* (New York: Macmillan, 1965), 422.

20. Mikhail Heller and Aleksandre Nekrich, *Utopia in Power* (New York: Summit Books, 1986), 204.

21. Robert Service, *The Bolshevik Party in Revolution* (New York: Barnes and Noble, 1979), 90.

22. J. Arch Getty, "Party and Purge in Smolensk: 1933–37," *Slavic Review* 42 (1983): 66. Getty makes the point that these activities, however vigorous, were "organizational-administrative operations" and should not be confused with subsequent "political witch hunts."

23. In July of 1941, the German Army overran the Russian city of Smolensk and captured party records for Smolensk and the surrounding region, administratively referred to as the Western region. After the war, the "Smolensk Collection" came under American control.

24. J. Arch Getty, *The Origins of the Great Purges* (New York: Cambridge University Press, 1985), 45–47; Getty, "Party and Purge," 64.

25. Getty, *The Origins of the Great Purges*, Table 2.1, 53.

26. Quoted in Getty, "Party and Purge," 66.

27. Getty, "Party and Purge," 72.

28. Carr, *The Bolshevik Revolution*, 203.

29. Ibid., 338.

30. Quoted in Carr, *The Bolshevik Revolution*, 344.

31. Nicholas Raisonovsky, *A History of Russia*, 4th ed. (New York: Oxford University Press, 1984), 494.

32. Alex DeJonge, *Stalin and the Shaping of the Soviet Union* (New York: William Morrow and Company, 1986), 244–47; Adam B. Ulam, *Stalin: The Man and his Era* (New York: The Viking Press, 1973), 322–23.

33. Raisonovsky, *A History of Russia*, 496, 502.

34. Fainsod, *Smolensk*, 55.

35. Fainsod, *Smolensk*, 144.

36. R. W. Davies, *The Socialist Offensive: The Collectivisation of Soviet Agriculture 1929–1930* (Cambridge: Harvard University Press, 1980), 204–9.

37. Commission of the CC of the CPSU (B), *History of the Communist Party of the Soviet Union* (Moscow: Foreign Languages Publishing House, 1950), 367.

38. Fainsod, *Smolensk*, 282.

39. Hough and Fainsod, *How the Soviet Union is Governed*, 152.

40. Robert Conquest, *The Harvest of Sorrow* (New York: Oxford University Press, 1986) 157–158, and see 217–307 for the Ukraine famine.

41. Ulam, *Stalin*, 343.

42. Fainsod, *Smolensk*, 244–50.

43. The CPSU (B), *History*, 379.

44. See Conquest, *The Harvest of Sorrow*, 217–307, and for Stalin's culpability, 328–29. There can be little doubt that Stalin deliberately pursued a policy of famine to break the back of the peasantry.

45. Hough and Fainsod, *How the Soviet Union is Governed*, 151.

46. In the *History of the CPSU* (Moscow, 1960) this is rendered as "Kulak Henchman." Quoted in Heller and Nekrich, *Utopia in Power*. I am indebted to Dr. Andrea Southard for the other possible interpretations of this term. It is worth noting in this connection that the Soviet biologist Trofim Lysenko, who is known for his unsuccessful attempts to apply Marxist-Leninist principles to the world of plant genetics, achieved the presidency of the Soviet Academy of Agricultural Science by labeling his superiors "Kulaks of Science." See Heller and Nekrich, *Utopia in Power*, 482.

47. Conquest, *The Harvest of Sorrow*, 119.

48. Officially, Kulak, middle peasant, and poor peasant represented economic classifications, the precise definition of which varied enormously with changes in policy. In practice, income and property were secondary considerations. Conquest, *The Harvest of Sorrow*, 118, cites a OGPU report that complains that the use of official tax lists to identify Kulaks "frequently did not correspond to reality."

49. Quoted in Fainsod, *Smolensk*, 250.

50. Geoffrey Hosking, *The First Socialist Society* (Cambridge: Harvard University Press, 1985), 153.

51. Conquest, *The Great Terror*, 549–51.

52. Ulam, *Stalin*, 301.

53. Heller and Nekrich, *Utopia in Power*, 228.

54. Quoted in Ulam, *Stalin*, 430.

55. The CPSU (B), *History*, 417; Heller and Nekrich, *Utopia in Power*, 282. Stakhanov's "overfulfillment" was achieved by providing him with a support crew and by shutting down all other work in his sector. The disruptive aspects of the Stakhanov movement became a bone of contention in the Central Committee.

56. Wolin and Slusser, "The Evolution of the Soviet Secret Police," 15; Hough and Fainsod, *How the Soviet Union is Governed*, 171.

57. Ulam, *Stalin*, 419.

58. Joel Carmichael, *Stalin's Masterpiece* (New York: St. Martin's, 1976), 9.

59. Hough and Fainsod, *How the Soviet Union is Governed*, 172; Conquest, *The Great Terror*, 52; Stalin is often implicated in the murder of Kirov, and Khrushchev in his address to the Twentieth Congress seems to suggest this. But, according to Getty, *The Origins*, 207–10, Stalin is not directly accused by anyone until almost twenty years after the event, and then by unreliable sources. Ulam, *Stalin*, 381–87, argues that Stalin had little to gain from having Kirov assassinated and that it is unlikely that anyone with Stalin's background would have encouraged the precedent of a successful assassination. All the same, Robert Conquest, *Stalin and the Kirov Murder* (New York: Oxford University Press, 1989), passim, has advanced a forceful and detailed argument that Stalin did engineer Kirov's murder.

60. Conquest, *The Great Terror*, 57–58.

61. Nikita Khrushchev, *The Anatomy of Terror: Text of Speech Delivered at the Party's 20th Congress* (Westport, Conn.: Greenwood Press, 1979), 25.

62. Conquest, *The Great Terror*, 367–419, discusses the show trials in depth; Robert C. Tucker and Stephan F. Cohen, *The Great Purge Trial* (New York: Grosset and Dunlap, 1965), provide extensive portions of the transcripts; Roy A. Medvedev, *Let History Judge* (New York: Knopf, 1972), 172, notes that the trial of Trotskyite-Zinoviet Terrorist Center was conducted without the encumbrance of defense counsel. In actual practice, none of the Moscow show trials were so burdened, but the fiction that the defendants had counsel was maintained at the second and third trials. These trials were attended by foreign observers. It was at the first show trial that the defendants "unexpectedly" implicated many of the prominent defendants of the second and third trials.

63. Ulam, *Stalin*, 412.

64. Tucker and Cohen, *The Great Purge Trial*, xv.

65. Conquest, *The Great Terror*, 367–419; Tucker and Cohen, *The Great Purge Trial*, 561–65.

66. Transcript quoted in Tucker and Cohen, *The Great Purge Trial*, 272–96.

67. Quoted in Conquest, *The Great Terror*, 418.

68. Quoted in Medvedev, *Let History Judge*, 171.

69. Service, *The Bolshevik Party in Revolution*, 175; Getty, *The Origins*, 117–18.

70. Getty, *The Origins*, 118.

71. Conquest, *The Great Terror*, 317.

72. Hough and Fainsod, *How the Soviet Union is Governed*, 177; Adam B. Ulam, *A History of Soviet Russia* (New York: Praeger, 1976), 130.

73. Irving L. Horowitz, *Taking Lives: Genocide and State Power*, 3d ed. (New Brunswick, N.J.: Transaction, 1982), 215.

74. Quoted in Fainsod, *Smolensk*, 233.

75. Ibid., 234–36.

76. Hough and Fainsod, *How the Soviet Union is Governed*, 174.

77. Ibid.

78. Medvedev, *Let History Judge*, 213.

79. Fainsod, *Smolensk*, 60.

80. Getty, "Party and Purge," 76.

81. Ibid.

82. J. Arch Getty and William Chase, "The Moscow Party Elite in the Great Purge," *Russian History* 41 (1978): 113.

83. Hough and Fainsod, *How the Soviet Union is Governed*, 174; Walter D. Connor, "The Manufacture of Deviance: The Case of the Soviet Purge 1936–1938," *American Sociological* 37 (1972): 405–9.

84. Conquest, *The Great Terror*, 465–66.

85. Getty, *The Origins*, 177–79.

86. Quoted in Getty, *The Origins*, 186.

87. Getty, *The Origins*, 186–88.

88. Zbigniew Brzezinski, *The Permanent Purge* (Cambridge: Harvard University Press, 1956), 119.

89. Conquest, *The Great Terror*, 466.

90. Getty, *The Origins*, 189.

91. Borys Levytsky, *The Stalinist Terror in the Thirties* (Stanford, Calif.: Hoover Institute Press, 1974), 19–20; Conquest, *The Great Terror*, 43–61.

92. George F. Kennan, *Russia and the West Under Lenin and Stalin* (Boston: Little, Brown and Company, 1960), 315–16.

93. Hough and Fainsod, *How the Soviet Union is Governed*, 170.

94. Roy A. Medvedev, *On Stalin and Stalinism* (New York: Oxford University Press, 1979), 111.

95. Khrushchev, *The Anatomy of Terror*, 42.

96. Sheila Fitzpatrick, "Stalin and the Making of a New Elite," *Slavic Review* 38 (1979): 396; Jerry Hough, *Soviet Leadership in Transition* (Washington, D.C.: The Brookings Institute, 1980), 38–40; Hough and Fainsod, in *How the Soviet Union is Governed*, 169, argue that: "There is a tendency for upward mobility to be associated with acceptance of the basic political system in any country, and there is every indication that this link was present in the Soviet Union for this group that Milovan Djilas pejoratively called 'The New Class.'"

97. Hough, *Soviet Leadership in Transition*, 46.

98. Ibid., 48.

99. Stephen F. Cohen, *Rethinking the Soviet Experience* (New York: Oxford University Press, 1985), 98.

100. Carmichael, *Stalin's Masterpiece*, 14.

101. Getty, *The Origins*, 206.

102. Cohen, *Rethinking*, 55.

103. At the 17th Party Congress (1934), Stalin castigated regional bureaucrats for their inability to ensure "fulfillment of decisions." He seems to have harbored a special loathing for "incorrigible bureaucrats and red-tapists." Getty, "Party and Purge," 72.

104. Quoted in Cohen, *Rethinking*, 103.

105. Typical of the literary effusions associated with Stalin's name, see Cohen, *Rethinking*, 101.

CHAPTER 10: THE HOLOCAUST

1. Joachim Fest, *Hitler*, trans. Richard and Clara Winston (New York: Harcourt, Brace and Jovanovich, 1973), 93, 89–106; and see also the discussion in Gordon Craig, *The Germans* (New York: G. P. Putnam's Sons, 1982), 66–72.

2. Gordon Craig, *Germany 1866–1945* (New York: Oxford University Press, 1978), 550.

3. Martin Broszat, *The Hitler State*, trans. John W. Hiden (New York: Longman, 1981), 1.

4. Hilberg, *The Destruction*, 1019.

5. Robert Lewis Koehl, *The Black Corps* (Madison: University of Wisconsin Press, 1983), 157.

6. Quoted in Alan Bullock, *Hitler: A Study in Tyranny* (New York: Harper and Row, 1962), 795.

7. Sarah Gordon, *Hitler, Germans, and the "Jewish Question"* (Princeton: Princeton University Press, 1984), 151.

8. See Gregory Bateson, *Mind and Nature* (New York: E. P. Dutton, 1979), 140, for the concept of morphogenesis. Thomas Mann wrote of German fascism (his term) that "it is a racial religion. . . . It is a pagan folk-religion, a Wotan cult; it is . . . romantic barbarism." As quoted in Charles Bracelen Flood, *Hitler, the Path to Power*, (Boston: Houghton Mifflin, 1989), 219.

9. Karl A. Schleunes, *The Twisted Road to Auschwitz* (Urbana: University of Illinois Press, 1970), 50.

10. Quoted in Herman Rauschning, *The Voice of Destruction* (New York: Putnam, 1940), 230; for a balanced evaluation of this thesis, see George G. Windell, "Hitler, National Socialism, and Richard Wagner," *Journal of Central European Affairs* 22 (1963): 479–97; see also, Gerald Fleming, *Hitler and the Final Solution* (Berkeley: University of California Press, 1984), 8–10.

11. See, for example, Hitler's astonishing interpretation of *Parsifal*, as quoted by Rauschning, *The Voice of Destruction*, 229. To Hitler the drama critic, *Parsifal* portrays the struggle between good and evil *blood*. On one of his many pilgrimages to Bayreuth, Hitler returned from Wagner's tomb and announced: "Out of *Parsifal* I make a religion." Quoted in Flood, *Hitler, the Path to Power*, 432.

12. Herman Rauschning, *Hitler Speaks* (London: Thornton Butterworth Ltd., 1939), 234.

13. Quoted in Fleming, *Hitler and the Final Solution*, 28–29.

14. Eberhard Jackel, *Hitler in History* (Hanover, N.H.: University Press of New England, 1985), 21.

15. Karl Bracher, *The German Dictatorship* (New York: Praeger, 1970), 334.

16. Gordon, *Hitler*, 149.

17. Ibid., 121; Robert Proctor, *Racial Hygiene* (Cambridge: Harvard University Press, 1988), 65–72.

18. Jackel, *Hitler in History*, 23.

19. Adolph Hitler, *Mein Kampf* (1925; reprint, Boston: Houghton Mifflin Co., 1943), 661.

20. Adolph Hitler, *Hitler's Secret Conversations* (New York: Octagon Books, 1972), 57.

21. Hitler, *Hitler's Secret Conversations*, 20, 32.

22. Hitler, *Mein Kampf*, 642–43, 654, 666.

23. Ibid., 661–62.

24. Gerald Reitlinger, *The SS: Alibi of a Nation* (1957; reprint, New York: The Viking Press, 1965), 8.

25. Koehl, *The Black Corps*, 49.

26. Quoted in Jeremy Noaks and Geoffrey Pridham, eds., *Documents on Nazism, 1919–1945* (New York: The Viking Press, 1975), 492.

27. Fest, *Hitler*, 114–15.

28. Koehl, *The Black Corps*, 285, n. 24.

29. Heinze Hoehne, *The Order of the Death's Head*, (New York: Coward McCann, 1970), 146–47; quoted in Hoehne, *The Order*, 148.

30. Koehl, *The Black Corps*, 180.

31. Broszat, *The Hitler State*, 333.

32. See Hilberg, *The Destruction*, Table 6–8, for a listing of SS Main Offices.

33. Hilbert, *The Destruction*, 1003.

34. Hans Buchheim, "The SS - Instrument of Domination," in Helmut Krausnick et al., eds., *The Anatomy of the SS State*, trans. Richard Barry et al. (New York: Walker, 1968), 167.

35. Koehl, *The Black Corps*, 103–56.

36. Ibid., 180–81.

37. Hilberg, *The Destruction*, 200–201, n. 28, notes an SS report stating that the SS had grown to nearly eight hundred thousand men; the majority of them were in combat field units. The administrative apparatus was comparatively small—less than forty thousand.

38. Hoehne, *The Order*, 405.

39. Hilberg, *The Destruction*, 951.

40. Robert Lewis Koehl, *RKFDV: German Resettlement and Population Policy 1939–1945* (Cambridge: Harvard University Press, 1957), 219; Koehl, *The Black Corps*, 192.

41. Koehl, *The Black Corps*, 199.

42. See the extensive discussion of the confiscation process in the camps in Hilberg, *The Destruction*, 947–61. Human hair was sent to industrial concerns to be made into felt. Blood, at times, seems to have been systematically drained from Jewish inmates for plasma. Hilberg, *The Destruction*, 954, n. 26.

43. Koehl, *RKFDV*, 37: Koehl, *The Black Corps*, 187.

44. Koehl, *RKFDV*, 106.

45. Hilberg, *The Destruction*, 68–69, 159–61; There were sixty-four thou-

sand Mischlinge of the first degree and forty-three thousand Mischlinge of the second degree within Germany, Austria, and the Sudetenland. Party officials brooded incessantly upon the hazard presented by this relative small but only moderately diluted pool of "Jewish" genes. Various conferences suggested various corrective measures—sterilization, "deportation"—but Hitler would not render a decision. Thus, the issue remained in limbo. And so, until the end of the regime, the ties of kinship linking people of "mixed Jewish blood" with "Aryan" Germany overrode ideology. Hitler chose not to risk a public confrontation with a determined phalanx of sturdy, wool-skirted German grandmothers. Hilberg, The Destruction, 417–30, and personal communication.

46. Hilberg, The Destruction, 71–73.

47. Ibid., 75–78.

48. See the extensive discussion in Hilberg, The Destruction, 83–188.

49. Gordon, Hitler, 125.

50. Hilberg, The Destruction, 177.

51. Schleunes, The Twisted Road, 241.

52. Gordon, Hitler, 123–24.

53. Donald McKale, "A Case of 'Nazi Justice'—The Punishment of Party Members Involved in the Kristallnacht, 1938," Jewish Social Studies 25 (1973): 233.

54. Hilberg, The Destruction, 43.

55. Ibid., 44.

56. Quoted in Schleunes, The Twisted Road, 246.

57. Hilberg, The Destruction, 167–68, quotes excerpts from these minutes. Heydrich proposed that Jews be marked with an "insignia," p. 177.

58. Hilberg, The Destruction, 5–14.

59. See the Introduction by Saul Friedlander to Fleming's Hitler and the Final Solution, vii–xxxii.

60. Broszat, The Hitler State, 282; Hilberg, The Destruction, 996.

61. The assertion by David Irving, Hitler's War (New York: The Viking Press, 1977), that Himmler, not Hitler, initiated the Holocaust and that Hitler was not aware of the Final Solution until 1943 has inspired a number of scholars to look closely at the bureaucratic process behind the Holocaust. Gerald Fleming, Hitler and the Final Solution, has gathered a mass of documentation on the origins of the Holocaust. From its inception on through to its final days the trail leads directly to Hitler.

62. Quoted in Fleming, Hitler and the Final Solution, 128.

63. Fleming, Hitler and the Final Solution, 129.

64. Quoted in Lucy Dawidowicz, The War Against the Jews (New York: Holt, Rinehart and Winston, 1975), 182–83.

65. Quoted in Fleming, Hitler and the Final Solution, 92.

66. Much of the clothing went to RKFDV resettlement camps, and the furniture ended up in the houses of Nazi officials. Ostensibly, the human hair was used to make special slippers for U-boat crews. In fact, German submariners had no need for special slippers; the actual need was to justify a ritual of degradation.

67. Quoted in Jackel, Hitler in History, 53.

68. Quoted in Hilberg, The Destruction, 1007.

69. Dawidowicz, The War Against the Jews, 199; and see especially the discussion in Hilberg, The Destruction, 407–16, on the deportation process.

In the first edition of The Destruction (New York: Octagon Press, 1961), Hilberg cites an SS order that dispatched fifty trains to "relocation centers" between 1 November and 4 December 1941 (p. 298).

70. Yehuda Bauer, A History of the Holocaust (New York: Franklin Watts, 1982), 314; Randolf Braham, The Politics of Genocide: The Holocaust in Hungary (New York: Columbia University Press, 1981), 606.

77. It should be noted that there were several attempts to ransom Jews before they fell victim to the Holocaust. According to David Wyman, The Abandonment of the Jews (New York: Pantheon, 1984), allied support for these endeavors ranged from nonexistent to feeble, and in the end result they came to nothing. In the best-known instance, Eichman, on Himmler's authority, proposed in May of 1944 that one million Jews be exchanged for ten thousand trucks (quantities of tea, cocoa, coffee, and soap were also requested). The trucks, insisted Eichman, were to be used only on the eastern front, suggesting that this was merely a device to split the allied powers. What is certain is that during the course of these negotiations, the Holocaust proceeded at an undiminished pace. Wyman, The Abandonment of the Jews, 243–46.

72. Hilberg, The Destruction, 416.

73. Martin Broszat, "The Concentration Camps 1933–1945," in Krausnick et al., The Anatomy of the SS State, 425.

74. Charles W. Sydnor, Jr., Soldiers of Destruction (Princeton: Princeton University Press, 1977), 26.

75. Quoted in Broszat, "The Concentration Camps," 433.

76. Broszat, "The Concentration Camps," 435–41.

77. Koehl, The Black Corps, 134; Broszat, "The Concentration Camps," 456. Broszat notes, p. 456, that "in various places" able-bodied males were preferentially arrested.

78. Hilberg, The Destruction, 871; Broszat, "The Concentration Camps," 498.

79. Robert Jay Lifton, The Nazi Doctors (New York: Basic Books Inc., 1986), 31; Proctor, Racial Hygiene, 66.

80. Gisela Bock, "Racism and Sexism in Nazi Germany: Motherhood, Compulsory Sterilization and the State," in Renate Bridenthal, Atina Grassman, and Marion Kaplan, eds., When Biology Became Destiny (New York: Monthly Review Press, 1984), 276.

81. Robert E. Conot, Justice at Nuremberg (New York: Harper and Row, 1983), 205.

82. Bock, "Racism and Sexism," 277.

83. Lifton, The Nazi Doctors, 25.

84. Conot, Justice at Nuremberg, 205. Colonial units made up much of this occupation force.

85. Gerald Reitlinger, The Final Solution (New York: Thomas Yoseloff, 1968), 132; Schleunes, The Twisted Road, 119, describes Gerhard Wagner as an old Freikorps man who owed much of his prominence in Nazi circles to the fact that Rudolf Hess was his patient. He was an outspoken advocate of euthanasia. In a research project that tells much about Nationalist Socialist "science," Dr. Wagner once attempted to identify "Jewish blood."

86. Dawidowicz, The War Against the Jews, 176.

87. Lifton, The Nazi Doctors, 45–78.

88. Ibid., 66.

89. Ibid., 66.

90. Ibid., 67.

91. Conot, *Justice at Nuremberg*, 206.

92. Fleming, *Hitler and the Final Solution*, 24.

93. Ibid.; Broszat, *The Hitler State*, 321.

94. Conot, *Justice at Nuremberg*, 211.

95. Lifton, *The Nazi Doctors*, 77.

96. Fleming, *Hitler and the Final Solution*, 24.

97. Lifton, *The Nazi Doctors*, 70.

98. Christopher Browning, *Fateful Months: Essay on the Emergence of the Final Solution* (New York: Holmes and Meier, 1985), 4.

99. Conot, *Justice at Nuremberg*, 209.

100. Lifton, *The Nazi Doctors*, 74–75.

101. Ibid., 97.

102. Bauer, *A History of the Holocaust*, 208.

103. Lifton, *The Nazi Doctors*, 96–102.

104. Browning, *Fateful Months*, 59.

105. Hilberg, *The Destruction*, 873.

106. Konnilyn G. Feig, *Hitler's Death Camps: The Sanity of Madness* (New York: Holmes and Meier, 1981), 268.

107. Hilberg, *The Destruction*, 189; Koehl, *The Black Corps*, 163–64; Nora Levin, *The Holocaust* (New York: Thomas Crowell, 1965), 150.

108. Levin, *The Holocaust*, 153.

109. Hilberg, *The Destruction*, 206.

110. Conot, *Justice at Nuremberg*, 215.

111. Jackel, *Hitler in History*, 51–58.

112. Hilberg, *The Destruction*, 288–90; Sydnor, *Soldiers of Destruction*, 321–23.

113. Hoehne, *The Order*, 358–59.

114. Hilberg, *The Destruction*, 286.

115. Ibid., 298, 343.

116. Ibid., 328–33. The man addressing Himmler was Obergruppenfuehrer von dem Bach-Zelewski, who was shortly thereafter admitted to a hospital suffering from intestinal complaints and hallucinations.

117. Browning, *Fateful Months*, 60, notes that Nebe's suggestion actually prompted a full scale experiment that even SS technicians considered a horrifying failure.

118. Hans-Adolf Jacobsen, "The *Kommissarbefehl* and Mass Executions of Soviet Russian Prisoners of War," in Krausnick et al., *Anatomy of the SS State*, 508–15; the text of order is provided on pp. 532–34.

119. Hilberg, *The Destruction*, 946; Conot, *Justice at Nuremberg*, 289–90.

120. Alexander Donat, *The Death Camp Treblinka* (New York: Holocaust Library, 1979), 272–76; Dawidowicz, *The War Against the Jews*, 180.

121. Reitlinger, *The Final Solution*, 137; A promotion request for Wirth submitted by Bouhler, dated 13 April 1943, states that since the beginning of the war, Wirth had been "serving in a special mission for the Fuehrer." In fact, Wirth's transfer from the SA to the Security Service dates to April 1938. At that time he is documented as being "at the disposal of the Fuehrer." Fleming, *Hitler and the Final Solution*, 25.

122. Hilberg, *The Destruction*, 884.

123. Feig, *Hitler's Death Camps*, 268.

124. Levin, *The Holocaust*, 306.

125. Hilberg, *The Destruction*, 878.

126. Feig, *Hitler's Death Camps*, 297.

127. Hilbert, *The Destruction*, Table 9–8; Martin Gilbert, *The Holocaust* (New York: Holt, Rinehart and Winston, 1985), 817.

128. Edward Crankshaw, *Gestapo* (London: Putnam, 1956), 180.

129. Donat, *The Death Camp Treblinka*, 70.

130. Feig, *Hitler's Death Camps*, 319; Hilberg, *The Destruction*, 893.

131. Reitlinger, *The Final Solution*, 313–19.

132. Feig, *Hitler's Death Camps*, 333–65.

133. Anna Pawelcynska, *Values and Violence at Auschwitz: A Sociological Analysis* (Berkeley: University of California Press, 1971), 31; Hilberg, *The Destruction*, 884, notes that there was a fifth gas chamber at Birkenau (Auschwitz II), which was used on a standby basis. He also confirms the two-thousand-person capacity of the larger gas chambers. It works out to a little more than one square foot per person.

134. Hilberg, *The Destruction*, 886–91. Zyklon B seems to have been specially concocted by the German chemical industry to kill people. The normal fumigant, Zyklon D, was for lice and rodents. Zyklon B was more efficient, from Commandant Hoess's point of view, because it killed people faster. There is no evidence that the death it brought was any less painful.

135. Hilberg, *The Destruction*, 870–71; Feig, *Hitler's Death Camps*, 344.

136. Quoted in Hilberg, *The Destruction*, 930.

137. Hilberg, *The Destruction*, 930; Feig, *Hitler's Death Camps*, 354, provides a much larger figure—150,000.

138. Reitlinger, *The Final Solution*, 497–98.

139. Gilbert, *The Holocaust*, 807.

140. Douglas Botting, *From the Ruins of the Reich* (New York: Crown Publishers Inc., 1985), 39–46.

141. Too many trains had been allowed to enter the camp. Conditions soon became so hideous (it was summertime) that even seasoned SS personnel were staggered, and the Sonderkommando refused to work (to kill them immediately would have left only the guards to deal with the problem). News of this impasse reached Globocnik, who, arriving on the scene, determined the dimensions of the crisis without entering the camp. The indefatigable Christian Wirth was given the task of removing the mountain of dead. The camp commander was transferred and the camp reorganized around larger gas chambers. Claude Lanzmann, *Shoa: An Oral History of the Holocaust* (New York: Pantheon Books, 1985); statements of *Unterscharfuehrer* Suchomel and state Prosecutor Spiess.

142. Hilberg, *The Destruction*, 978.

143. Sydnor, *Soldiers of Destruction*, 330–35.

144. Hilberg, *The Destruction*, 975.

145. Ibid., ix.

146. George Kren and Leon Rappaport, *The Holocaust and the Crisis of Human Behavior* (New York: Holmes and Meier, 1980), 9.

147. Hilberg, *The Destruction*, 996; Broszat, *The Hitler State*, 342.

148. Benno Müller-Hill, *Murderous Science*, trans. George R. Frazer (New York: Oxford University Press, 1988), *passim*; Proctor, *Racial Hygiene*, 289.

149. Quoted in DeJonge, *Stalin*, 382.

150. Hilberg, *The Destruction*, 272–74.

CHAPTER 11: MORAL LANDSCAPES AND THE PERSISTENCE OF EN-
CHANTMENTS

1. Quoted in Roger Daniels, *Concentration Camps USA: Japanese Americans and World War II* (New York: Holt, Rinehart and Winston, 1972), 76. Warren repeated this line of reasoning on several occasions and was evidently influenced by the cogitations of General DeWitt. In his report on the evacuation of Japanese Americans from Military Area I (the West Coast), DeWitt states: "The very fact that no sabotage has taken place to date (February 14, 1942) is disturbing and confirming indication that such action will be taken." Lieutenant General J. L. DeWitt, *Final Report, Japanese Evacuation from the West Coast, 1942* (Washington, D.C.: U.S. Government Printing Office, 1942), 255.

2. House Reports, Report No. 2124, *National Defense Migration* (Washington, D.C.: U.S. Government Printing Office, 1942), 255.

3. For example, the Western Growers Protective Association. There were many such organizations; all foursquare for removal. The managing secretary of the Salinas Vegetable Grower-Shipper Association could not have been more candid: "We're charged with wanting to get rid of the Japs for selfish reasons . . . we do. It's a question of whether the white man lives on the Pacific coast or the brown man. They came into this valley to work, and they stayed to take over. . . . They undersell the white man in the markets." Quoted in Frank J. Taylor, "The People Nobody Wants," *The Saturday Evening Post*, 214 (9 May 1942).

4. Quoted in Peter Irons, *Justice at War* (New York: Oxford University Press, 1983), 68.

5. Powers, *Secrecy and Power*, 249.

6. Quoted in Irons, *Justice at War*, 203.

7. Quoted in Michi Weglyn, *Years of Infamy* (William Morrow, 1976), 47.

8. Weglyn, *Years of Infamy*, 34.

9. Irons, *Justice at War*, 133. Local chapters of the ACLU did, however, initiate test cases.

10. Irons, *Justice at War*, 82.

11. *United States Reports*, vol. 323 (Washington, D.C.: U.S. Government Printing Office, 1945), 216, 220.

12. Daniels, *Concentration Camps USA*, 73; Weglyn, *Years of Infamy*, 87.

13. Daniels, *Concentration Camps USA*, 71.

14. Ulam, *Stalin*, 413.

15. Ulam, *A History of Soviet Russia*, 436; Tucker and Cohen, *The Great Purge Trial*, 6.

16. Navasky, *Naming Names*, 319–24, elaborates the thesis that the committee's Hearings were essentially rituals of degradation. See also Walter Goodman, *The Committee* (London: The History Book Club, 1969), 358.

17. "Card Carrying Communists" were scarce goods during the McCarthy Era; something to be husbanded. In 1954, for instance, J. Edgar Hoover recommended that the Justice Department *not* prosecute too many Communists— only the most important. It would not do, in other words, to totally exhaust this valuable commodity. Michael R. Belknap, *Cold War Political Justice* (Westport, Conn.: Greenwood, 1977), 156. Hoover's expressed fear was that public trial would unmask his informants and thereby undermine his efforts to bolster the fading public perception of a hidden conspiracy. Hoover was well aware,

by the admission of his assistant, William Sullivan, that "the Party didn't amount to a damn." Quoted in Belknap, *Cold War Political Justice*, 175.

18. Even as late as 1943, SS officers were removed from positions of responsibility if an eighteenth-century Jewish ancestor came to light. Koehl, *The Black Corps*, 359, n. 65.

19. Jan Tomasz Gross, *Polish Society under German Occupation* (Princeton: Princeton University Press, 1979), 49; Richard C. Lukas, *The Forgotten Holocaust: The Poles under German Occupation* (Lexington: University of Kentucky Press, 1986), 220.

20. Max Weber, *Economy and Society*, ed. Guenther Roth and Claus Wittich (New York: Bedminster, 1968), 404. The quote is taken from Weber's discussion of the world of ideas, which according to Wolfgang Schluchter, *The Rise of Western Rationalism* (Berkeley: University of California Press, 1981), 26, n. 4., prefigures Weber's theory of disenchantment. No one better understood that the march of rationalization was "haunted by the ghosts of dead religious beliefs."

Bibliography

Adams, Ames Truslow. *The Founding of New England*. Boston: Atlantic Monthly Press, 1921.

Adler, Les K. "The Politics of Culture: Hollywood and the Cold War." In *The Spector*, edited by R. Griffith and A. Theoharis. New York: New Viewpoints, 1974.

Allen, Frederick L. *Only Yesterday*. 1931. Reprint. New York: Harper and Row, 1964.

Aronson, Elliot. "Persuasion via Self-Justification: Large Commitments for Small Rewards." In *Retrospectives on Social Psychology*, edited by L. Festinger. New York: Oxford University Press, 1980.

Bateson, Gregory. *Mind and Nature*. New York: E. P. Dutton, 1979.

Bauer, Yehuda. *A History of the Holocaust*. New York: Franklin Watts, 1982.

Bayley, Edwin R. *Joe McCarthy and the Press*. Madison: University of Wisconsin Press, 1981.

Beck, F., and W. Godin. *Russian Purge and the Extraction of Confession*. New York: Viking, 1951.

Beik, William. "Popular Culture and Elite Repression in Early Modern Europe." *Journal of Interdisciplinary History* 1 (1980): 97–103.

Belefrage, Cedric. *The American Inquisition*. New York: Bobbs-Merrill, 1973.

Belknap, Michael R. *Cold War Political Justice*. Westport, Conn.: Greenwood, 1977.

Ben-Yehuda, Nachman. *Deviance and Moral Boundaries*. Chicago: University of Chicago Press, 1985.

Black, Max. *Models and Metaphors*. Ithaca: Cornell University Press, 1962.

Bendix, Reinhard. *Kings or People*. Berkeley: University of California Press, 1978.

Bock, Gisela. "Racism and Sexism in Nazi Germany: Motherhood, Compulsory Sterilization and the State." In *When Biology Became Destiny*, edited by Renate Bridenthal et al. New York: Monthly Review Press, 1984.

Boserup, Ester. *Population and Technological Change*. Chicago: University of Chicago Press, 1981.

Bossy, John. "The Counter-Reformation and the People of Catholic Europe." *Past and Present* 47 (1970): 51–70.

Botting, Douglas. *From the Ruins of the Reich*. New York: Crown, 1985.

Boyer, Paul, and Stephan Nissenbaum. *Salem Possessed*. Cambridge: Harvard University Press, 1974.

————. *Salem Village Witchcraft: A Documentary Record of Local Conflict in Colonial New England*. Belmont, Calif.: Wadsworth, 1972.

Bracher, Karl. *The German Dictatorship*. New York: Praeger, 1970.

Braham, Randolph. *The Politics of Genocide: The Holocaust in Hungary*. New York: Columbia University Press, 1981.

Brattle, Thomas. "Letter of Thomas Brattle," 1692. In *The Narratives of the Witchcraft Cases*, edited by George Lincoln Burr. New York: Charles Scribner's Sons.

Bremer, Francis J. *The Puritan Experiment*. New York: St. Martin's, 1976.

Brody, David. *Labor in Crisis*. Philadelphia: Lippincott, 1965.

Brown, Roger. *Social Psychology*. New York: Free Press, 1965.

Browning, Christopher. *Fateful Months: Essay on the Emergence of the Final Solution*. New York: Holmes and Meier, 1985.

Broszat, Martin. *The Hitler State*. Translated by John W. Hiden. New York: Longman, 1981.

————. "Hitler and the Genesis of the Final Solution." *Yad Vashem Studies* 13 (1979): 73–125.

————. "The Concentration Camps 1933–1945." Translated by Richard Barry et al. In *Anatomy of the SS State*, edited by Helmut Krausnick et al. New York: Walker, 1968.

Brzezinski, Zbigniew. *The Permanent Purge*. Cambridge: Harvard University Press, 1956.

Bullock, Alan. *Hitler: A Study in Tyranny*. New York: Harper and Row, 1962.

Burner, David. "1919: Prelude to Normalcy." In *Change and Continuity in 20th Century America*, edited by John Greaman et al. Columbus: Ohio State University Press, 1968.

Burr, George Lincoln, ed. *Narratives of the Witchcraft Cases*. New York: Charles Scribner's Sons, 1914.

————. "The Literature of the Witchcraft Cases." *Papers of the American Historical Association* 4 (1890): 27–66.

Calef, Robert. *More Wonders of the Invisible World*. 1700. In *Narratives of the Witchcraft Cases*, edited by George Lincoln Burr. New York: Charles Scribner's Sons, 1914.

Candeloro, Dominic. "Louis F. Post and the Red Scare of the 1920s." *Prologue* 11 (1979): 41–55.

Caridi, Ronald J. *The Korean War and American Politics: The Republican Party as a Case Study*. Philadelphia: University of Pennsylvania Press, 1968.

Carleton, Don E. *Red Scare!* Austin: Texas Monthly Press, 1985.

Carmichael, Joel. *Stalin's Masterpiece*. New York: St. Martin's, 1976.

Caro Baroja, Julio. *Inquisición, Brujeriá y Criptojudáismo*. Barcelona: Ediciones Ariel, 1972.

————. *The World of Witches*. Chicago: University of Chicago Press, 1965.

Carr, E. H. *The Bolshevik Revolution*. New York: Macmillan, 1952.

Caute, David. *The Great Fear*. New York: Simon and Schuster, 1978.

Chambliss, William J. "Toward a Political Economy of Crime." *Theory and Society* 2 (1975): 149–70.

Clark, Stuart. "King James' Daemonology: Witchcraft and Kingship." In *The Damned Art*, edited by Sydney Anglo. London: Routledge and Kegan Paul, 1977.

Coben, Stanley. "A Study in Nativism: The American Red Scare of 1919–1920." *Political Science Quarterly* 79 (1964): 52–75.

—————. *A. Mitchell Palmer: Politician.* New York: Columbia University Press, 1963.

Cockburn, J. S. "The Nature and Incidence of Crime in England: A Preliminary Survey." In *Crime in England 1550–1800*, edited by J. S. Cockburn. Princeton: Princeton University Press, 1977.

Cohen, Albert. *The Elasticity of Evil: Changes in the Social Definition of Deviance.* Oxford: Basil Blackwood, 1974.

—————. *Deviance and Social Control.* Englewood Cliffs, NJ: Prentice-Hall, 1966.

Cohen, Stephen. *Rethinking the Soviet Experience.* New York: Oxford University Press, 1985.

—————. *Bukharin and the Bolshevik Revolution.* New York: Knopf, 1973.

Cohn, Norman. *Europe's Inner Demons.* New York: Basic Books, 1975.

—————. *The Pursuit of the Millenium.* New York: Oxford University Press, 1970.

Collins, Randall. *Conflict Sociology.* New York: Oxford University Press, 1975.

Commission of the CC of the CPSU (B). *History of the Communist Party of the Soviet Union.* Moscow: Foreign Languages Publishing House, 1950.

Connor, Walter. "The Manufacture of Deviance: The Case of the Soviet Purge 1936–1938." *American Sociological Review* 37 (1972): 401–13.

Conot, Robert. *Justice at Nuremberg.* New York: Harper and Row, 1983.

Conquest, Robert. *Stalin and the Kirov Murder.* New York: Oxford University Press, 1989.

—————. *The Harvest of Sorrow.* New York: Oxford University Press, 1986.

—————. *The Great Terror: Stalin's Purge of the Thirties.* New York: Macmillan, 1968.

Craig, Gordon. *The Germans.* New York: Putnam, 1982.

—————. *Germany 1866–1945.* New York: Oxford University Press, 1978.

Crankshaw, Edward. *Gestapo.* London: Putnam, 1956.

Craven, Wesley. *The Colonies in Transition.* New York: Harper and Row, 1968.

Crosby, Donald. *God, Church and Flag: Senator Joseph R. McCarthy and the Catholic Church 1950–1957.* Chapel Hill: University of North Carolina Press, 1978.

Currie, Elliott. "Crimes Without Criminals: Witchcraft and Its Control in Renaissance Europe." *Law and Society Review* 3, no. 1 (1968): 7–32.

Dallin, Alexander. *German Rule in Russia 1941–1945.* New York: Macmillan, 1957.

Daniels, Roger. *Concentration Camps USA: Japanese Americans and World War II*. New York: Harper and Row, 1972.

Davies, R. W. *The Socialist Offensive: The Collectivization of Soviet Agriculture 1929–1930*. Cambridge: Harvard University Press, 1980.

Dawidowicz, Lucy. *The War Against the Jews 1933–1945*. New York: Holt, Rinehart and Winston, 1975.

DeJonge, Alex. *Stalin and the Shaping of the Soviet Union*. New York: William Morrow, 1986.

Delumeau, Jean. *Catholicism Between Luther and Voltaire: A New View of the Counter-Reformation*. Philadelphia: Westminster Press, 1977.

Demos, John. "Underlying Themes in the Witchcraft of Seventeenth-Century New England." *American Historical Review* 75 (1970): 1311–26.

Donaldson, Gordon. *Scotland: the Shaping of a Nation*. London: David and Charles, 1974.

Donat, Alexander. *The Death Camp Treblinka*. New York: Holocaust Library, 1979.

Easlea, Brian. *Witch Hunting, Magic and the New Philosophy*. Atlantic Highlands, NJ: Humanities Press, 1980.

Edelman, Murray. *Politics as Symbolic Action*. Chicago: Markham, 1971.

Epstein, Scarlett. "A Sociological Analysis of Witch Belief in a Mysore Village." *Eastern Anthropologist* 12 (1958): 234–51.

Erikson, Kai. *Wayward Puritans*. New York: Wiley, 1966.

Evans-Pritchard, E. E. *Witchcraft Oracles and Magic Among the Azande*. Oxford: Clarendon Press, 1937.

Ewen, C. L'Estrange. *Witchcraft and Demonism*. London: Heath Cranton, 1933.

———. *Witch Hunting and Witch Trials*. London: Kegan Paul, Trench, Trubner, 1929.

Fainsod, Merle. *Smolensk Under Soviet Rule*. Cambridge: Harvard University Press, 1958.

Favret-Saada, Jeanne. *Deadly Words*. Translated by Cathrine Cullin. New York: Cambridge University Press, 1980.

Feig, Konnilyn. *Hitler's Death Camps: The Sanity of Madness*. New York: Holmes and Meier, 1981.

Fest, Joachim. *Hitler*. Translated by Richard and Clara Winston. New York: Harcourt, Brace and Jovanovich, 1973.

Festinger, Leon. *A Theory of Cognitive Dissonance*. Stanford, Calif.: Stanford University Press, 1957.

Fitzpatrick, Sheila. "Stalin and the Making of the New Elite." *Slavic Review* 38 (1979): 379–403.

———. *Cultural Revolution in Russia, 1928–1931*. Bloomington: Indiana University Press, 1978.

Fleming, Gerald. *Hitler and the Final Solution*. Berkeley: University of California Press, 1984.

Flinn, Michael. *The European Demographic System 1500–1820*. Baltimore: The Johns Hopkins University Press, 1981.

Flood, Charles Bracelen. *Hitler, the Path to Power*. Boston: Houghton Mifflin, 1989.

Forbes, Thomas. *The Midwife and the Witch*. New Haven: Yale University Press, 1966.

Foster, Stephan. *Their Solitary Way*. New Haven: Yale University Press, 1971.

Freeland, Richard M. *The Truman Doctrine and the Origins of McCarthyism*. New York: Knopf, 1972.

Fried, Richard M. *Men Against McCarthy*. New York: Columbia University Press, 1976.

Gaddis, John Lewis. "Was the Truman Doctrine a Real Turning Point?" In *Succession or Repression: Realities of the Truman Presidency*, edited by Jack Stuart. New York: Simon and Schuster, 1975.

Gengarelly, William Anthony. "Resistance Spokesmen: Opponents of the Red Scare 1919–1921." Ph.D. diss., Boston University, 1972.

Gerhard, Dietrich. *Old Europe: A Study of Continuity, 1000–1800*. New York: Academic Press, 1981.

Getty, J. Arch. *The Origins of the Great Purges*. New York: Cambridge University Press, 1985.

—————. "Party and Purge in Smolensk: 1933–1937." *Slavic Review* 42 (Spring 1983): 60–79.

Getty, J. Arch, and William Chase. "The Moscow Party Elite in the Great Purges." *Russian History* 5, no. 1 (1978): 105–15.

Gilberg, Martin. *The Holocaust*. New York: Holt, Rinehart and Winston, 1985.

Goldstein, Robert Justin. *Political Repression in Modern America*. New York: Schenkman, 1978.

Goodchild, Peter. *J. Robert Oppenheimer: Shatterer of Worlds*. Boston: Houghton Mifflin, 1981.

Goodman, Walter. *The Committee*. London: The History Book Club, 1969.

Gordon, Sarah. *Hitler, Germans and the "Jewish Question."* Princeton: Princeton University Press, 1984.

Griffith, Robert. "American Politics and the Origins of McCarthyism." In *The Specter*, edited by Robert Griffith and Athan Theoharis. New York: Franklin Watts, 1974.

Gross, Jan Tomasz. *Polish Society Under German Occupation*. Princeton: Princeton University Press, 1979.

Hale, John. *A Modest Inquiry into the Nature of Witchcraft*, 1702. In *Narratives of the Witchcraft Cases*. Edited by George Lincoln Burr. New York: Charles Scribner's Sons, 1914.

Hall, David D. *Worlds of Wonder, Days of Judgment*. New York: Knopf, 1989.

Haller, William. *Foxe's Book of Martyrs and the Elect Nation*. London: Jonathon Cope, 1963.

Hansen, Chadwick. *Witchcraft at Salem*. New York: Signet, 1970.

Harper, Alan D. *The Politics of Loyalty*. Westport, Conn.: Greenwood, 1969.

Harper, Edward B. "Fear and the Status of Women." *Southwestern Journal of Anthropology* 25 (1969): 80–91.

Haskins, George Lee. *Law and Authority in Early Massachusetts*. New York: Macmillan, 1960.

Hawley, Ellis W. *The Great War and the Search for a Modern Order*. New York: St. Martin's, 1979.

Heikkinen, Antero. *Paholaisen Liitolaiset*. Helsinki, 1969. English summary, 374–94.

Heilbronner, Robert L. *Marxism: For and Against*. New York: Norton, 1980.

Heller, Mikhail, and Aleksandre Nekrich. *Utopia in Power*. New York: Summit Books, 1986.

Hempel, Carl G. "The Functions of General Laws in History." *Journal of Philosophy* 39 (1982): 35–48.

Henningsen, Gustave. "The Greatest Witch Trial of All: Navarre, 1609–1614." *History Today* 30 (1981): 36–39.

—————. *The Witches' Advocate*. Reno: University of Nevada Press, 1980.

—————. "Informe sobre tres años de investigaciones etnologicas en España." *Revista de Antropología* 1 (1971): 61–90.

Hibbert, Christopher. *The Days of the French Revolution*. New York: Morrow, 1981.

Higginson, John. "An Epistle to the Reader." 1702. In *Narratives of the Witchcraft Cases*, edited by George Lincoln Burr. Charles Scribner's Sons, 1914.

Hilberg, Raul. *The Destruction of the European Jews*. 2d ed., 3 vols. New York: Holmes and Meier, 1985.

—————. *The Destruction of the European Jews*. New York: Octagon, 1961.

Hitler, Adolf. *Hitler's Secret Conversations*. Translated by Norman Cameron and R. H. Stevens. 1953. Reprint. New York: Octagon Books, 1972.

—————. *Mein Kampf*. Translated by Ralph Mannheim. Boston: Houghton Mifflin, 1943.

Hockett, Homer Cary. *Political and Social Growth in the United States*. Vol. 1. New York: Macmillan, 1933.

Hoehne, Heinze. *The Order of the Death's Head*. Translated by Richard Barry. New York: Coward-McCann, 1970.

Holmes, Ronald. *Witchcraft in British History*. London: Frederick Muller, 1974.

Holmes, Thomas J. *Cotton Mather: A Bibliography of His Works*. Cambridge: Harvard University Press, 1940.

—————. *Increase Mather: A Bibliography of His Works*. Cambridge: Harvard University Press, 1931.

Horowitz, Irving L. *Taking Lives: Genocide and State Power*. 3d ed. New Brunswick, NJ: Transaction, 1982.

Horsley, Richard A. "Further Reflections on Witchcraft and European Folk Religion." *History of Religion* 19 (1979): 71–95.

Hosking, Geoffrey. *The First Socialist Society*. Cambridge: Harvard University Press, 1985.

House Reports - 77th Congress, 2nd Session. Vol. 8. Report No. 2124. *National Defense Migration*. Washington, D.C.: U.S. Government Printing Office. 1942.

Hough, Jerry F. *Soviet Leadership in Transition*. Washington, D.C.: The Brookings Institute, 1980.

—————. "The Cultural Revolution and Western Understanding of the Soviet System." In *Cultural Revolution in Russia*, edited by Sheila Fitzpatrick. Bloomington: Indiana University Press, 1978.

Hough, Jerry F., and Merle Fainsod. *How the Soviet Union is Governed*. Cambridge: Harvard University Press, 1979.

Hutchinson, Thomas. *The History of the Province of Massachusetts*. Vol. 2. 1764. Reprint. Cambridge: Harvard University Press, 1936.

Institoris, Heinrich, and Jacob Sprenger. *Malleus Maleficarum*. 1486. Translated by Montague Summers. New York: Benjamin Blom, 1970.

Interchurch World Movement: The Commission of Inquiry. *Report on the Steel Strike of 1919*. New York: Harcourt, Brace and Howe, 1920.

Irons, Peter. *Justice at War*. New York: Oxford University Press, 1983.

—————. "The Cold War Crusade of the United States Chamber of Commerce." In *The Specter*, edited by Robert Griffith and Athan Theoharis. New York: New Viewpoints, 1974.

—————. "America's Cold War Crusade: Domestic Politics and Foreign Policy, 1942–1948." Ph.D. diss., Boston University, 1972.

Irving, David. *Hitler's War*. New York: Viking, 1977.

Jacobsen, Hans-Adolf. "The *Kommissarbefehl* and Mass Executions of Soviet Prisoners of War." Translated by Richard Barry et al. In *Anatomy of the SS State*, edited by Helmut Krausnick et al. New York: Walker, 1968.

Jackel, Eberhard. *Hitler in History*. Hanover, NH: University Press of New England, 1985.

Jackson, R. M. *The Machinery of Justice in England*. New York: Cambridge University Press, 1977.

Jensen, Joan M. *The Price of Vigilance*. Chicago: Rand McNally, 1968.

Jernegan, Marcus W. "The Province Charter." In *Commonwealth History of Massachusetts*, edited by Albert Bushnell Hart, vol. 2. New York: Russell and Russell, 1966.

Juviler, Peter H. *Revolutionary Law and Order*. New York: The Free Press, 1976.

Kamen, Henry. "500 Years of the Spanish Inquisition." *History Today* 31 (1981): 37–41.

—————. *The Iron Century, 1550–1660*. New York: Praeger, 1971.

—————. *The Spanish Inquisition*. New York: The New American Library, 1971.

Karlsen, Carol F. *The Devil the Shape of a Woman: Witchcraft in Colonial New England*. New York: Norton, 1987.

Kennan, George. *Russia and the West under Lenin and Stalin*. Boston: Little, Brown, 1960.

Kieckhefer, Richard. *European Witch Trials: Their Foundation in Popular and Learned Culture, 1300–1500*. Los Angeles: University of California Press, 1976.

Kiernan, V. G. *State and Society in Europe, 1550–1650*. New York: St. Martin's, 1980.

Kittredge, George Lyman. *Witchcraft in Old and New England.* Cambridge: Harvard University Press, 1929.

Koehl, Robert Lewis. *The Black Corps.* Madison: University of Wisconsin Press, 1983.

—————. *RKFDV, German Resettlement and Population Policy 1939–1945.* Cambridge: Harvard University Press, 1957.

Kren, George, and Leon Rappaport. *The Holocaust and the Crisis of Human Behavior.* New York: Holmes and Meier, 1980.

Khrushchev, Nikita. *The Anatomy of Terror: Text of Speech Delivered at the Party's 20th Congress.* Westport, Conn.: Greenwood, 1979.

Langbien, John H. *Torture and the Law of Proof.* Chicago: University of Chicago Press, 1977.

—————. *Prosecuting Crime in the Renaissance.* Cambridge: Harvard University Press, 1974.

Lanzmann, Claude. *Shoa: An Oral History of the Holocaust.* New York: Pantheon, 1985.

Larner, Christina. *Enemies of God.* Baltimore: The Johns Hopkins University Press, 1981.

—————. "Crimen Exceptum? The Crime of Witchcraft in Europe." In *Crime and the Law,* edited by V. A. C. Gatrell et al. London: Europa Publications, 1980.

—————. "James VI and I and Witchcraft." In *The Reign of James VI and I,* edited by A. G. R. Smith. New York: St. Martin's, 1973.

Latham, Earl. *The Communist Controversy in Washington.* Cambridge: Harvard University Press, 1966.

Lauderdale, Pat. "Deviance and Moral Boundaries." *American Sociological Review* 41 (1976): 660–76.

Lea, H. C. *A History of the Inquisition of the Middle Ages.* New York: Harper, 1955.

—————. *Materials Toward a History of Witchcraft.* Philadelphia: University of Pennsylvania Press, 1939.

Leggett, George. *The Cheka: Lenin's Political Police.* Oxford: Clarendon Press, 1981.

Leuchtenburg, William E. *A Troubled Feast, American Society Since 1945.* Boston: Little, Brown, 1975.

—————. *The Perils of Prosperity, 1914–1932.* Chicago: University of Chicago Press, 1958.

Levin, Murray B. *Political Hysteria in America.* New York: Basic Books, 1971.

Levin, Nora. *The Holocaust.* New York: Thomas Crowell, 1965.

Levytsky, Borys. *The Stalinist Terror in the Thirties.* Stanford, Calif.: Hoover Institute Press, 1974.

Lifton, Robert Jay. *The Nazi Doctors.* New York: Basic Books, 1986.

Lindsmith, Alfred R., et al. *Social Psychology.* Hinsdale, Ill.: Dryden, 1975.

Lofland, John. *The Dramaturgy of State Executions.* Montclair: Patterson Smith, 1979.

Lovejoy, David S. *The Glorious Revolution in America*. New York: Harper and Row, 1972.

Lovell, Bernard. *Emerging Cosmology*. New York: Columbia University Press, 1981.

Lukas, Richard C. *The Forgotten Holocaust: The Poles Under German Occupation*. Lexington: University of Kentucky Press, 1986.

Macfarlane, Alan. *Witchcraft in Tudor and Stuart England*. London: Routledge and Kegan Paul, 1970.

McKale, Donald. "A Case of 'Nazi Justice': The Punishment of Members Involved in the *Kristallnacht, 1938*." *Jewish Studies* 25 (1973): 228–38.

Mair, Lucy. *Witchcraft*. New York: McGraw-Hill, 1969.

Marwick, Max. "Witchcraft as a Social Strain Gage." In *Witchcraft and Sorcery*, edited by Max Marwick. New York: Penguin, 1970.

Mather, Cotton. *The Wonders of the Invisible World*. 1692. In *Narratives of the Witchcraft Cases*, edited by George Lincoln Burr. New York: Charles Scribner's Sons, 1914.

——————. *Memorable Providences, Relating to Witchcraft and Possessions*. 1689. In *Narratives of the Witchcraft Cases*, edited by George Lincoln Burr. New York: Charles Scribner's Sons, 1914.

Medvedev, Roy. *On Stalin and Stalinism*. New York: Oxford University Press, 1979.

——————. *Let History Judge*. Translated by Colleen Taylor. New York: Knopf, 1972.

Merton, Robert K. "Social Structure and Anomie." *American Sociological Review* 3 (1938): 672–82.

Midelfort, H. C. Erik. "Heartland of the Witchcraze: Central and Northern Europe." *History Today* 31 (1981): 27–31.

——————. "Witch Hunting and the Domino Theory." In *Religion and the People, 800–1700*, edited by James Obelkevich. Chapel Hill: University of North Carolina Press, 1979.

——————. *Witch Hunting in Southwestern Germany: 1562–1684*. Stanford, Calif.: Stanford University Press, 1972.

Miller, Perry. *The New England Mind*. Cambridge: Harvard University Press, 1953.

Monter, E. William. "French and Italian Witchcraft." *History Today* 30 (1980): 31–35.

——————. "Historical Demography and Religious History in Sixteenth-Century Geneva." *Journal of Interdisciplinary History* 9 (1979): 399–427.

——————. *Witchcraft in France and Switzerland*. Ithaca: Cornell University Press, 1976.

Morison, Samuel Eliot. *The Puritan Pronaos*. New York: New York University Press, 1936.

Morey, Adrian. *The Catholic Subjects of Elizabeth I*. Totowa, NJ: Rowman and Littlefield, 1978.

Morris, Terrence. *Deviance and Control: The Secular Heresy*. London: Hutchinson, 1976.

Moseley, James G. *A Cultural History of Religion in America.* Westport, Conn.: Greenwood, 1981.

Muchembled, Robert. "The Witches of Cambresis: The Acculturation of the Rural World in the 16th and 17th Centuries." In *Religion and the People, 800–1700,* edited by James Obelkovich. Chapel Hill: University of North Carolina Press, 1979.

Muller-Hill, Benno. *Murderous Science.* Translated by George Fraser. New York: Oxford University Press, 1988.

Murphy, Charles J. V. "McCarthy and the Businessmen." *Fortune* 49 (1954): 180–94.

Murphy, Paul. "Sources and Nature of Intolerance in the 1920s." *Journal of American History* 51 (1964): 60–76.

Murray, Robert K. *Red Scare: A Study in National Hysteria.* Minneapolis: University of Minnesota Press, 1955.

Nadel, S. F. *Nupe Religion.* New York: Schocken, 1970.

Nagel, Ernest. *The Structure of Science.* New York: Harcourt, Brace and World, 1961.

National Popular Government League. *Report Upon the Illegal Practices of the United States Department of Justice.* Washington, D.C.: NPGL, 1920.

Navasky, Victor. *Naming Names.* New York: Viking, 1980.

Noaks, Jeremy, and Geoffrey Pridham, eds. *Documents on Nazism, 1919–1945.* New York: Viking, 1975.

Noggle, Burl. *Into the Twenties.* Urbana: University of Illinois Press, 1974.

Notestein, Wallace. *A History of Witchcraft in England, 1558–1718.* 1911. Reprint. New York: Russell and Russell, 1965.

Ollard, Richard. *This War Without an Enemy.* New York: Atheneum, 1976.

Oshinsky, David M. *A Conspiracy So Immense: The World of Joe McCarthy.* New York: The Free Press, 1983.

—————. *Senator Joseph McCarthy and the American Labor Movement.* Columbia: University of Missouri Press, 1976.

Panunzio, Constantine. *The Deportation Cases of 1919–1920.* 1921. Reprint. New York: Da Capo, 1970.

Parker, Geoffrey. *Europe in Crisis, 1598–1648.* Ithaca: Cornell University Press, 1980.

Pawelcynska, Anna. *Values and Violence at Auschwitz: A Sociological Analysis.* Berkeley: University of California Press, 1979.

Payne, Robert. *The Rise and Fall of Stalin.* New York: Simon and Schuster, 1965.

Peters, Edward. *The Magician, the Witch and the Law.* Philadelphia: University of Pennsylvania Press, 1978.

Pollack, Frederick, and Frederick William Maitland. *The History of English Law.* Vol. 2. Cambridge: Cambridge University Press, 1923.

Post, Louis F. *The Deportation Delirium of Nineteen-Twenty.* Chicago: Charles H. Kerr, 1923.

Powers, Richard Gid. *Secrecy and Power: The Life of J. Edgar Hoover.* New York: The Free Press, 1987.

Preston, William. *Aliens and Dissenters*. Cambridge: Harvard University Press, 1963.

Pritchard, Arnold. *Catholic Loyalism in Elizabethan England*. Chapel Hill: University of North Carolina Press, 1979.

Proctor, Robert. *Racial Hygiene*. Cambridge: Harvard University Press, 1988.

Raisonovsky, Nicholas V. *A History of Russia*. 4th ed. New York: Oxford University Press, 1984.

Rauschning, Herman. *The Voice of Destruction*. New York: Putnam, 1940.

——————. *Hitler Speaks*. London: Thornton Butterworth, 1939.

Reeves, Thomas C. *The Life and Times of Joe McCarthy*. New York: Stein and Day, 1982.

Reitlinger, Gerald. *The Final Solution*. 2nd ed. South Brunswick, NJ: Thomas Yoseloff, 1968.

——————. *The SS: Alibi of a Nation*. New York: Viking, 1965.

Remy, Nicholas. *Demonolatry*. 1595. Translated by E. A. Ashwin. Reprint. New York: Barnes and Noble, 1970.

Reynolds, Paul Davidson. *A Primer in Theory Construction*. Indianapolis, Ind. Bobbs-Merrill, 1971.

Rigby, T. H. *Lenin's Government: Sovnarkom 1917–1922*. New York: Cambridge University Press, 1979.

Robbins, Rossell Hope. *The Encyclopedia of Witchcraft and Demonology*. 1959. Reprint. Bonanza Books, 1981.

——————. Introduction to *Witchcraft: Catalogue of the Witchcraft Collection in Cornell University Library*. Edited by Martha Crowe. Millwood, NY: KTO, 1977.

Rogin, Paul Michael. *The Intellectuals and McCarthy: The Radical Specter*. Cambridge: MIT Press, 1967.

Rovere, Richard H. *Senator Joe McCarthy*. New York: Harcourt, Brace, 1959.

Russell, Jeffrey B. *A History of Witchcraft, Sorcerers, Heretics, and Pagans*. New York: Thames and Hudson, 1980.

——————. *Witchcraft in the Middle Ages*. Ithaca: Cornell University Press, 1972.

Schattschneider, E. E. *The Semisovereign People*. Hinsdale, Ill.: Dryden, 1975.

Schlesinger, Arthur M., Jr. *The Politics of Upheaval*. Boston: Houghton Mifflin, 1960.

Schleunes, Karl A. *The Twisted Road to Auschwitz*. Urbana: University of Illinois Press, 1970.

Schluchter, Wolfgang. *The Rise of Western Rationalism*. Translated by Guenther Roth. Berkeley: University of California Press, 1981.

Schneier, Edward. "White Collar Vigilantism: The Politics of Anti-Communism in the United States." In *Vigilante Politics*, edited by Peter C. Sederberg. Philadelphia: University of Pennsylvania Press, 1976.

Sebald, Hans. "Franconian Witchcraft: A Discussion of Functionalism." *Deviant Behavior* 2 (1981): 349–69.

——————. *Witchcraft: The Heritage of a Heresy*. New York: Elsevier, 1978.

Seignobos, Charles. *The Rise of European Civilization*. New York: Knopf, 1938.

Selby, Henry A. *Zapotec Deviance*. Austin: University of Texas Press, 1974.

Service, Robert. *The Bolshevik Party in Revolution*. New York: Barnes and Noble, 1979.

Shipton, Clifford K. "A Plea for Puritanism." *American Historical Review* 40 (1935): 460–67.

Soman, Alfred. "Criminal Jurisprudence in Ancien-Regime France in the 16th and 17th Centuries." In *Crime and Criminal Justice in Europe and Canada*, edited by A. Knafla. Waterloo, Ont.: Wilfred Laurier University Press, 1981.

——————. "The Parlement of Paris and the Great Witch Hunt (1565–1640)." *Sixteenth Century Journal* 9 (1978): 31–44.

Starkey, Marian. *The Devil in Massachusetts*. New York: Knopf, 1949.

Sydnor, Charles W., Jr. *Soldiers of Destruction*. Princeton: Princeton University Press, 1977.

Tanner, William R., and Robert Griffith. "Legislative Politics and 'McCarthyism': The Internal Security Act of 1950." In *The Specter*, edited by Robert Griffith and Athan Theoharis. New York: Franklin Watts, 1974.

Taylor, Frank J. "The People Nobody Wants." *Saturday Evening Post*, 214 (9 May, 1942).

Theoharis, Athan. "The Escalation of the Loyalty Program." In *Succession or Repression: Realities of the Truman Presidency*, edited by Jack Stuart. New York: Simon and Schuster, 1975.

——————. *Seeds of Repression*. Chicago: Quadrangle Books, 1976.

Thomas, Keith. *Religion and the Decline of Magic*. New York: Charles Scribner's Sons, 1971.

Thomas, M. Halsey, ed. *The Diary of Samuel Sewall*. New York: Farrar, Straus and Giroux, 1973.

Thomas, M. Wynn. "Some Metamorphoses of Salem Witchcraft." In *The Damned Art*, edited by Sydney Anglo. London: Routledge and Kegan Paul, 1977.

Trevor-Roper, H. R. *The European Witch-Craze of the Sixteenth and Seventeenth Centuries*. New York: Harper and Row, 1969.

——————. "The General Crisis of the 17th Century." *Past and Present* 16 (1959): 31–66.

Tuchman, Barbara. *A Distant Mirror*. New York: Knopf, 1978.

Tucker, Robert C., and Stephen F. Cohen. *The Great Purge Trial*. New York: Grosset and Dunlap, 1965.

Turk, Austin T. *Political Criminality: The Defiance and Defense of Authority*. Beverly Hills, Calif.: Sage, 1982.

——————. "The Sociological Relevance of History: A Footnote to Research on Legal Control in South Africa." In *Law and Deviance*, edited by Michael Armer and Allen D. Grimshaw. Beverly Hills, Calif.: Sage, 1973.

——————. *Criminality and the Legal Order*. Chicago: Rand-McNally, 1969.

Ulam, Adam. *A History of Soviet Russia*. New York: Praeger, 1976.

——————. *Stalin: The Man and His Era*. New York: Viking, 1973.

————. *The Bolsheviks*. New York: Macmillan, 1965.

United States Reports. Vol. 323. Washington, D.C.: U.S. Government Printing Office, 1945.

Upham, Charles W. *Salem Witchcraft*. 1867. Reprint. New York: Frederick Unger, 1959.

Vadney, Thomas E. "The Politics of Repression, A Case Study of the Red Scare in New York." *New York History* 49 (1968): 56–73.

Verbruggen, F. *Looking for Leon Festinger in the 18th Century*. Ghent: University of Ghent, 1974.

Vold, George B. *Theoretical Criminology*. New York: Oxford University Press, 1958.

Wallace, H. Lew. "The McCarthy Era." In *Congress Investigates: A Documented History 1792–1974*, edited by Arthur M. Schlesinger and Roger Bruns, vol. 5. New York: Chelsea House, 1975.

Wallerstein, Immanuel. *The Modern World System*. Vol. 1. New York: Academic Press, 1974.

Weber, Max. *Economy and Society*. Edited by Guenther Roth and Claus Wittich. Translated by Ephraim Fischoff et al. New York: Bedminster, 1968.

Weglyn, Michi. *Years of Infamy*. New York: William Morrow, 1976.

Wiener, Carol Z. "The Beleagered Isle: A Study of Elizabethan and Early Jacobean Anti-Catholicism." *Past and Present* 51 (1971): 27–62.

Wilson, Monica. "Witch Beliefs and Social Structure." *American Journal of Sociology* 56 (1951): 307–13.

White, Lynn, Jr. "The Spared Wolves." *Saturday Review of Literature* 37 (1954): 23–35.

Windell, George. "Hitler, National Socialism, and Richard Wagner." *Journal of Central European Affairs* 22 (1963): 479–97.

Wolin, Simon, and Robert M. Slusser. "The Evolution of the Soviet Secret Police." In *The Soviet Secret Police*, edited by Simon Wolin and Robert M. Slusser. New York: Praeger, 1957.

Wyman, David. *The Abandonment of the Jews*. New York: Putnam, 1984.

Yanov, Alexander. *The Origins of Autocracy*. Berkeley: University of California Press, 1981.

Yarmolinsky, Adam. "How a Lawyer Conducts a Security Case." *The Reporter* 10 (1954): 18–22.

Ziff, Larzer. *Puritanism in America*. New York: Viking, 1973.

Index

303